Praise for
Thirty-Seven-Year Abduction
Memoir of a Gay Mississippi Author
Finding Himself Again

"As a victim of childhood sexual abuse and someone who has mentored other abuse victims as they struggled to write their painful memoirs, I thought I'd heard it all. I believed that nothing else could shock me. Then I read Thirty-Seven-Year Abduction by Milan Sergent. If Sergent had written a horror novel, he couldn't have horrified and saddened me more than this, his memoir of child and adult abuse. I'm not talking about what we usually think of as rape or sexual molestation. Milan's rape was the long-term violation of a human being, his essence, and his right to be who he was born to be; a gay man. His 37 years of rape began as a result of what, for me, are the archaic religious beliefs of his parents. They continued when a desperate Milan tried to redeem himself in his and everyone else's eyes through a regular male-to-female marriage and by joining a Pentecostal church.

Thirty-Seven-Year Abduction rivals the best impossible-to-put-down books I have ever read. Milan Sergent has a superb command of language and beautiful control of his pacing and characterization. How he absorbs us into his emotions and makes us feel his deep, ongoing pain is powerful …. My final thoughts on this poignant, gut-wrenching memoir are that I will never forget it. Read it!"

—Viga Boland for *Readers' Favorite*

"Thirty-Seven-Year Abduction: Memoir of a Gay Mississippi Author Finding Himself Again by Milan Sergent is a harrowing story; real-life ones always are, especially when you've been through everything he has. Now a critically acclaimed author, this is his story, no-holds-barred, and it makes for a tough read, understanding how one person has gone from nothing to everything through sheer determination. It is gritty and will bring tears to your eyes at some point … I take my hat off to Sergent for sharing his life with us."

—Anne-Marie Reynolds for *Readers' Favorite*

"In an attempt to stop his son from being gay, Sergent's father drove the family from one end of the country to the other in search of a place to isolate his son from everyone and everything.... Thirty-Seven-Year Abduction by Milan Sergent describes the abuse he faced as a child that only worsened through adolescence and into adulthood. The truth about hidden love and life is heartbreaking as Sergent recounts the mental, physical, psychological, and emotional abuse he suffered at the hands of those who were supposed to love and protect him unconditionally. I applaud the author's bravery and convictions and how he searched for ways to flourish in the face of so much controversy about his sexuality. I recommend this memoir to adults who love true stories that take you through the trenches of society and prove that the human spirit can draw inspiration and succeed regardless of what is considered to be normal."

—Amy Raines for *Readers' Favorite*

"This heartfelt memoir explores the author's journey to face many tragedies and difficulties, particularly in escaping the horrors of gay conversion therapy.... Milan Sergent highlights critical issues in this raw, unapologetic memoir. Books like this remind us of the massive uphill climb for full LGBTQ+ rights, visibility, and fair treatment across every country. I was very impressed with the author's candor and narrative style. It pulls no punches in explaining the full range of horrors that gay conversion therapy inflicts upon young minds when they're just trying to be themselves, be happy, and be loved. The narrative felt like a dear friend pouring their heart out, and I felt for Sergent and his journey to freedom and self-love. Overall, I would not hesitate to recommend Thirty-Seven-Year Abduction to anyone who enjoys accomplished and heartfelt memoirs and anyone looking to broaden their horizons about LGBTQ+ rights and social issues surrounding the topic."

—K.C. Finn for *Readers' Favorite*

"It was difficult to read about all the tactics parents and others used to scare their children and teens away from homosexuality. The cruelty of certain situations and experiences will move readers to tears. Thirty-Seven-Year Abduction is a good selection for LGBTQ+ teens and adults as it may help them feel more confident about revealing their true selves."

—Courtnee Turner Hoyle for *Readers' Favorite*

Thirty-Seven-Year Abduction

Memoir of a
Gay Mississippi Author
Finding Himself Again

Thirty-Seven-Year Abduction

Memoir of a Gay Mississippi
Author Finding Himself Again

A MEMOIR OF
MILAN SERGENT

Cryptic Quill Publishing LLC.

Published by
Cryptic Quill Publishing LLC

ISBN 13: 978-1-954430-14-3

Library of Congress Control Number: 2023909317

Table of Contents

PROLOGUE

AS soon as I learned of my parents' plans to isolate me in the wilderness, I kept a journal. When I found a way to escape, I was so ready to leave the past behind that I burned the daily updates in a wood heater, but the memories remained seared in my brain. Years after my suicide attempt, I contacted a religious website specializing in spiritual abuse. Desperate for help, I sent them an email mentioning some of my awful experiences, and they replied, "Hardly believable, but thanks." The administrator blocked me from accessing the website. I was glad I wasn't still suicidal. People believe in flying horses and the talking snake and donkey in the Bible. But I discovered they don't often believe victims' stories of abuse unless they experience it themselves. I began to realize that most people are privileged enough to live in a secure bubble, a dull one perhaps, but as for certain other people, well, for them, truth can be stranger than fiction. Following the principle that when life hands you lemons, you make lemonade, I turned my biography into a work of fiction in what became the *Candlewicke 13* fantasy series for young adults. Book two of the series earned two international book awards, which amused me as that book paralleled my family trying to isolate me in the wilderness. This memoir, however, is the true story of what happened to me.

After thirty-seven years from the day of the abduction, I have decided to risk everything, including my secret, safety, and recent career as an author writing under the pen name Milan Sergent. I do so mainly to protect my identity. I realized far too late that honesty is always best, no matter how painful to oneself or others. I know now that my mission is to help the marginalized, not just members of the LGBTQ community, but the countless multitudes who have had their lives ravaged or scarred by hate and by religion and those who use it to control and oppress others. I was naïve to think I could turn to humankind for help or God.

I have tried to recreate events, locales, and conversations from my memories. In order to maintain their anonymity in some instances I have changed the names of individuals and places. Besides chronology and timelines, I may have changed some identifying characteristics and details such as physical properties, occupations, and places of residence. I also decided to cut many other unpleasant parts of my life to avoid bogging down this memoir and to avoid further disbelief.

CHAPTER 1

"YOU see this scar, Son?" Mother stood in the kitchen and hooked her thumbs around the waistband of her pants. I froze near the sliding glass door where I had been playing with my baby turtles, scooting them over the linoleum floor, foolishly assuming they were little racing cars. I questioned where the baby turtles came from. I didn't want to look up at Mother, but by the tone of her voice, this was important. She continued to ease her pants down to her pubic hair, showing me the cesarean scar.

"The doctor cut me open. You came out of me. You belong to me, Son, and I will never ever abandon you."

On the outside, I was a quiet and overly mannered boy, well-trained to smile pretty. On the inside, I was becoming increasingly acquainted with a nearby cage called loneliness. Father was always working, and with no friends to play with, I watched the supernatural soap opera "Dark Shadows" before I started kindergarten. I developed a consoling fascination with ghosts and imagined that spirits of the dead were watching as a protective host. The day when loneliness trapped me in its cage, I had little care except for getting stuck by the spiky leaves of the yucca plant while playing on the wagon wheel in my front yard on Burton Street in West Jackson, Mississippi.

Avoiding the spikes.

The sun in 1970 stung my unprotected pale skin as I tried to sing the hippy peace and harmony anthem, "Aquarius (Let the Sunshine In)." Besides having buzzed hair, I had no cause to feel different from other boys. I was captivated by their long hair and colorful clothes I saw everywhere—clones of the boys in The Monkees. I had a stuffed monkey, but it wasn't nearly as cute, especially after Mother had to pin it to the clothesline to dry.

As soon as I understood the meaning of words, my parents taught me that they loved me and, more importantly, that Jesus loved me. I learned the Golden Rule and that Christians must love their neighbors as themselves, and they must turn the other cheek when someone hits them. All was safe and well in my world. I had no idea I would soon be dropped off at kindergarten, much less big schools. My heroic parents were sitting on the trunk of their sky-blue Chevrolet Impala in the driveway, enjoying the sunshine, when a boy stomped down the street, sat on our ranch-style fence, dropped his pants, and began to poop in our yard. Shocked by his brazenness, I eased away from the wagon wheel and moved beside my parents.

"Hey, kid!" the boy yelled at me. "Come over here so I can punch ya in the nose." He shook his fist at me and snarled. Judging by the poop hitting the ground, his grimace wasn't from constipation.

My heartbeat raced triple time. I didn't know this boy, so why the heck was he threatening me?

"What do I do?" I asked my parents, firmly expecting Father to rip his leather belt from around his hairy waist while charging at the boy who was now dropping yet another turd onto our freshly mowed lawn. If Father had beaten me with a belt for saying the word "fart," he would surely spank the hell out of the brat and then make him apologize.

"Well, go over there and beat 'im up, Son," my dad said with his head up, smiling at the sun's rays.

This was a gut punch. I didn't even know how to defend myself, much less beat up someone. What if the kid murdered me? Did my mommy and daddy not care if that happened? Parents always tell the truth to their children. Jesus, Santa, the Tooth Fairy, and the Easter bunny were all still very real. But so much for loving your neighbor as yourself and turning the other cheek. The Christian-love bubble I lived in had hidden holes.

At seventeen, the betrayal continued when my parents signed me up for the military draft the split second I was of age to preregister.

"But why don't girls have to register? They demand equal everything," I said, sure that aliens had taken over my parents. I could just see the girls who taunted me in school, laughing as I got blown to bits in some war. I thought parents were supposed to be protectors of their children, not hand them over to the leaders to get blown to bits over an issue of oil and greed, especially when the same leaders won't allow the endangered young soldiers to buy a beer or cigarette until twenty-one.

"It's the law. All boys have to register for the draft by eighteen," Mother said with steely-eyed determination, steering the car to the military office.

I began realizing that the U.S. was the plaster saint of mixed messages. With parental and state permission, children could engage in holy matrimony by age fourteen as long as they don't send a risqué photo to their fiancé until they're seventeen, or they'll be charged with a crime, and their young lives will be over. While I signed the draft papers, I knew my life would be over, too, if I told my parents my secret. They would've kicked me out at fourteen if I had told them I was gay, which I almost did. Either I would've been living on the streets like many homeless gay kids, or they would've tried beating it out of me until I disavowed who I was.

As Mother drove the car back home, I had a gut feeling my whole life was actually in a slow process of being murdered—snatched from the flames "for the greater good," as many people, including my parents, believe.

It had always been easy for Mother and Father to discard loved ones from their lives. I had never even seen my older and younger sisters' graves. They died not long after birth. I almost died as a baby, as well, but desperate for a child, my mother kept shaking me until I would start breathing again. For most of my youth, I wished I had died. When I was four years old, I had a brother for a few short months. Mother's alcoholic brother, Sam, had separated from his wife and claimed he wasn't able to take care of his three-year-old son, Davy. Sam intended for us to become Davy's permanent family, and the talk of adopting him made me so happy I couldn't sit still. Having a brother had been the most thrilling but scarce memory of my childhood. Even going to the grocery store to find a particular cereal that Davy would eat excited me.

"Rounie-oos!" he yelled. Unfortunately, that was about the only thing he had been used to eating on a daily basis—a stark comparison to Mother weaning me on collard greens.

Davy and I both enjoyed having a sibling in those few short months because we went on a wild binge, and Father didn't beat me with his belt as much with my new brother there. Davy tried to smother himself by shoving red holly berries up each nostril to the point he couldn't get them out, and I panicked, fearing I would lose yet another sibling to the stingy Grim Reaper. Mother managed to pull the berries out with a pair of tweezers that had annihilated her eyebrows. I wonder if the neighbors across the street saw Davy and I moon them through our bedroom window.

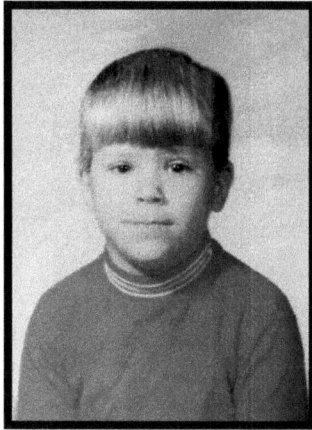

Mother tried to cheer me up by making me wear
her gold cross necklace for a second photo.
It didn't work.

After a week or two, Sam sobered up for a triumphant weekend and, on that whim, decided he couldn't live without Davy. After my newest sibling's final departure, I wept inconsolably and returned to my lonely shell, slowly becoming the little adult they expected. As they had done with my sisters, my parents never spoke about Davy again or tried to see him.

CHAPTER 2

BY the hot April morning of 1984, during my senior year of high school, my parents had swiftly sold the only home I had known since starting grade school. A packed utility van sat in the driveway of our two-bedroom, asbestos-shingled home on Willow Terrace in South Jackson. Throughout the neighborhood, azalea blossoms covered the landscape like a wedding cake in shades of pink, white, and lavender.

Despite keeping my secret locked inside and isolating myself for years in my bedroom to avoid my parents, they were figuring out my sexuality but denying it with their faith. Since no war was shipping off teenage boys, they had concocted a devious fourth plan that didn't involve correctional violence or kicking me out. It involved a hidden hole in the ground and the biblical scripture they loved in the book of Jude, where Christians are commanded in most translations to save people by "snatching them."

In their rush against my hormones, they had practically given away all of our possessions in a garage sale—everything—gone like my three siblings. Besides the main necessity, the Holy Bible, the only personal essentials we could keep had to fit in one army duffle bag per person, which Father tied to the van roof under a garish blue tarp that rattled in the wind. He had just quit his job at a printing shop where he worked as a bindery man. He was an expert at binding anything.

Trying to lighten up and do her part as a biblical helpmeet,

Mother sold her recently upgraded diamond wedding ring and the only possession her dead mother, Lorna, had given her: a ruby necklace and matching earrings.

I had countless dreams that seemed like nightmares because I was trying to salvage my cherished belongings: Celebrity posters, photo albums, school memorabilia, records, clothes, and furniture. There was space in the van for so much more of our irreplaceable possessions. But I realized Father associated many of these objects with the sin into which he believed I was further sinking. Like the ancient Israelites fleeing slavery in Egypt, he wanted to keep the chains of bondage far from my flexible wrists.

A few people realized something wasn't adding up with my family, but the body count was. Our two fur babies were the latest family members Father had decided to remove from his life.

"The shelties will be too much baggage for the hike into the wilderness. It could take several weeks to get deep enough into the mountains. I don't think the dogs will survive the snows there," Father had assured us, scraping his knives against a sharpening stone with scary perseverance.

The reason involved more than the snow. My parents became distraught when our male dog, Milo, only ever tried to hump other males, both humans and dogs. It didn't help when Milo tried to nurse another dog's litter of puppies. I thought it was the sweetest thing ever, but Mother and Father refused to believe that same-sex behavior occurred in over four hundred and fifty animal species. According to them, science and all of its findings were an enemy of God until my parents desperately needed medical assistance, that is.

"I don't want kids seeing this." Mother turned her back to Milo and swabbed her sweaty brow with her hand.

Father gritted his teeth and tried isolating Milo in the back of the garage storage room. "I may have to have 'im put to sleep. The Apostle Paul does suggest in the Bible that even some animals sinned. They're part of the whole creation that suffers because of the fall."

The Bible also implicated a talking snake for humankind's downfall, and Father could've easily been that snake. I worried about my loyal gay sheltie vanishing sooner because of Father's righteous venom.

Mother surprised me when she broke down and sobbed the day

before when a family took our dogs away to their new home. At least the dogs had a new home, and Father didn't have to kill Milo. I had no idea of the final location my parents planned their biblical "snatching" of me to be except to the wilderness, where they intended to live in a hole in the ground with a pipe driven through the underground dwelling for light. Father's plans had gone oddly under-discussed—around me, at least. I did overhear him talk.

"We'll need to live underground in case helicopters or planes fly over the wilderness and spot us."

My parents had been studying what they called "eschatological charts" that resembled a horoscope of monsters they claimed were foretold in the Bible's Book of Revelation, along with the two-thousand-year-old "soon" promise of the Lord's return and the horrible judgments following the frightful occasion. But underneath Father's sudden fear of monsters, I sensed it was a smokescreen for their actual plans. The man was afraid of nothing except what he saw me becoming. He once walked up to a seven-foot rattlesnake and pinned its head down with a wooden stick, killing it. Later as he skinned it and removed the undigested rat from its stomach as if it were a bonus, I begged him not to make me eat it. "It's just chicken nuggets," he later lied after serving me snake for dinner. The greasy, gristly taste remained with me long after I had fallen off the barstool at the kitchen table.

Underneath his veneer of integrity, to which he boasted, Father could lie when he thought it was for the best. I was barely eighteen. Sure, I had thought of fleeing my gradual abduction, if only for my safety. It wasn't the only time. I had nightmares and daydreams of running away on many occasions in my childhood. But what could I do now? While the men were concealing the guns and knives inside the van, I was still reliving my final walk of shame into the principal's office at the beginning of my senior year, months earlier at McKenzie High School. The perplexed expression on Principal Harrigan's face when I gave him the watered-down version of why I had to drop out at such an odd time convinced me that he had a few concerns.

"You are so close to graduating. You need to reconsider this, Milan," said Harrigan.

"It won't do any good completing my education. My parents are moving to the wilderness. They don't plan on ever seeing another living soul again."

I was disappointed that Principal Harrigan wasn't nosy and had asked the right questions or contacted social services—not that anyone could have rescued me from my father and his plans at that point. I must've been the most dunce boy in Mississippi, for it finally occurred to me as I walked out of my school and onto Fairhope Street for the last time that my parents had never attended one PTA meeting or even discussed the subject of college with me. It wasn't even in my thoughts as it should be. My ambitions had become paralyzed a few years earlier. I had fantasized about becoming a singer or musician in a band, to circulate the emotional pain, or an actor, so I could pretend I was someone other than a weird boy born nailed to a cross.

"Oh, Son! Real Christians cannot pursue such worldly occupations. Some of those people are homosexuals, especially those Hollywood people. It's out of the question. You'll compromise your morals, and your soul will be in jeopardy," Mother had said, stirring dinner in a boiling pot on the stove. "Put your hand near this flame; go ahead."

I eased my hand near the flames flickering out the side of the boiling pot, regretting ever mentioning any desired occupation.

"That's what the fires of Hell will feel like for those types of people," she continued, "except the flames will burn them for all eternity."

For a woman against worldly occupations, Mother loved to tease people that she was "a stripper" before clarifying that she stripped photo negatives in a printing shop. The saying "not a real Christian" was always used to justify everyone's moral failings, especially the most embarrassing ones. I was beginning to wonder if I'd ever meet a real Christian except for my parents.

"I don't understand, Mom. Singers and actors aren't any worse than half of your friends and family; they're always divorcing and remarrying. Even the music director got caught with another woman. I still can't believe we have to go to that church. They split because they don't wanna let Black people attend. Besides, I don't think there's anything wrong with gay or Black people."

Another reason I didn't want to go back to church happened a year earlier at a Baptist youth retreat in Gulf Shores, Alabama. The boys had stayed in one apartment with bunk beds, and the girls stayed in another. On the bus ride there, the girls layered on red lipstick and left as many kiss prints on the boys as they could, except for me. The boys excluded me as well, but I didn't understand why. They had been pantsing and pranking one another all summer, putting hair removal cream down select boys' underwear while they were sleeping. The girls had been sneaking photos of the boys in the showers and talking about who had the biggest, or worse, smallest dicks. A handsome college-aged guy named Jason was the boys' chaperon and our Sunday school teacher. He came strutting out of the bathroom wrapped in just a towel while the boys were asking him what it was like to have sex with girls.

"I can't lie and say it isn't great. But Christians are supposed to wait until marriage," Jason said dutifully … saving his reputation.

I was sitting on a lower bunk when another boy snatched Jason's towel off him, exposing his perfect ass framed in its golden tan line. While I was staring at two fleshy globes, the meaning of the universe opened up to me. Those pale globes deserved a place in the galaxy.

"What do you think about all of *this*, Milan?" Jason asked after turning around to expose his genitals in front of my face.

I wasn't sure if Jason was asking me what I thought of his glorious physical endowments or what I thought of the conversation. With all eyes on me, I thought my heated blush would set me aflame. I figured out that his publicly exposing himself to me was all a test that the boys had orchestrated to see if I were gay. He was tempting a starving sweet tooth with a cream-filled donut fresh from the oven. Unsure of what else to do at that moment, my upper body collapsed back onto my bunkbed where I had been sitting on the edge.

"I could care less, really," I grossly lied but did so in a bored tone, worried that my arousal in my thin polyester shorts was saying otherwise. I had no idea a male body could be that beautiful underneath clothes, for I hadn't seen many naked men. The next evening, I sat in a chair next to Jason for the packed Baptist assembly in the auditorium, and Jason said, "Nothing personal," and moved one more chair away from me.

Before leaving the youth retreat, Kerri Lyons kicked my right shin as hard as she could for no reason. She was a precocious girl who once led the worship service by singing "Personality" by Lloyd Price. But the ministry didn't slide that cheeky tune into the morning service because of Kerri's personality; it was the silver strings her affluent parents had pulled. That same year, the youth group accused a sweet girl from our church of being a lesbian and forced her out of her daycare position. With the gay witch hunt, and a slight limp in my right leg, I was growing more uncomfortable there each Sunday.

Mother pointed her stirring spoon at me. "Oh, Son! You mean you don't see anything wrong with homosexuality? You need to get on your knees and pray. You don't think or feel that way. The Bible says, 'we Christians must die so that Christ may live through us.' We are commanded to die daily—crucify our flesh, our wants, and desires. You cannot belong to the world and Christ at the same time."

I realized then that the "I must die" scripture my church taught advocated suicide of everything certain people were—for the greater good. I should've had the courage to run away at that moment. Unfortunately, I was born with the sinful inclination to question such things. I also learned the scripture, "If your hand offends you and keeps you from going to Heaven, cut it off."

"But that would undoubtedly cause you to bleed to death," I had to suggest. My parents and many others considered wrist cutters Hellbound with no hope of redemption if they committed suicide. Only my Devil-possessed heart realized that all evil actions started in the brain. So, if my brain offends me, am I to chop it off as well to make sure I get to Heaven? If all else fails, am I to get a gun and blow my sin originator off my shoulders? I had thought about doing that, too, when Father ritualistically forced me to man up and go deer hunting with him. I often sat on the cold, wet ground from dawn to dusk with the cold barrel of the gun pointed under my chin. If it went off on its own, I could kill my brain, the source of my homosexual thoughts and desires I dared not confess. And then I wouldn't suffer any more bullying at school either. Everyone would win.

I almost did lose my head. Instead of the piano lessons at my begging, Father gave me a motorcycle and no helmet. The first time I tried to ride it in the backyard, I crashed headfirst into a huge pine tree and nearly got a concussion. The Barrett sisters, who allegedly lived in a roach den a few houses away, saw the accident and came running.

"Oh my God! Are you okay?" one of them asked while my vision blurred. I would've been fine if a cute boy hanging out of a pair of blue-jean cutoffs had come running to check on me instead.

My parents had ceased church attendance because of politics. As the saying went, they were on and off like a water faucet.

"We stopped going to church because you didn't want to go, Son," Father later said as if I ever had any sway in the family when it was God's will that always seemed to be in harmony with the intentions of Rowan and Brigitte Sergent. The exodus to the mountain wilderness would soon kill any muscular temptations that might rob my soul. The utility van would prove to be mere angel wings to fly us into another realm where we would hide underground from evil humanity until we died, or the Rapture happened. Father wasn't sure which one would occur first, so he wouldn't take any chances. He had all the bestsellers that predicted the pending Rapture, including *The 1980's: Countdown to Armageddon* by Hal Lindsey.

CHAPTER 3

A painting I did of Grandmother Evelyn.
She hated it.

ODDLY, on the day of the snatching, only a few of Father's Christian acquaintances knew of his plans. For some reason, Mother didn't tell any of her friends and family that we would never see them again, which further added to my anxiety. My paternal grandmother, Evelyn, stood on the front steps of our newly sold home, her snow-white hair shining gloriously in the morning sun. I had already hugged her goodbye forever before she requested one final word with my father.

"Please, please, please, God. Let her change his mind," I prayed silently.

"Now, Mom, you know I love you, but the Lord is firmly leading me to do what I must do. You won't see us again until Jesus splits the eastern sky, and we meet in the clouds. We are going to be so far back in the wilderness we won't have an address. There won't be any way of contacting us."

After Grandmother dried her eyes and drove away, another car pulled into our driveway. Mitch Odom, my only real friend from middle through high school, got out of the front passenger's seat. Mitch called himself "the Lone Wolf" and was the oldest son of a military-minded family. Our friendship started with a bang in the ninth grade. After gym class, the final school bell rang, and he walloped me on the back of my head with his schoolbooks, and I almost passed out. I found him minutes later, standing on the front school lawn, waiting for his ride home. I asked him why he hit me, and instead of getting into a fistfight that I had feared, he apologized. Neither of us was good at sports, so by tenth grade, we took ROTC to get out of gym class.

By eleventh grade, Mitch and I would go to the fancy new Metrocenter Mall on Friday nights and play games such as Tron or Pacman at Diamond Jim's arcade. Usually, later, we would go back to my house and watch flashy music videos on MTV or cruise around the streets of South Jackson. I was stunned that he came to say goodbye. He waddled up to me with legs wide apart and held his hand out, but we ended up in an awkward hug. We were an odd mix, Mitch with his old man hair plastered in a side part and me in my homemade sun visor covered in magazine clippings to match the one Boy George wore. I was touched by his farewell gesture and badly wanted to tell him of my fears about Father's plans.

"You're moving to the wilderness, huh? That sounds so cool, dude," Mitch said as he leaned against the hood of his dad's car.

I nodded my head as expected. For a Lone Wolf like Mitch, about to join the Special Forces as soon as he graduated, vanishing into the wilderness would probably seem an adventure. This was where I began seeing the dividing line in our friendship. I had only joined ROTC to avoid being bullied in sports or during gym. He truly loved the military. I was busy battling my own warfare with my parents and society than being interested in guerrilla warfare.

After Mitch and his father drove away. Father cranked the engine. It was time to begin our exodus. He had converted the dreary bluish-gray utility van to sleep five people. The other van inhabitants were Hansel Philips, the son Father wanted, and Hansel's new bride, Karen. The two were about six years older than me and had few possessions. Like this exodus to the wilderness, they had come into my life in an equally sudden and shocking way.

A few pensive months earlier, I had just returned home from school, and after plopping my schoolbooks on the kitchen table, I got a phone call from Mother at her "stripper" job.

"Milan, you need to go to the woods near the backyard and say hello to Hansel, he's from Columbia, and he works with your dad. He is building a teepee back there and plans to live in it!"

"Are you kidding me? Why would anyone do that?" I replied, thinking it was a joke.

"He and his girlfriend, Karen, grew up in and out of foster care. Hansel needs to save money because he can't afford to pay rent on an apartment ...," Mother replied.

In disbelief, I hung up the pea-green rotary dial phone, then walked to the backyard, still expecting that the invitation was a joke. How many times in this modern age does one come home to a young man building a teepee in your backyard? Instantly a friendly Southern voice echoed from the woods.

"Hey! I'm Hansel Philips. You probably think I'm crazy!" Hansel wasted no time as he emerged from the frame of the teepee, he had already constructed at the edge of the woods that were split in half by a broad creek several yards behind him.

I do not remember what I said. The whole situation was odd, but Hansel impressed me with his kindness. He was a short young man with a broad face, a goofy smile, and a bush of dark-brown hair. He puffed out his chest and shoulders until they dwarfed his legs and hips. I felt instantly sorry for him. How could anyone seem happy about living in a tiny teepee in the woods, and why would anyone need to?

Father knew how to play to our compassion to wedge his preferred son into the family. As if there were no other woods in the state of Mississippi except beside our house. Two days had barely passed before the men, and I, constructed Hansel a wooden shed in our backyard, which earned Mother's approval—it was much better than that miserable teepee in the rain. The third week came, and my father's plans were reaching fruition. He sold my bed, replacing it with bunk beds. By the sixth week, my parents sold the dining room furniture Mother had always wanted and had recently bought, and Hansel had his own bedroom. I found Hansel's presence a relief because he buffered the turbulent relationship between Father and me. I believe Hansel figured out I was gay at once.

"Ya know, most of the Village People are gay, right?" he said while flipping through my record collection. For some reason, he stood on his head, using the wall to support himself. I tried not to gawk at his muscles, especially since he tended to wear only tight jeans or sweatpants and no underwear. I also didn't want to admit to knowing the sexuality of the singers of "YMCA" and "Macho Man." Over time I began to realize that most of my musical favorites, including The B-52's, were predominantly gay.

Hansel sat beside me on my bed and kissed Boy George's painted lips on my treasured Culture Club picture book cover. I was stunned. Was this some sort of signal, or was my father using Hansel to bait me somehow? The next day he gave me an old record he had of "The Rocky Horror Picture Show" and told me about attending the late-night showings where many attendees cross-dressed. I got chills when Hansel made a habit of sneaking up behind me and biting my arms or neck lightly. His hot breath in my ear when he pressed against me and whispered caused sensations I never knew I had—like being on the best tingly drug. I was afraid I would melt at his feet. I wondered when he would try to see me naked, and sure enough, when I was showering, he broke into the locked bathroom under the pretext of pouring a glass of icy water on me. Was my desperate need somehow soliciting him, or was this all in Father's plan, a test, a trick to lure me into the wilderness? If anything, it made me realize the intimacy that was missing in my life.

Despite these odd and rare bonding moments, Hansel was far more like Father. He loved the forest and hunting. I am sure he already knew of Father's plans of moving to the wilderness before he built the teepee, and he wanted Father to include him, to take him away from his nowhere life. Hansel's mother still lived in Colombia, and his father, a Caucasian American, died in military combat. Hansel's mother couldn't afford to take care of him by herself. While in foster care, Hansel met Karen Faircloth, and they became lovers.

Karen was a rather simple young woman; she was lanky with big wavy blonde hair and freckles. According to Karen, dementia ran in the Faircloth family, and so far, she had eluded the fated disease. She was daffy and warm and spoke with a quirky baby-doll voice. Usually, she sat around reading romance novels, cracking all the bones in her body while chain-smoking. She set the trashcan on fire on two occasions with her discarded cigarette butts. Her idea of wiping up any spill was to use the tablecloth or potholder instead of a paper towel, but she would giggle, and everything would wash over, and Father wouldn't give it another thought.

Karen and Hansel soon married, and on the wedding day, Hansel stood out in the front yard in his tuxedo, cracking a whip in the air. Scotty Inglewood, the neighborhood bully across the street, never threatened to beat me up again after seeing Hansel and all his martial arts on display, so that worked in my favor. The afternoon after the wedding it was like a funeral in my house. I surprised myself by crying in my sleep. I realized I had developed a mild crush on Hansel. After returning from the honeymoon, which I was sure they had already consummated many times in their courtship, the newlyweds moved into what once was our dining room. Everyone smoked except for me, so the house stayed in a fog as it had since I was a baby, but the front door now opened and closed more than a seedy hotel. Hansel and Karen became my parents' best friends and didn't have to answer to them or receive any discipline as I did. Hansel went from being like a brother, morphing instead into Father's wingman, where they would consult about family matters that did not include my mother or me. From the moment they made plans to move, I kept a memoir detailing everything including the huge garage sale to get rid of anything unnecessary.

My parents sat in the front two seats of the van while Hansel and Karen sat behind them in the passengers' seats. I sat on the top padded bunk bed in the back of the van as we drove away from our house for the last time. The only thing we were sure of was that we were heading north.

CHAPTER 4

DRIVING past my old middle school on Green Hills Drive and then my old high school on Fairhope Street, so many memories filled my head. I tried to understand never seeing another living soul again, except for my parents, Hansel, and Karen. I thought of all the friends I never had and would still somehow miss and the school dances I never attended except alone in my bedroom with a Disco record spinning. I thought of my bullies and wondered who their next victims would be. I was positive the excuse "boys will be boys" originated in the Magnolia State's capital. I learned the saying was a dog whistle encouraging destructive male behavior. And what many males enjoyed the most was emasculating other males. I was terrified when I first began seeing all of the "endowed" pickup trucks driving around with castrated deer testicles hanging from their antennae and mirrors, even from trees. "Redneck Christmas balls," they called the prized trophies from their hunting kills. Men trying to out-man the other males for bigger "truck nuts" started hauling soccer-ball-sized scrotums swinging from their bumpers. I was more shocked to learn that people other than my father loved to eat pretty much any testicles put before them, naming these delicacies everything from cowboy caviar to meatballs topped with cream sauce to yummy lamb fries.

Acceptance into the violent pack was determined by one's ability to "take it" anywhere on one's body and at any time, especially when boys like me weren't naturally aggressive or as big as the others in the pack. If the bros weren't calling you a motherfucker, you risked getting branded a "fag," two words they include in every sentence. And I found it difficult to believe these same straight boys actually loved female genitalia considering their constant slanderous use of the words "cunt, axe wound, twat, pootytang, stench trench, and you fuckin' pussy," as if there could be nothing worse. I eventually discovered these boys learned to act this way because they were taught that women and gay men don't worship the constraints of toxic masculinity and need to either submit or be dehumanized.

The parents of these boys weren't much better; too often they drove vehicles with bumper stickers that gloated that their children beat up honor students. That might've been a factor as to why I kept a lower grade-point average—to escape the terrorists pushing for an uprising against smart boys and girls. Later I perceived that it was just a part of the anti-intellectualism, anti-science, and anti-rationalism movement to dumb down society. Then, all over the city, I began seeing bumper stickers that said, "Real men love Jesus."

"Does that mean men who aren't Christian are pantywaists, Dad?" I had asked.

"Yup, and it's the damned truth," Father had grunted.

Eventually, I learned the whole "Real men" thing was more about guys with issues of love between two men and their fears of what society thought of middle-aged altar boys in satin choir robes, lifting their hands, singing "I love you, sweet Jesus," praise songs to the ultimate Him who demands adoration and confessions of their most embarrassing shortcomings.

Throughout my school years, I couldn't begin to tally the number of "Dutch rubs," "Indian burns," pantsings, titty twisters, and ball swats I had suffered. Despite how many modern parents overreact to sex descriptions and naked images that existed on church ceilings for two millennia, they had no clue how kinky and naughty their kids were being before they even reached puberty—the sexual realities of what their little bundles of joy inevitably faced once they broke out of their stained-glass bubbles.

Around sixth grade, the obsession most boys had about gay people, and the types of sex they had, was exhausting. As if love between gay people was a non-factor. With the boys I knew, only the sex act was worthy of dwelling on, especially butt sex, and oh, how they loved anal jokes. Eventually, they just had to try it secretly and wanted anal and oral sex with any girl willing, especially fitness girls with some muscle and extra booty for "cushioned pushin'." When the boys in my schools discussed the same anal act performed between two guys, they tried to make it as gross as possible by calling it "fudge packing." When the boys performed oral sex on girls, or they did the same on them, they called it "hot as hell," but when two women or men did the same act, they degraded it as "rug munching" or "pole smoking," yet the ultimate fantasy the boys talked about was to watch two or more women have sex.

"A mouth is a mouth, and an asshole is an asshole. They have no genders," I was desperate to tell the hypocrites who wanted to criminalize and kill gay people like me while letting straight people engage in the exact same sex acts they stole from homosexuals. What blood-chilling audacity.

By middle school, my classmates and I knew more about sex than our parents did, but if we confessed this, we'd risk punishments, freakouts, or embarrassment. I will never forget the hairless boys in the school locker room, strutting around, tugging on their cocks, "self-fluffing," so their sex organs would look good and long for the eyes of the other guys—who had better not notice, "Not in a weird way." That was always their alibi for their naked male bondings, their younger years of self-discoveries and experimenting to see if they were the only "perv." Boys never seemed happier than when they were naked together, especially during sleepovers, offering helpful hands, comparing and testing the limits of their penises and nuts, their giggly truth or dares. And when they were older, they were easily coerced into stiff-necked group circle jerks and down-low daisy chains—for the team captain or some chick's voyeuristic fantasy "and nothing more." The usual inhibition killer was there needed to be a photo or video of a woman's tits nearby, a pussy proxy, licensing them to engage in repetitive homosociality. And that was before the schoolboys went off for more hot male bonding at the college and pro-level establishments. There the alcohol-fueled, naked everything from hazings to "pulling train" had been perfected to a deeper, harder, girthier level. All the while the fraternal order guarded the debauchery by an oath of execution. I thought Father would want me to go to college where the hazing deaths have an excused history.

Like most victims of bullying, I never told anyone, especially with so many parents proud of their little monsters' behavior. Another thing I had to keep quiet was an attraction to Dean Duke, the school heartthrob and one of the star players on the football team. After the coach made me use the weights in the locker room, Dean straddled my face in his skimpy white shorts while I was on my back, lifting leg weights. I knew he wasn't trying to help build up my legs; it was all a sexual interrogation, and he was watching to see where my gaze landed. I shut my eyes before my body gave me away.

On the first day of football practice my freshmen year, I entered the boy's side of the gym with the rest of the team. The football coach had warned boys like me that other boys would rape them, only he didn't use the word rape; it was implied in the methods he described.

"Now, I just want to give you boys a heads up; there's a lot of rivalry and hormones in competitive sports," said the coach with his game-show-host smile. "When you get four or more guys piled on top of ya, lots of things can happen. You might get your privates bitten, pantsed, or a thumb up your butt. So, if ya aren't man enough to handle horseplay, then ya need to sign up for band or get ya a set of pompons and become a cheerleader."

A hopeless sinking moved through me at that moment, especially when the boys snickered. I had learned that the word gymnasium translated as "a school for naked exercise" in Greek, which was everyone's favorite group activity next to the long history of naked male sports. I had hoped middle school would be less painful than elementary school as far as the physical bullying and institutional gymnophobia, but it had been worse—far worse—especially during gym class.

Lost in the wilderness, I would never have sex or know love. I also wouldn't have the ninth-grade quarterback yelling at me in front of the whole team on the bus ride back to school after a losing game, "Hey, Milan, why don't you come back here and suck my big juicy dick?"

The entire bus had grown silent, awaiting my response. With my football helmet beside my thigh padding, I didn't move a muscle on the squeaky seat. I had never been the target of such a vulgar public demand from one boy to another until that moment. Other than to get their secret daily porn fix, I couldn't understand why so many boys loved pinning another boy down, exposing his nakedness, and shoving their lube-free fingers and makeshift dildos up his ass. Yearly world news reports were full of them using anything they could find: golf balls, rusted rebar, jump-rope handles, pinecones, gun barrels, pencils, screwdrivers, or discarded ammunition requiring a bomb squad to remove. But bullies really got off on using longer objects as thick or thicker than the average erect penis: Tennis rackets, javelins, flashlights, hockey sticks, hairspray and deodorant bottles, or the trusty mop and broom handles. For a bunch of self-professed straight guys, I suspect they got off on it and spent their evenings jerking off in their bedrooms, revisualizing the pain, pleasure, and humiliation they had caused.

Even mighty, manly men such as the Vikings could shove their cocks in another man, as long as it was to humiliate and degrade him and not just for pleasure. It has been the standard for far too many straight men of morals forever, especially rough men in prison. Every time these mighty men need sex, they pretend to be enraged at the candy-assed boys they're sticking it to. *No wonder they always appear so grumpy.* That trick must've worked so well during all those years at sea.

History had taught us well: Real men stake new territory. Sissy boys stick a stake up their own territory.

"It's good old locker-room tomfoolery. You equal-rights clowns have gone too far," too many people say.

I detested the excuses they made for bullies. School teachers should be allowed to use DNA test kits in the abusers' homes after their mattresses stop squeaking. They'd see how the bullies' memories of their brutalities drive their testosterone and fuel their "tomfoolery" fantasies. That's why they keep fooling around with Tom. In the Bible Belt of America, there were plenty of Christians on that packed school bus, but none of them, not even the bus driver, tried to stop or rebuke the sexual abuse I was facing. Of course, I was the only kid throughout my school years who didn't drool and yell with excitement when I saw a fistfight break out. I found it so disturbing that it made me sick. Pastors loved boxing and wrestling, even inviting idols of competitive violence to perform and speak in their churches. Where was the Christian love everyone claimed was our purpose for living? I was yet again that little boy taught to turn the other cheek while playing near the spiky yucca plant in my front yard on Burton Street. Only the bullies on the bus didn't want to punch me in the nose, and I wasn't ready to spread both cheeks. I couldn't take on the whole football team, especially when they were huddled in the back seats with the star player who had instigated the demand that I please him sexually.

Ask and you will receive!

"Oh, God, please, please help me. I beg you. I'm sorry for whatever I've done. Please make them stop," I prayed for the hundredth time.

Sorry, Milan, but you know the saying. Everything happens for a reason.

Love hurts.

Entering the dressing room beside the middle-school gym, I was always sure I had entered a torture chamber or large tomb. Water puddling on the floor and the faint hissing of pipes signaled that the toilet bowls had overflowed again. I figured the boys had shoved more jock straps down them to hide the evidence of their anal "roughhousing," anything to leave their victims exposed and vulnerable. But all would be forgiven by the next team prayer spectacle on the field.

How many missing pairs of underwear will it take before parents realize something is wrong and order a school inspection?

I often hid as best I could behind my open locker door as the other boys continued to file inside. I began glancing around for any potential dog-pilers before easing off my jeans and into my shorts and t-shirt.

"All right, fellahs, which head would ya rather stick in a girl's pussy?" asked the wide receiver, holding his crotch with a glassy-eyed gaze.

"We know that don't include you, Milan," the running back said, adding talcum powder to his sneakers before slapping the size-twelve shoes together in front of my face, choking me in a cloud of powder. My heart sucked up into my throat as I remained behind my locker door with burning eyes, wondering what else I could pray, beg God to do to keep me safe.

"I'd rather stick my dickhead in a chick, but those big juicy tits— hell, I can blow my nut 'tween a set of those big time. Know what I'm sayin'?" replied the running back before slamming his locker door.

Dean Duke tossed his blond hair off his forehead and strutted around in his jock strap as though his pale ass was made of diamonds and his balls were as big as baseballs. "I ain't funny or nothing, but speaking of tits, have any of y'all noticed David Eastridge's nipples?"

A couple of other boys laughed as if they, too, had noticed David's nipples. The air in my chest constricted. As much as I tried not to think about it, my nipples were larger than average for a boy.

"Fuck no, dude! Shit, only fags be noticin' other guys like that," said Jerome Mangum as we all stomped our way up the concrete steps before gathering in the gymnasium.

"Dude, ya can't help but notice his nipples; they nearly poke your eyes out if you get near him. A few days ago, he and McElhanney were the last to come out of the locker room, and David's nipples were as long and hard as a girl's, except they were all wet and shiny like McElhanney was sucking on 'em."

"Maybe they were squirting milk. Isn't that what happens when fags get their period?" asked another boy.

They had hushed their nasty talk when the gym coach walked across the polished wood floor with his clipboard and silver whistle. His tennis shoes squeaked with every step—a sound I now hated. The blood in my veins was pulsing then. The boys had to know I was in the back of the line as they walked toward the right side of the basketball court, where they gathered for the coach to perform the roll call.

I had become self-conscious about my butt, how I styled my hair, held my wrists, and even the way I walked or ran. I had dreams that my legs had become paralyzed while trying to climb the school stairs and wasn't so sure it might not be happening with the shin splints and leg cramps that had kept me awake at night. Was it growing pains, fear of a feminine manner of walking, or the damned football practices I had to do?

Basketball practice was no better. During gym classes, several girls were always perching like vultures up in the bleachers on the left side of the basketball court, waiting for half of the boys (chosen for team skins) to strip off their t-shirts and toss them on the floor. The girls got excuses to sit out gym class because they were having their monthly periods. I wished to God that I had an excuse to avoid this humiliation from yet another act of forced nudity that males couldn't act touchy about. I questioned my guilt for being embarrassed about my nipples. I could always see the shame on the faces of the few boys who were fat or had noticeable growths of male breast tissue from a condition called gynecomastia.

"Dude, you need a bra!" was just one of the usual comments I had suffered back in elementary school, but at least my chest had flattened by middle school.

Surprise, surprise, the gym teacher, lingering on the sidelines, chose Dean Duke as the captain to divide the boys into two teams for basketball. I inevitably stood unchosen and isolated from the players while the captains worked out which team had to take the soggy leftovers. The teacher watched the pecking order he could've prevented but, as always, wouldn't dare take traditional joys away from the toxic alphas.

Across the gym, the cheerleaders were practicing some cheers. At least one girl always managed to jump to the top of the girl pyramid and lift her foot above her head, giving the whole gym a good view of her crotch and flexibility as cheerleaders do. A few of my classmates whistled at the pompon pussy parade.

"Wow. And she won't even let me hold her hand," one boy said.

I had seen similar lissome cheerleaders in my parents' school yearbooks as well—the wholesome traditions passed down from the good old days, as they called them. The crotch flashings were a small reward for the football team to beat the shit out of the opposing team in case their prison rape re-enactments, designed to punish fags like me, didn't elevate their testosterone high enough to kick the opposing team's asses.

More than anything, I now feared being on the skins' team and having to strip off my shirt. *Oh, please, God, not now. Not after what Dean just said about boys with big nipples.* I had eased my eyes over at David to see how he was coping with all that had happened.

The team captain for the shirts turned his head away as he raised a hesitant arm at David. "*Ehhh*, I'll pick David, I guess," he said with a sigh.

By default, I minced over to team skins. If I hesitated to strip off my shirt in front of the whole school, it would only draw more attention to myself. I never had to worry about the basketball team ever passing the ball to me, which had worked well as I wasn't coordinated enough to dribble the ball, much less move about with it. I always shuffled along, trying not to cause any fouls, following the shielding movements of other boys on the team.

Days later, Dean Duke, the school heartthrob, had gotten up from his desk in the middle of English class and deliberately shoved his crotch in my face after sharpening his pencil. The ribbed fabric of his beige corduroy pants was rough against my nose.

I wouldn't miss the taunts about running like a girl or threats to beat me up. Fearing things would only get worse, I quietly quit the team and never told my parents all that had happened. They never came to any of the games anyway, and I only joined to try to please my father and the assistant coach, who was impressed with my thick ankles and height. The truth was, I would have much rather been a cheerleader instead. On the quiet weekends or when no one was looking, I spent my middle-school years collecting blue and white streamers from the cheerleaders' pompons that had shed onto the classroom floors and schoolyard. Crinkled plastic prizes I bound together with rubber bands and shook while imagining myself cheering for my sexy teen bullies. Could a male or pessimist have become a cheerleader?

At what point during the abuse did the innocence—the person I should've become—die? If only I could go back to those months or years before becoming obviously gay. I like to imagine how I, such a loving and gentle boy, might've prevented it. Most teens would become abusers themselves, but somehow to survive, or perhaps from all my desperate grabbing for any repressed childhood memories, I began reliving the abuse, picturing in my masochistic fantasies the visual and physical thrill my sadistic abusers had while tormenting me. In a twisted way, this gave me control over my abusers. It shoved in God's face the graphic reminders of what He let happen to me while busy in the Heavenly clouds, guiding the cleats of football teams who had the most fan prayers for the win. Miraculously one team always did beat the other, and God always got forgiven for helping "pulverize, stomp," and ultimately "beat" the losing team as the fans had requested on their handmade banners.

In the back of the van, I removed my journal from my leather gym bag with my school's name and team mascot on the front. At least I got to keep some reward for my suffering—the last worldly possession I would ever be allowed to have. But how long before the paper ran out—before my pencil became a nub? Would I end up like the cave dwellers and scratch crude pictures of my life on some subterranean rock wall?

CHAPTER 5

I got a sinking feeling when I realized that Father didn't load any medical supplies in the van. He did not consider what would happen if we were to need emergency medical attention in the wilderness. Then again, perhaps he meant to forget. A thumping noise alerted Father to pull into a roadside truck stop no more than twenty-five miles on the exodus.

"Hansel, it looks like we have a flat tire," Father said to his new partner in crime before they jumped out of the van and went into the truck stop. Karen stared quietly at the flat tire as if it might be an illusion. I sat on the edge of my seat; certain it was an omen. Already people were gawking at us as though we were nomads.

The sky should've been thundering and the air tornadic to match my worries, but the weather was typically warm and sunny after we replaced the tire and resumed our drive north, not stopping again except for gas. Father and Hansel swapped turns driving as the other one slept until we reached the border of Colorado near dusk. When we piled out of the van at a hotel, we were still wearing shorts and tee shirts, and the locals were bundled up in coats and winter apparel. Everyone stared at us as if thinking, "What are these hicks doing in their shorts in the snow?"

"Father didn't anticipate the huge climate change, just three state border crossings from Mississippi," I wanted to yell as we dashed for the hotel room, shutting out the snow flurries.

"Milan, you're going to have to sleep on the floor because your dad only paid for two beds," Mother said as we prepared for sleep. Hansel and Karen took the only other available double bed.

That night I had the most unusual dream, a dream so absolute, so prophetic that it would forever leave its imprint. In the dream, I held a large, sealed book given to me by an unseen entity. The room stood in blackness to the point that I couldn't see anything but pale candlelight illuminating a small area around my body where I stood. The book appeared at first bound in ancient leather, peeling back, coming loose in places from its sheer antiquity. I broke the seal without hesitation, and upon opening the book, I discovered that it contained pages and pages of dead people. Then I realized the leather was human skin, a type of yearbook of the deceased.

Perhaps this was a sign of my pending death. For the old, dull, lonely life I drifted through was ending with each passing mile and each passing day. Mother saw that she was losing her son and longed to have children untarnished by puberty again.

"Listen, Hansel and Karen: I need you to have me some grandbabies when we get to the wilderness," Mother blurted out at the dinner table weeks earlier.

"Hansel, you're a short fellah, and short fellahs are known to have itty-bitty tallywackers. So, you're gonna hafta get on the ball," Father said, smirking at Hansel while chewing his meatloaf.

I nearly strangled on my dinner. Though a grin broke Hansel's face, I could tell he was as mortified by the discussion as I was.

"Just place a pillow under Karen's hips when you have sex. It'll help with the conception process," Mother added while Karen giggled.

My parent had the power to break their own rules; they believed Heaven favorably weighed their indiscretions on the scales of righteousness. To them, it was the homosexuals and unmanly who would ultimately pay in Hell. I still have intestinal scars from when Mother summoned me into the living room right before we left Jackson.

"Milan, sit down; there's something I need to tell you." She sat tense in her recliner, her eyes fixed straight ahead as if she had found out she had days to live.

"Son, your father and I are not able to have sex anymore."

I was speechless by her revelation. I was unaware of why Mother told me this embarrassing personal information or how she expected me to alleviate the situation. After a long awkward silence, I responded.

"Well, you still love each other, and that's all that matters."

My mother sat emotionlessly and quietly as someone stoned on the drug of bitter yearning. *Had I given the wrong answer?* I had to release that moment, disconnect, or I feared she would trap me somehow—a bigger trap than the wilderness cave they planned to live deep inside.

They couldn't have sex anymore, and now they were trying to stop me from ever having the sex I wanted. I felt as though they had once again violated my sexual boundaries. After all, I was not supposed to have any boundaries. One thing I knew for sure now was that everyone had needs; only Father could not act upon his needs, only run from them.

I realized part of the reason why Father was so angry all the time. He was annoyed that he couldn't get sexual satisfaction. Throughout my developing years, his wrath toward me had been a major release from that frustration. Planted in my head was that frustration equaled sex, and sex equaled pain and degradation. After my parents suspected I had been masturbating using their body massager, I looked over my shoulder as I surrendered my bottom to them and awaited the painful humiliation of Father's leather belt he would snatch from his waist.

"My father always told me, 'If you touch it more than twice, you're playing with it,'" my dad said, cracking his leather belt across my exposed bottom. "Pray that God'll deliver you from this perversion! Your body is a temple of the Holy Spirit, and you have violated your temple, Son."

I had just whacked off Jesus Himself according to Dad's holy logic. *But it's impossible to cause the sacrificial lamb to sin.* Maybe the Holy Spirit fled my perverted body and returned to John Calvin; yes, all cozy inside the bowels of the beloved leader of the Protestant Reformation, who burned at the stake five hundred people accused of witchcraft—roasted them alive so they couldn't fly around on their witchy brooms and steal vulnerable souls for the Devil.

I often looked over my shoulder during sobbing breaks in my prayers in those days to see if the strike of the belt had reached its last crack and the torture would end. Filtered through my tears, my parents' grimaces might've been eager grins, giving me the creeps, while they gazed at the belt in front of my red-welted ass as though the object was some sacred dildo, the igniting match of a bonfire of witches.

When I had reached puberty, Mother taunted me at the breakfast table in front of my dad.

"I'm going to sneak into your room when you're asleep and pull down your underwear and look at your pubic hair," she insisted with a smirk.

I became that preschool kid again, playing with my baby turtles while Mother showed me her C-section scar and instilled in me that I was her property. This time I wanted to run out the kitchen door and get help from the first stranger who would open his door, but all I remembered saying was, "No, you can't!"

Seeing this was humiliating me, Father flashed his bottom teeth in a snarl. "She's your mother, and she can look at your pubic hair whenever she wants to!"

Another morning during breakfast, I was half-asleep, and my mother told some joke about a chicken and its pecker breaking off, and I was afraid to laugh. Father thought I was being disrespectful because I did not laugh. God forbid I did not laugh. He snatched me off the barstool and dragged me through the kitchen until I smashed my head on the oven. He then forced me to bend over the bed while he snatched off his belt and taught me the ways of righteousness.

Sleep I found uncomfortable, worrying about Mother gazing at the goods beneath my underwear at night. And the times she asked why my bed was squeaking when all I was doing was trying to sleep. I began having nightmares of having sex with her, making me want never to crawl into bed again. I cannot even describe the sick feeling this left me trying to shake. It wasn't the only impropriety my parents sanctimoniously committed; other embarrassing things were too disturbing to confess. I think I blocked out many of them, but the lesser offenses included Mother listening through my bedroom or bathroom door, which I was never allowed to lock.

"Son, you aren't doing anything nasty in there, are you?" she would ask, leaving me to feel that even using the toilet was sinful. Father joined in Mother's twisted games one evening, snickering and glaring at me in a most intimidating manner.

"Son, have you gotten your masturbatory license yet?" he asked the moment I walked into the smoky living room.

I pretended I didn't know the word, not after my father had once begged to be discharged from the Navy years earlier. According to him, all the sailors were perverts. I assume Father reached this conclusion because of the "gooey socks" he claimed the men kept under their mattresses. He got the discharge, and now he was after mine.

I worried their sick mind games were getting worse. If I were to keep the last fragment of myself, I would have to lock my passions and opinions inside my soul. Too many adults obsessed over what children were doing with their sex organs. By eleventh grade, my science teacher, Mr. Barrymore, accused a girl of masturbating while she had her head pressed against her arms on her desk. From my position behind her in the classroom, it appeared as though she was taking a nap to get rid of a headache and nothing more.

"Masturbation is homosexuality, kids! And homosexuality is a sin that will send you to Hell," he growled.

The man couldn't've been qualified to teach science but probably was given the position to keep him on staff as many underpaid public high school coaches were. Mr. Barrymore naturally took a dislike to me and was always doing his best to find something to entrap me. When students went up to his desk to pick up their test papers, I had to gently hold my papers until he completely let go of his gripped end, or he would go off on me. "Don't you snatch that paper out of my hand, Milan. I'll jump all over you."

I survived science class, thankfully, but would I survive my parents' insane gay-conversion experiment they planned for me?

CHAPTER 6

THE next morning as we all woke up in the Colorado hotel, I was a little stiff from sleeping on the floor, so I wrapped myself in a blanket and hobbled to the bathroom to get my shower in case it was my last before we crammed into an airtight hole in the ground. While Mother and Karen shared the hotel vanity to do their hair, Hansel and Father had left to check out the mountainous region.

"There are dadburn hotels and mansions all over the place here. You just can't see 'em through the trees until it gets dark, and they turn on their lights," Father said with a snort upon returning to the hotel room. "We're gonna have to keep heading north. Colorado ain't gonna give me the permanent seclusion we need."

After breakfast, we packed our shorts and t-shirts and dressed in readiness for the torrents of chilly air.

"What is that blowing around on the ground?" I asked.

"It's tumbleweed," replied Father.

"That's what I thought," I said. The only thing blowing around on the ground where I was from was garbage, so I likened tumbleweeds to nature's trash.

When we drove off from the hotel with the jackalope mounted on the café wall, Father tried to convince Hansel that there was no such animal as a jackalope and that the taxidermist took the horns of an antelope and mounted them on a jackrabbit. Hansel, however, remained convinced that it was real and that we were coming into a strange new world full of unusual creatures.

As we inched over more mountain cliffs, I began to feel another touch of fear creeping into my stomach. Not an anxiety about what we left behind, but the unknown territory was so overwhelmingly foreign, rugged, and lonely. I had traveled out of Mississippi many times in my young life, but the mountains seemed endless, as though they would devour us.

"Be careful, Rowan, you're gonna go over the edge. Do you think the van will continue to hold out?" Mother cried, trying not to look down the mountain drop-offs. Father appeared unconcerned, almost hypnotized, the deeper he drove into the mountains. Karen slumped back in her seat, reading her romance novel and smoking. Whatever was going on in her head, we never knew.

That morning after I lost count of the mountain passages that had vanished into the horizon, the realization that this was happening came into my consciousness like a harsh reality. *How could I ever find a companion lost in the wilderness?* I would always be alone. Mother had Father and Hansel had Karen, but I was the odd one out. Unbelievably, I started hoping the predicted evil cataclysm Father used as a cover for my abduction was about to overtake the world. That way, we wouldn't slowly wither alone in the wilderness, unable to find our way out. The pecking order usually went by age and health. Being the group's youngest, how would I survive on my own after they all died?

"When we all get to Heaven, we'll be just as we are now, living in our private mansion in the clouds together," Father said as he romanticized the eastern sky tumbling softly over the snow-capped mountains. I laughed silently, wondering why he was so sure God wouldn't force him to live eternally in his parents' Heavenly mansion as their subservient child. No, he was the man with the plan, the man in God's right hand. Look out, Antichrist. Father would keep his son's soul safe from the gay lifestyle even if he had to kill us all in the process! He didn't seem to understand that the outside world had nothing to do with who I was on the inside. You cannot isolate or destroy decadence, but it can relocate.

Like my boring life, the landscape repeated itself in a twisted maze. Our top-heavy van edged along the towering Rocky Mountains, teetering dangerously around every winding curve. The atmospheric pressure changes from the extreme ascension caused our ears to stop up, which was fine with me; I couldn't hear Father preaching. The drop in humidity, along with the climb, felt as though we were soaring to Father's Heavenly mansion. When the landscape leveled off, Karen broke from the glassy-eyed fixation on her romance novel for the first time in hours.

"I thought buffaloes were extinct!" she shouted, pointing toward the left driver's window over Father's plaid shoulder.

"No, Karen, the government declared buffalo an endangered species at one time," Mother informed her.

It surprised me that Mother knew this because I never saw her read, except for the Bible and a few steamy romance novels. She claimed she didn't read trash literature. But she left for my hungry eyes to find the only magazine she had ever brought home. I soon realized why she had done this: The magazine featured an article about a young man who was skateboarding home with a frugal sack of groceries for his bride until a gang of alleged homosexuals captured him and took turns raping him bottom up in a back alley, supposedly destroying his marriage and his desire to wear shorts again. With renewed resolve, I continued to wear the only pair of shorts my parents had bought me until Father accused me of giving the Scroggins family glimpses of the goods while we were shelling butterbeans in a heatwave.

The occasional glimpses of wildlife broke the monotony of the long travel and endless snow-covered landscape, where dozens of avalanche caution signs welcomed us into the outskirts of Yellowstone National Forest. I fell asleep in the back of the van by then but awoke hearing all the excitement. I did not expect to see a significant tourist attraction for some reason, so I was all ablaze with expectations. Father didn't plan on touristy detours; then again, he did not know exactly where he was going. He followed the map to the Yellowstone Park tourist center.

"Closed for the season?" everyone said disappointedly after we brushed a foot of snow off what we suspected was the business sign among the rolling mounds of white ice. Darkness soon wrapped its eerie cloak around us. The moonlight beamed down through the trees, and the snow was luminous from its reflection.

"It's getting late, and we haven't seen a hotel nowhere," Mother whined.

"A'ight then," grunted Father. "I'm gonna find somewhere and park for the night."

He kept control of the wheel in the coarse snowy regions, not fully trusting Hansel. In his eyes, I was not man enough to control the van. Mother offered to drive but never did. Karen saw enough of the bleak scenery and resumed ogling the next chapter in her romance novel under the light of her burning cigarette.

"This is so unlike Jackson. We haven't seen another vehicle for over an hour," Mother said, stretching her legs and applying another coat of lip balm.

"Just think, Brigitte, we ain't a-gonna have to worry about traffic no more. We can hitch a ride on the backs of deer," Father said on his midnight course, crossing the border into a small region the Montana locals called Beyond Hope. By this time, we were in the heart of the Bitterroot. For miles and miles, we passed little white crosses on the side of the desolate highway. Everyone knew the crosses were death markers from accidents along the treacherous road.

"I don't like the looks of this!" Mother sighed as she sank lower into the front passenger's seat. "What if we run out of gas or something? I haven't seen a store for miles."

This didn't faze Father in the least, though I'm sure he hoped Mother wouldn't allow lack of faith to sink in its pitchfork while its glowing red eyes cast an unflattering light on his uncertainty. Escaping to the wilderness was not exactly Mother's lifelong dream. Still, she trusted her little macho man and allowed him to remain her spiritual leader, as many Southern women are groomed to do.

If what Mother said was true about them not being able to have sex anymore, then perhaps Father wanted me around to pacify Mother to keep her off his back, I rationalized. He wanted me there to fill in for him emotionally and physically but not have any adult authority. He reserved authority for himself; it was his last bit of masculinity. We were the Sergent Family Trinity: the father, sacrificial son, and holy mother. I learned that my mission as the third person in the trinity was to be eternally enmeshed to the holy mother.

When Mother was a young girl raised by her grandmother, she desperately wanted children. She had even built an altar in her youth with her chipped Jesus statue and mismatched dolls. In the middle of this circle, Mother would kneel, fold her hands to match the gold-printed hands on the Bible cover, and pray for two girls and one boy. She lied about her age to get a job at a hamburger restaurant in downtown Jackson where she met my father. Being underaged, Mother had to obtain permission to marry when Father struggled to get a college education, working long hours at the newspaper company. Mother's soon pregnancy was a surprise for Father; he had to get a second job, and his college education began to suffer. Sadly, Courtney died of crib death after six weeks in my mother's arms. Mother plunged into a deep depression. Seeing her in this state was killing Father, so he realized that the only way she would fill the deep void in her life was to have a baby. The doctors warned Mother that it was dangerous for her to get pregnant due to earlier complications. She should've listened because I was born prematurely a year later, and they named me Milan Sergent.

The doctors kept me in an incubator until they thought I could safely leave the hospital. With the piling medical and funeral bills, the debt forced Father to quit college. Mother soon became pregnant a third time with Mara Delyn, who managed to survive six months before succumbing to crib death. I never knew exactly why Mother's family blamed her for both girls' deaths. The deep vexation between them became evident because Mother rarely spoke with her family.

A self-portrait as a ghost boy and the girl Mother preferred.

Finally seeing a place to pull off the side of the highway, Father pulled in and parked the van. If there were a rest area sign, it remained covered in ice. The eerie night seemed timeless. The moon graced the snowy woods with a luminescent blue haze, allowing us to see a white van parked near us covered in almost a foot of snow.

"Oh goodness. It looks like someone abandoned that vehicle," said Karen as she sprang from the van to stretch and pop her joints after the long drive. Hansel and I headed toward the forest to empty our bladders.

"Look, Hansel, there are two sets of footprints in the snow." I followed them from the abandoned van a good distance into the woods. Hansel walked on ahead and noticed something in the snow.

"It's a ten-dollar bill," Hansel said with a worried rattle in his voice. He pocketed the money before he, too, noticed that the footprints ended there.

"Oh great," I said. "We have an abandoned van, footprints that mysteriously end, and it looks like a phantom stranger robbed and killed someone. Here we are in the middle of nowhere, with no one to call for help."

"Oh, Milan, calm down, it's probably a couple of skiers, and they walked over here to take a leak, and the money fell out of their pocket," Hansel replied while I searched for evidence of yellow snow.

Climbing back in and locking the van doors, we tried not to let our imagination play on in our heads. While Mother and Karen prepared the beds, I tried to find some music on the local radio stations. I paused on a channel playing "Modern Love" by David Bowie. With the song's ambiguous lyrics and Bowie's fluid sexuality, I was reminded of the liberation I would never have. I wanted to live in a world of Bowies, Pete Burns, Culture Club, Adam Ant, Haysi Fantayzee, Leigh Bowery, and the androgynous British Blitz Kids or New Romantics who had taken over the music scene in the early eighties. They spent much of their days doing their makeup and clothes, turning themselves and music into works of art. Father made me channel the station to a less controversial New Age station that relaxed and sailed us away from any apprehensions they had while playing poker in the back of the van before bed. *This is a naughty change,* I thought. Mother was an expert at the game Solitary, but if the cards did not start with a promise, she would swipe them all up and re-deal a new hand.

The sci-fi edge of the following few songs reminded me that we were unaware guests in a possible murder mystery. I always turned the radio dial to another channel if the oldies song "Born to Lose" was playing because Mother swore it was written about her, and her mood would seem to become as barren as the snow-buried landscape now surrounding us. Mother had been desperate to prove that she wasn't barren. She wanted girls but settled for me.

Even the wildlife was hibernating in dark recesses far removed from human eyes. I laughed as the thought occurred to me; *in the coming months, we will be like the early settlers, settling on anything that crawls on the earth's putrid surface for food.*

CHAPTER 7

EACH passing morning confirmed the reality that we were homeless drifters heading off into the unknown. Still wearing Tuesday's rags, we slowly became one with the rugged terrain. Father pulled breakfast out of one of the plastic bags under the foldout beds as Karen poured our water into the red plastic cups with our names written in permanent black marker. After a cheap meal of powdered donuts and water, Father started going over the plans he and Hansel had secretly been discussing.

"Since we ain't gonna have no gas or electricity, we need to live underground. I know caves stay at a moderate temperature year-round. We'll have to survive as self-sufficient as possible."

"When we run outta bullets, we can hunt with wooden spears. And I'm sure there'll be plenty of streams where we can fish," Hansel added.

"I can eat tree bark if'n I gotta," said Father. "The Rapture is gonna happen soon, and we'll be much safer in the woods than in a city. The Bible plainly says that in the end times, it'll be like Sodom and Gomorrah. People'll behave like brute monsters, and God'll unleash monstrous locust creatures from the belly of the earth to punish 'em." Father's eyes glazed over as he repeatedly warned us of God's pending judgments. "The creatures will endlessly torture those that have the Mark of the Beast. People will try to kill themselves from the torments, but God won't let 'em die. That way, they'll suffer even more until the Day of Judgment. Then God's gonna toss the unbelievers by their ankles into the lake of fire. I'm convinced the end is near, and we'll be safer underground or at least away from others until old Gabriel blows his trumpet, and we fly up to meet Jesus in the air."

As Father cranked the van, the images of his prophetic warning would not leave my mind. Then I laughed under my breath. *What if Gabriel gets hip with the times and strums an electric guitar to herald the Rapture Father anticipated?* But it wasn't funny, and I sat in the back of the van, silently wishing he would admit that it was all his and not God's plan to keep me from living my life.

Sensing that I was pensive, Father said, "Perk up, Milan. You're worse than a woman on the rag."

Yeah, and you're worse than a doomsday prophet with a following, I thought as we pulled away from the rest area.

Behind my unlocked bedroom door growing up, I dreamed up dances and little skits complete with makeshift costumes. I even made a blond wig out of yellow yarn and tried to get my four friends to participate. I couldn't understand why they acted disinterested, except for Leigh Scroggins, who was equally shy and awkward when it came to dressing in tacky costumes to become a muse in my theater of freaks.

In my living room, with Leigh's parents and my parents watching, I had played a safe old record my parents had: "I'm Gonna Sit Right Down and Write Myself a Letter." We dared blow a kiss to the audience and slap our hips during the song's line about a kiss on the bottom of the letter.

"Did you know you priss, and you smack your lips when you talk, Milan? Well, you do," said Leigh's mother, sitting on the sofa that evening with a grin broadening her face as wide as her thin afro. "Now, I'm not being critical," she added with a throaty chortle while I stood in stunned silence in front of the television. That was the only reaction to the performance except for my parents sitting in their recliners with lost eyes, puffing cigarette smoke into the suffocating silence that had overtaken the room.

We soon resumed our customary church attendances, and Father had a worrisome nightmare involving me. Biblical prophets were known to see the future through dreams, and Father made the gay nightmare he had had about me seem more catastrophic than Armageddon. The dream disturbed him so severely that he refused to reveal any specifics. I often wondered why he had to say anything at all except to get me anxious and repentant, perhaps. The nocturnal sprites had placed a leveling weight upon the scales of justice because I had many nightmares that I was trying to flee his sadistic wrath. We were never close, and yet for a boy too afraid of him to ever rebel, it seemed I infuriated him simply by breathing. When he didn't slap my face, he often beat me viciously with a belt until I became a sobbing puddle on the floor, begging for mercy. I could still feel my underwear being snatched over my trembling ass cheeks on full display on the edge of my childhood bed with a neatly tucked bedspread, especially if I had wet the bed and was desperate to hide the uncontrollable fact. As I waited in the bent position, I remembered a movie my parents had watched featuring a naked woman bent over, getting "screwed." The submissive role where you must bow before the master and get what you deserve.

I had hoped my stuffed animals would rescue me from that fate. Batman and Superman never had their underwear snatched down. I could still see Dad ease away from me and unbuckle his belt from around his waist. The leather buried and buried in my burning flesh as I broke into tearful, screaming sweats.

"No, please, Daddy! I'm sorry," I had pleaded time after time, smack after smack. Oh, the humiliation when I realized my parents were getting a full view of my ass cheeks bouncing apart between every skillfully landed swat near my stinging crack. My balls swung dangerously close to the pounding strap while they dangled over the bend of the mattress. The occasional slapping sounds my sex flesh made after Dad's belt and Mom's hands had swatted my nakedness was degrading, and I grew to dislike them for it. When I started going through puberty, they finally figured out that I should be spanked with clothes on. I realized it was never for my feelings or modesty; they saw I was getting old enough to discover how they were sexualizing their violent brand of discipline—that I might hold them accountable. Why is pubic hair always the time parents lose interest in continuing the abuse and start grounding kids instead?

The frozen expression on Father's face during the beatings so closely resembled that of Jack Nicholson's drunken and wildly murderous character in "The Shinning" as he brandished his bottom teeth like a rabid dog. Inevitably, after the beatings, I would have to enter a disconnected state of humanity, kiss his stubbly cheek, and tell him that I was sorry for causing him to beat me.

"Son, you are upsetting your father," Mother gave voice to Father's concerns as she was roller-setting her hair at her bedroom dresser. I had been sitting cross-legged on the floor, admiring the contents of her box of jewelry as if it were a pirate's chest. "He's concerned about your masculinity."

I realized the truth at that crushing moment. I understood the reason my father was rejecting me. He despised that he still had to love me, and it cut through my fragile soul. I realized I would never be what he wanted. Being myself wasn't good enough; it had never been good enough. I also realized that whatever was wrong with me must be clear to others as well as that same year of 1980, when I was desperate to be popular, my freshmen classmates had voted me "Most Mysterious." I don't recall that category ever existing until I came along, probably because there wasn't a "Most Homo" category.

I began to wonder if other people had a deeper insight about me than I had about myself—if I was mentally challenged or just blinded to how I looked and behaved. While most people in my region celebrated their Southernness, I didn't even feel American. Most everything I preferred was British. Namely, I hated my accent, which was a nervous monotone slur, given that I was born tongue-tied, but thankfully Father noticed it while bottle-feeding me, and I underwent corrective surgery. Later in life, I adjusted my elocution by learning to soften the growling nasal Rs and practicing crisp consonants according to the standard British accent. Even my manner of walking appeared suspicious, and occasionally students let me know it.

"You sorta float when you walk," one boy said, snorting through his nostrils. Another boy demonstrated my way of walking. He swished around like a little flower girl limply dropping pink rose petals down the aisle at a wedding.

That same pivotal year, "The Blue Lagoon" was released, and I was mesmerized not by the beauty of Brooke Shields but by how hot Christopher Atkins was, running around the island in only a loincloth with his golden blonde curls and golden tan. I don't think I blinked through the entire movie. Every inch of him stirred buried sensations in me. It took a few days, weeks perhaps, for me to fully grasp the meaning of what was happening to me and that it wasn't the norm—that I was aware of. I couldn't confess any of this to anyone. In 1980 the only out gay person I knew about was Elton John. The students at my middle school loved to pass along rumors about other rock legends' sexuality, namely stories about a pint of undigested cum being found in one male singer's stomach or another. I knew what gays were from the occasional dance shows, art documentaries, and movies my parents watched, namely "A Different Story" with Perry King, another actor I found attractive. Even though I lived in the capital city of Mississippi, I felt stuck in the boonies. I knew there was a gay world thriving in cities like New York with its Studio 54 scene, which I wanted to be a part of, as well as in San Francisco, and London. People said gays were evil and Hellbound, and though those films resonated with me, it didn't, until "Blue Lagoon," occur to me that I was gay and that my parents had watched these movies with me to gauge my reaction—to test their nagging suspicions about my sexuality.

Obsessing days and lonely nights, my attraction to boys had grown. I spent many hours in bookstores, leafing through select books and magazines, desperate to find just one photo of a naked male, constantly looking over my shoulder as if I were engaging in criminal activity. At night, my pitiful pillow suffered abuse while I imagined it was a companion to whom I could tell my every secret thought. The pang of loneliness ate at me, and with each passing day, I grew curious to be intimate with another boy—to see him naked, to feel his body heat. I felt so awkward and ugly that I was certain no boy would consciously ever want to have sex with me, even if he were gay. *But what if he were unconscious? He wouldn't protest then.* This devious thought took me by the hand while gazing out the living room window one lonely morning during a summer break that seemed eternal. I spotted an older teenage boy wearing nothing but red short-shorts and a glistening tan, skateboarding down the steep incline of Willow Terrace. When he went back up the hill for another turn, I rushed out the kitchen door, through the backyard, and into the woods beside my home that led to the edge of the road. With my heart pounding, my lust for him drove my thoughts to throw a large rock and knock him out, and then I planned to drag him into the woods, or so I thought.

I remained in a state of turmoil as I knelt behind the tall bushes and field grass. He was swiftly approaching the clearing a few short yards from me. As I prepared to throw the large rock, my consciousness overtook me, and I saw the beauty of his life, his soul. My body froze.

"No, I won't do such a thing!" I scolded myself, so I dropped the rock and returned home in disbelief that I had even considered such a disturbing thing—me, a boy who didn't believe in hurting anyone, a boy who never fought back even while I was being bullied in school or at home.

Sleep began to evade me. The fact that I came as close as I did to attacking that skateboarder left me feeling that I had shackled my soul somehow. I was drifting further outside of society in my search for others like myself. Now that goal was soon to be impossible.

CHAPTER 8

T RAVERSING north in the utility van, Father began searching for a gas station and a place to get a "rib-sticking" breakfast. It surprised me that he made allowances for hotels and restaurants when we were soon to live forever primitive. Perhaps he was biding time with his plan, making it seem like a vacation until he trapped me in squalor.

Several miles from the rest area lay a quaint little village, frozen in the late 1960s. Several women wore beehive hairdos and polyester blouses with wide collars. Father fueled up at the lonely gas station, and directly beside it was a log cabin restaurant where we had a decent breakfast of pancakes and sausage.

"Would you prefer oleo with your pancakes?" the waitress asked.

"No, but butter would be nice." In my youthful inexperience, I didn't know oleo and butter were the same, and the waitress thought it was funny. After a contemplative breakfast, Father approached the cash register and started a conversation with a man who introduced himself as the restaurant proprietor. During the chat, Father began to feel out the owner's knowledge of any wilderness area in either Northern Montana or the surrounding areas that were remote and available for public occupation—"free" occupation.

"What if someone were to just wander far back into the vast mountain wilderness and live on all this here wasted land?"

"The government sanctioned most of the mountain wilderness as protected national forest land; if not, it is someone's private property, sir. You wouldn't believe the number of idiots who think they can still stake their claim to property like the early settlers did. The authorities circle these parts with aircraft, looking for illegal trespassers, and if they catch them, they either get shot or thrown in jail."

"It's a shame that the government owns all of God's green earth. They aren't ever going to use this much wilderness, so you'd think they'd at least sell some of it at an affordable price before they'd do that," Father responded. His countenance dropped, and his lips disappeared behind a grimace.

"I hear ya," repeated the owner. "But if they catch you living on private or government property, it ain't gonna be pretty."

Father somehow didn't predict those cold, hard, yet logical facts. He had sold everything we had ever owned and dragged his family across the United States. No other choice remained. Only now, I had gruesome images of the government or people hiding from the government gunning down my family as soon as our heads popped out of the hole in the ground.

"Well, let me ask you this," Father said, shifting his body closer to the counter. "Is there anywhere I can find a vast area of land so I can live secluded that won't cost me my firstborn child? I'm even thankin' about Canada."

"Northern Idaho or Alaska is definitely your best choice for isolation," the restaurant owner said as if he had expert knowledge of the entire country. "The Canadian government controls all mountain property in Canada, so they can take it from you at their discretion. Idaho is on the western side of the continental divide, so it has a milder climate than Montana does. Believe me, man; the winters on this end are pretty damn tough."

Father took up much of the restaurant owner's time. Was this the dramatic turning point in his plans as to exactly how secluded our future would become? Was Big Brother, the system, holding out its iron claw, preventing Father from isolating me? I'm sure he must have felt a little foolish. Would he bury the Book of Revelation under the Book of Plan B? Whatever he and Hansel discussed after that day, I remained unaware. Even Mother's attitude seemed to make a sudden flip. She approached me outside the restaurant while Father settled the bill.

"Your dad doesn't ever consult with me about anything anymore now that he has Hansel. I have no clue what he plans to do now, and I'm going to tell him how I feel about it."

Truth be known, I think my mother "wore the pants in the family," as Father suggested one day. If Mother became unhappy, everything would become miserable. Whether she actually confronted Father, as she claimed, I'll never know. After this episode, Father became noticeably hostile toward me, as if it were somehow my fault that he was having problems isolating me. Hansel also became distant and less friendly.

For some reason, when Mother was in one of her moods, she would avoid looking at me and tell people that she had no family left. A few years earlier, we discovered that she was possibly a twin. Doctors found teeth and bone fragments in Mother during a hysterectomy. The day we left Jackson, she tossed several handfuls of prescription bottles into the trashcan.

"Didn't the doctor say you have to keep taking your hormone tablets?" I asked, staring into the filthy can in disbelief.

"We might as well get used to it. We'll be so far back in the wilderness we won't be able to refill any prescriptions," Mother had said. Perhaps these factors help contribute to her depression and mood at times.

Later that morning, after leaving the log cabin restaurant, the dreadful next phase still in its infancy, Father set his destination for Idaho. I crouched anxiously in the back of the van, writing in my memoir. My pen drifted off the page as the van swerved violently.

"What does that damned nut think that he is a-doing?" Father yelled as he honked the horn. "Rave on, McDuff. Hell ain't half crowded!" We had narrowly escaped a crazed motorist ramming us off the mountain highway. The restaurant proprietor warned him to drive carefully in that area because there were a lot of Hell's Angels and other motorcycle gangs. Rumored tales of motorists' entanglements with the Angels abounded among the mountain locals. I, for one, didn't want to get in their way or especially have Father run over a Hell's Angel in his rush to beat the Devil.

"I guess I'm gonna hafta look for a real estate agency in the area," sighed Father as though he had stabbed God in the back.

I'm sure the words "real estate agency" was a punch in Father's steely gut. He couldn't even find a lake to sink the van into as he had planned. The lakes and streams were all frozen and impossible to find buried under the snow. Even if we had tried to wander as far back as possible into the mountains of the National Forest, we would have had to tunnel through snow higher than our heads and would've frozen to death in no time. Father couldn't even bring himself to admit this.

The crooked beak of time struck three o'clock when we arrived at the Idaho tourist information center. This was a baby step for Father, who trudged into the building.

"Milan, are you going to get out of the van or not? You haven't said two words since we left Montana," Mother complained, stretching her legs.

I climbed out of the van and checked my appearance in the passenger side mirror for what I did not know; perhaps it was the prospect that there might be another teenage boy in my future after all.

"All right, I'm ready," I said before being the last to enter through the tourist center door.

"Oh look, Brigitte. They have gobs of books on Idaho!" Karen said.

"Help me find one with lots of pictures of the area," my mother replied. While we were all examining the books, Father approached the woman at the information desk.

"Hello, my name is Linda. Can I help you?"

"Yeah, I am looking to relocate here, from Jackson, Mississippi, possibly." Father always got a thrill announcing his Southern heritage as though it would impress the rest of the world. I usually wanted to crawl under a rock when he played his nasal accent like a trumpet.

"We heard Idaho had a lot of mountain property the government isn't hoarding. What we're looking for is enough mountain property that we can build on and have lots of privacy. I know we need to go to a real estate company, but perhaps you can tell us where the best region in this here state for that type of property might be?"

The expression on Linda's face was a bit patronizing at first, and then she smiled and said, "As you can tell by looking through this book on Idaho, this is a richly diverse and beautiful state. However, what you want would probably be in the northern tip of the state—

say around Coeur d'Alene and the region north of Lake Pend Oreille. Here's a map of the area." Linda smoothed out the map across the desk and then, using a pink highlighter pen, circled the area where we were and drew a line along the route to Coeur d'Alene.

"Follow the pink line, and you'll be there in a couple of hours. There's also a great seafood restaurant on the highway near the city," Linda concluded.

Karen handed the same book to Father that Linda had shown him, and he paid for the book, took the map, and we all piled back in the utility van. Driving on, we followed the highlighted roads. The area was beautiful as we arrived in Coeur d'Alene, though Father did not see enough mountains.

"Let's stop here and eat, then I am gonna start looking for a real estate company," he said with a hint of ruin stifled behind a fake cheerful tone.

I dared not question my parents' unspoken change in plans. They would become angry and claim that I misunderstood everything as usual. I laughed to myself, remembering a time when Father was trying to minimize the dents in the wooden armrest of his recliner using dusting spray, a terrycloth hand towel, and a steam iron. While Mother was in the bathroom, he was going to surprise her with his magical technique. Instead of dusting spray, Father accidentally used air freshener, and the towel stuck to the chair arm. Remembering how he almost hit me in the face for laughing was not magical.

Another time Father thought he had used spray deodorant after his morning shower, but it was oven cleaner. Later that afternoon, when he was working at the printing company, the oven cleaner activated from his body heat. Remembering the funny things about him helped when he tried to come across as infallible. Usually, he had a stern, unapproachable look on his face, and he was never tolerant of children behaving childishly as far as frivolous behavior goes. However, sometimes Father could be even sillier than the behavior he couldn't tolerate. Such as the time he skipped through Metrocenter Mall, imitating a little girl shortly after exiting Spencer's. I was checking out the glow-in-the-dark posters, desperately wanting one of Christopher Atkins in his clingy loincloth, but to please my parents, I settled for a Cheryl Ladd poster that did nothing for me but depleted my allowance. Naturally, Mother made me hide Cheryl's exposed cleavage by thumb-tacking a spread deck of playing cards over the offending bit of flesh. While in the gift store, Father saw that his dentures were glowing green from the black lights, so he went up to everyone, grinning half out of his mind.

"Milan, it's good to see you smiling," Mother said as we entered Molly's Seafood Palace. The place was decorated like the 1950s and was nearly empty but appeared clean. After the hostess seated us in the red vinyl chairs, Father saw a real estate guide stand at the front entrance and sent me over to get a couple. Manically flipping through the guides, we did not even glance at the menus before the server rushed to the table.

We ordered, and as soon as Mother tasted the oysters, she called the server over and belligerently complained that she had eaten a lot of seafood before and that those were not oysters on her plate. The manager came out of the kitchen and assured her they were oysters and that he could show her the can that they came from.

The realization came to me that day that everybody needed somebody to feel superior to, let their frustrations out on, and blame for their own demons. All that the poor server got for a tip was an insulting penny. While Father settled the bill, I darted to the van to avoid their wrath.

"Can you believe those turkeys? Who ever heard of oysters from a can?" Father hissed, defending Mother, as he slammed the van door.

"Food up here tastes bland. It's like they don't use any seasoning," Mother added.

I thought it hypocritical that here was a couple who planned to eat tree bark to survive, and on the first day in Idaho, they went bonkers over oysters in a can. Father would now have to spend his limited money to buy enough land to dig a hole. In the meantime, he expected the royal treatment for those precious last dollars he shelled out.

The Idaho snow had melted in the lower altitudes, but off in the distance, we could see an occasional, white-tipped mountain peak. The day was getting late, and at this point in our exodus, we began losing track of time and days. My parents had sold their wristwatches, but time was paying us back.

"I think we should head north toward those mountains, and then we'd better find a place to lodge. We can scout out the area tomorrow," Father said, trying to appear in control as his mind scrambled for his next plan.

We were near the border of Canada and Washington State. After driving from one end of the country to the other, I wondered if he would find enough secluded woods where he'd never see another person again. If Idaho didn't work, all that was left for him to consider was Alaska, which to me, might as well have been the North Pole.

CHAPTER 9

A steady rain fell when we finally reached Sandpoint, Idaho, that evening. Locals called the area "The Great North-Wet," because when it wasn't snowing, it was usually raining, as we were about to discover. Spotting a French-style mountain chalet, Father stopped and got a room with a little kitchen in case we needed to stay a while to search for property. The chalet had a peculiar musty odor and a hideous popcorn-textured ceiling with silver glitter sprinkled all over it. *What is that stuff, Disco asbestos?* I thought to myself. A rabbit-eared television sat on a small table, and a funny lampshade made out of egg cartons with marbles stuck in the holes hung from a welded horseshoe chain. Was this dingy chalet offering us the last bit of luxury we would ever experience?

Following a decent night's sleep, I awoke to the smell of bacon cooking in the kitchen. After inhaling an appetite-suppressing cigarette and his recited prayer at the breakfast table, Father became outraged and accused me of hogging the bacon, which embarrassed me so dreadfully that I became scared to eat. I became the enemy of whatever his mind was suffering during this time. Perhaps he wanted to save the extra protein for the real men who were doing the work of hunting for our property. I should've remembered I had been raised to graciously refuse a glass of water if someone offered it.

Without inviting me, Father and Hansel left to find the nearest real estate company while Mother and Karen occupied themselves with cigarettes and the static on every television channel. The new frontier was depressingly lonely and uninhabited as I walked down the mountain highway from the chalet. I had thoroughly planned to run away this time, so I continued walking a long distance. The surroundings stayed the same: dense forest for miles and miles. I feared a grizzly bear or pack of wolves would jump out from either side of the highway and eat me, so I began to get nervous. No one was going to drive by and offer to rescue me as it was. And if they did, where could I possibly live at this point? If the authorities returned me to my parents, I feared their rage even more. How far was my father willing to go to keep me from living the life he feared?

According to Grandmother Evelyn, in September 1962, many Southerners' comfort levels heated up because Black citizens were beginning to boldly branch out and taste the rights properly extended to any American citizen. For this reason, Father had stormed off to Ole Miss University with a shotgun just because James Meredith was trying to enroll and live his best life. All mayhem had erupted on the Oxford campus, requiring federal troops and U.S. Marshals to step in amongst the carnage. The aftermath left two people dead, including French journalist Paul Guihard, who died from a gunshot wound to his back. By the time the military gained control, the protesters had grievously wounded forty-eight soldiers and twenty-eight U.S. Marshals.

Just what actions my father took when he arrived at the university is still a mystery. I'm sure he considered Meredith's enrollment, like me graduating and doing something unmanly for a living, an act of brazen insubordination. I'm sure Father fired a few shots during the bloody pandemonium. Flashing back even further, it seemed my father's mind battled something more profound than his contempt for human rights, as he spent most of his youth isolated in the woods near his home in the foothills of the Appalachian Mountains. Father was a skilled hunter and convinced many that there indeed was a Bigfoot as he tore through the hills, hoodwinking the locals. As a teen, he drove a knife through his bedroom wall when his mother forbade him to go camping with his latest girlfriend. And then he told stories about throwing a classmate out the school window, sending a mountain goat plummeting to its death, and some story about a group of friends drilling a flame-heated corkscrew down the urethra of a suspected rapist's penis.

Either way, Father was impetuous and unpredictable. He had done things I would never dream of doing. But somehow, I was the one whose soul was in danger of eternal damnation no matter how gentle and well-behaved I was—perhaps my being a boy with those attributes secretly triggered many people, especially Father. I was constantly trying to figure it out.

Feeling like a plucked chicken, I returned to the chalet and communicated with my only friend—my memoir. I couldn't journal most of my thoughts and details of my life in case my parents read my memoir, which they probably did anyway. They did have eyes in the back of their heads since before the time I found a *Playboy* magazine under the bridge beside our home and hid it under my mattress. A few days later, ten minutes before bedtime, Mother decided to swap my mattress with theirs. And then there was the time I "played doctor" with my school friends who were brother and sister. My short, overweight mother somehow managed to lean across the sink where she was washing dishes, peer straight down through the high window, and see us curious kids near the edge of the house. The shaming she gave me could melt an ice cream cone in one second.

"Wait until I tell your father what you did," she loved to say and would almost always beg him to spank me.

Then there was the time I cut the seat out of my tighty whities to see how I would look in a jockstrap before joining the football team. As if it were X-rated contraband, I hid the ruined underwear in a drawstring pouch, which usually held this annoying laughing box Father detested—until he didn't. "Ho-ho-ho! Ha-ha-ha!" He burst into my room at the butt-crack of dawn. My eyes blinked open at the sight of his hairy arm fishing around the top of my closet. To my horror, his hand honed into the exact spot where the damned thing was. Two seconds later, he ripped my makeshift jockstrap out of the pouch with a snarl. He tolerated nothing silly, so I knew he didn't want to take the gag gift to work to impress his boss, as he claimed. He and my mother were on constant surveillance for any behavior they remotely suspected to be gay. Perhaps that's why I caved in and joined the football team, to get an ass-revealing jockstrap.

Instead of writing about my plans to escape from my parents that morning, I wondered what my old classmates were doing with their freedom: Enrolling in college? Deciding what fraternities were the best? I was sure they'd think poorly of me for dropping out of school. "Dropping out" would be easier to explain to my classmates than the fact that my parents had abducted me from my life and home and carted me into the wilderness. But what would it matter? It would add an extra layer to the mystery my schoolmates saw in me. The wilderness banishment would undoubtedly live up to their expectations.

Later that afternoon, the men trudged back to the chalet from the hunt. I resolved that I would develop the savoir-faire of a Tibetan monk next time a plate of anything edible was sitting in front of me. Even though Father would put more butter on his biscuit than the size of the biscuit itself, I would be careful not to rob it of its fumes by sniffing it.

"I told the agent we'd meet 'im at the property in half an hour. It's only a little ways up the road from here, and there's a cabin already on the property," Father said, removing his baseball cap to scratch his balding head.

"Oh, goodie. I hope it has an indoor toilet!" Karen laughed between puffs of smoke and her joint popping.

We drove up the long dirt road and saw a well-built but small A-frame cabin. The inhabitants had deserted the property, and the real estate agent had not made it yet, so we climbed out of the van to have a preview. I headed straight to the cabin while Father and Hansel inspected the acreage. Not far from the cabin, down the winding dirt path, stood a cedar outhouse with license plates for roofing shingles. Upon further inspection, Hansel saw a marijuana plant growing out of the ground, which confirmed his assumption that the place had a sinister feel. Meanwhile, back at the A-frame, I noticed someone left the front door unlocked, so I called Mother and Karen to see if they thought we should go on in the building. Karen peered into the window, which only reached to her chin.

"It looks as if nobody's living here, so I don't see how it would matter," Mother said, pulling the door open and stepping inside. It was like walking into a ransacked closet with dried clumps of feces scattered on the floor, of what origin we didn't know. Also on the floor was a pair of men's white underwear. That was enough for my mother's sin-sniffing sensibility, so she said, "Let's go!"

I tittered behind Mother and Karen through the lattice invasion of vegetation. The shriek of startled birds caused Karen to lose two out of every three steps. "Aaah, what was that?" she screamed and leaped back to the van just as the agent drove up.

I kept wanting to swat the mosquitoes on Father's ears and neck, but encephalitis and malaria be damned, he wanted to show his toughness and leave them to feast. He greeted the agent and promptly told him that he had already looked over the property and that it wouldn't do.

"Come here and tell me what this is." Father went back down the path to the garden of decadence. "Is this what I thank it is?"

Taking off his sunglasses, Matt, the real estate agent, squatted down by the plant, breaking off a handful of leaves.

"Yep, it's Mary-Jo-Wanna! I don't know if you're from here, but this is the drug capital of the U.S. Marijuana growers live throughout these parts."

"Hmm, I never heard that," Father said with a frown. Hetero Heaven was a palace of pot. "But I'm a-gonna need more land than this and more privacy. I'm not interested in an existing home on the property. I'd rather build underground, so can we see something else?"

"I'm sorry to tell you, Mr. Sergent. Unless you plan on bringing in some major equipment and dynamite, you might want to reconsider building underground. These mountains have very little soil; it's almost pure rock everywhere. And on the budget you gave me I don't think you're gonna get far."

Father's chin twitched. "Well, do ya got any property with a cave?"

"Not that I know of," said Matt, taking a harder look at his property listings.

"You were wanting secluded acreage. We have a listing here which seems within your budget. Let's see … yes, the listing shows forty wooded acres on Whiteraven Mountain in Sandpoint, about an hour or so northeast. If you want, you can leave your van back at the chalet, and I'll drive you."

"Thanks. That sounds like a winner to me," replied Father, having to chalk off yet another part of his scheme to isolate me. I couldn't imagine living in a dirt hole as he had planned anyway. I thought it was disingenuous when, to save face, he relabeled his plans to burrow like foxes as merely "building underground."

"I will follow you back to the chalet, then we'll head on up to the property." Max handed Father a printout of the property listing before walking back to his truck.

After meeting back at the chalet, we all left with Matt to see the mountain property. We barely squeezed six people in his car, and within a few minutes of driving, the last signs of the farmlands were fading into the distance. We turned left onto a graveled side road, and off in the distance were several peaks rising and falling, one of which was Ruby Ridge. The weather was warmer that afternoon with a misty rain. After turning on the bumpy, winding gravel road, it was about forty minutes before we reached the base of Whiteraven Mountain. Matt paused his vehicle beside a gray metal box jutting from the weeds.

"Over there's your community mailbox. This is the end of the county-maintained road. There are no phone, water, or electric lines past this point. There are only six property owners from here on up, and everyone is responsible for maintaining the dirt road," the agent said before we entered the mouth of the mountain.

The dirt road was rough and bumpy, overcast by heavy clusters of white birch and cedar from both sides of the muddy banks of the meandering path. On rare occasions, the engulfing trees cleared out of the way while ascending the mountain, and the view was incredible. At unexpected times, the drop-off was steep and dangerous. The snow was still melting off the highest peaks, so the dirt road was soggy in places. Plush cedars obstructed one of the first properties we passed, and a tall gate nearly obscured a strange cedar construction that jutted high over the dirt bank upon lumber stilts. Behind the gate were two vicious-looking dogs barking menacingly. On the following property, nothing but the dirt entry drive was visible. Then we drove over an old log bridge that carried us over Whiteraven Creek. Soon the incline became nail-biting steep, but luckily, Matt drove a vehicle equipped for rugged terrains.

"I hope our van can make it up here!" Hansel's wide eyes angled as hard as they could to see what lay behind every turn.

"Me too," Father replied with an animated semblance of concern.

The next property was out of viewing range unless you glanced back as you passed. Up in the distance, someone had an old street sign named Sterling Avenue stuck in the ground on a wooden post just for appearance. I wouldn't have been less shocked to see a chandelier in a swamp. The next property joined the available forty-acre land we came to inspect after the three-mile mountain climb. The neighbors had built the cabin partially on the road, so we slowed down beside it to see what they had to offer. A vertical timber shed shoddily connected to a small travel trailer. As we shuddered from the debacle before us, out came a witchy-haired woman. Following her were seven barefoot kids in tattered clothes. Her eyes hardened on the new intruders. The welcome committee creeped us out, but our attention turned to the next road entry.

"Well, here we are, Mr. Sergent." Matt pointed out the beginning of the property line.

Passing through the overgrown tree-lined entry, a swamp obstructed the road as we made our way around the next curve. Matt parked in front of the swamp to avoid getting stuck. "We'll have to walk the rest of the way; the rain has washed out the road from here."

After stepping carefully out of Matt's car to avoid sinking in the mud, everyone moved to the highest edge of the road where it was dryer, and then we walked on ahead.

"Mosquitoes are the state bird here." Matt swatted the air around his head with his hand.

"I've never seen hummingbirds get this close to humans before," Hansel told the agent.

"Well, we definitely have a lot of them here, too," Matt replied.

"Are we the last property on the mountain?" Father asked.

"According to my map, there is one more north of this one. Their last name is Hedgpeth, and—"

Father pulled the agent to the side to have a whispered conversation about the mountain residents. I gathered enough from the exchange to realize he was concerned about the people I might have access to.

"… No, the Hedgpeths come up from California once a year and stay for a month or two. They have a trailer, but you can't see their place from here, Mr. Sergent."

"Do you know if there's a well or lake on this property?" Father asked the agent while he inspected the swamp on the road.

"Not that I know of, and the creek doesn't pass through these forty acres either. But from the looks of this standing water, I would suspect there's an underground spring somewhere in the vicinity if you dig deep enough," the agent said as we walked to the eastern border next to the Hedgpeths' property. The altitude was the highest point on Whiteraven. The distant mountains resembled some enchanted far-off islands.

"Oh, man! This view would be incredible if we cut down these trees. We could build a cabin right here, Hansel," Father said assuredly, though I could not see my reflection in the snow-covered hills the way they were seeing the majestic grandeur in a mountaintop of bushes. But I was becoming more hopeful that we wouldn't all have to squeeze inside a hole or head to the North Pole.

"You will be getting a great deal on this much mountain property. We rarely get a prime listing such as this, because mountain property is becoming scarce," Matt said while Father stood contemplating the view.

Upon hiking the entire perimeter of the forty acres, which consisted of four mountain peaks and valleys, the journey seemed like four hundred acres. Father broke his limber vow, turned to Matt, and said, "We'll take it, I guess."

CHAPTER 10

THE next day after purchasing the forty acres, Father and Hansel were ready to build the gay-conversion camp. After buying a chainsaw and all the necessary hand tools and supplies, we made the twenty-five-mile drive from town to the base of Whiteraven Mountain. We first checked to see if our mailbox key worked, then we ascended the narrow dirt road, dodging ruts and potholes like bullets in a warzone. The three-mile climb took an eternity because of this.

Less than one mile up, the van became stuck in a mud hole. Everyone climbed out of the van except Mother, and we all pushed as she hit the gas pedal, covering us in mud. I cannot remember how we finally got unstuck, but as soon as we did, we spent the next hour or so hauling rocks and stones off the side of the road to fill in the mud holes until we could get a culvert and bury it in the road right over the mud pit.

Although we had only ascended halfway up the mountain, these exhausting efforts wrought no appreciation from the other mountain residents. After several road patches, the van finally reached our property. The rain was unrelenting, yet before the van could pass over to the other side of our land, we had to put in another culvert to drain off the swamp that had accumulated.

As for the time to adapt, it was indeed upon us that first day when we realized we would no longer be taking hot baths to wash off the mud and grime. "Cold showers keep fleshly temptations away," my parents had instructed me since puberty. Father determined where he would keep the boxy van parked, and then we pitched a tent in front of it. The rain came and went periodically as we began setting up the campsite. We stretched a plastic tarp over the posts, making a protective roof to have a fire while it was raining. On the back of the van, we used more of the blue tarp to wall in a small area so we could sponge bathe with privacy. We placed a small travel toilet seat over a shallow hole we dug until we could mine out a more permanent outhouse.

The first night we roasted hotdogs on the fire for dinner. We heated our bath water in a metal bucket over the campfire and took our first lukewarm sponge bath in the night air filled with mosquitoes, embracing dust with every wipe of the common washcloth. Occasionally a strong wind would catch the bare bones of the makeshift bathroom when we were sponge bathing or squatting on the portable toilet. It couldn't be better than being on a nudist beach in a hurricane.

My parents started sleeping in the tent after that first night while Hansel, Karen, and I slept in the utility van. Hansel was always trying to snatch my pants and underwear down when I had my arms full, or he was still trying to bite me. Every time I would near sleep, he kept shining the flashlight at me—no care being for our limited battery supply. I was too exhausted to give him a show. Hansel, however, was wound up like a seven-day clock and probably wanted me to sleep out in the woods to give him and Karen sex time. I sure as hell wasn't sleeping in the tiny tent with my parents.

Exhaustion still gripped us the next morning, yet soon after breakfast, we started searching for a water source. Instead of prayer, Father went the old-fashioned divination route, carrying around a water-witching stick he had fashioned from a tree branch but to no advantage. We logically dug to the side of the road where the most water puddled.

With every strike of the shovel and pickaxe against stone, we eventually hand-chiseled twenty feet below the earth's surface, excavating many large boulders. After water began to fill the dig, we lifted and dropped giant concrete rings down the deep well to hold in the water. Everything was bleak at this point in my life. Endless days of chopping bushes, misty rain, and mud wore on us like a cold, wet shroud.

"What they need to do is send Boy George up here, and I can make a real man of him," Father had said when he discovered I still had a photo of the singer in his frock, bowler hat, and beribboned braids. I was sickened at his hostility and what he might do to a human who wasn't hurting anyone. It was yet another warning of what he might do to me. At least his plans to get us all hopelessly lost in the wilderness where I couldn't leave had failed.

The rainy season was finally easing up, and we needed food and supplies. Going to town for something as simple as toothpaste was a big adventure but seeing any semblance of civilization was refreshing. Even though it was only about sixty miles round trip, it would take half a day's travel because of the rugged mountain passage. I tried memorizing the roads and area for whenever I worked up the nerve to run away.

The following week we began clearing off the trees and underbrush. Father and Hansel were the official chainsaw operators, while I was given a handsaw, hatchet, and machete. Mother and Karen gathered the cut underbrush and smaller tree limbs and put them in a pile I burned as we went along. Occasionally sparks from the fire drifted far from the clearing, igniting a small blaze, which I would quickly pound out with a shovel and dirt. Because of the trees and high winds, fires were a potential hazard in the Rocky Mountains, especially in the dry season. Father did not want to rent a backhoe or any mechanical equipment; he wanted to do things the long, cheap, and manly way. Along with all the chopping and hauling, the flames from the fire and the sun's smoldering rays were taking a toll on me.

"Milan, quit being lazy and get to work; you aren't doing your part," Father yelled from up the hill.

"Yes, I am!" I shouted, lamenting the day I was born.

"Don't use that tone of voice with me. I oughta knock your teeth out! We're busting our asses off, and you haven't done anything!" Father yelled. His eyes were icy steel, and I resented him more than ever. The men appeared to be doing much more work because they were chain-sawing trees down everywhere. The gas-powered blade did most of the work for them while I had to use a hatchet and hack the trees to death. Father didn't consider me man enough to use the power tools, but I was not woman enough to gather sticks with Karen, who occasionally came out of the van from her romance novel breaks.

"I talked to Rowan and told 'im that he was bein' way too hard on you," Hansel said, feeling a tinge of empathy later that afternoon.

"He's always been this way, Hansel. We've never gotten along, and I'm tired of him yelling at me. But that's going to change soon because I'm going to leave," I replied, gazing up at Hansel with misty eyes under cover of a shade tree.

"Where are you going to stay?" Hansel asked, keeping his voice down so Father wouldn't know he was splitting allegiance.

"I might hitchhike to San Francisco and stay at the YMCA," I replied, stirring the dusty dirt with a stick as if I were reading my fate in tea leaves.

"You can't go to San Francisco. That's where all the gay people live," said Hansel.

"So! They aren't going to hurt me," I said. *How dare Hansel tell me what I can't do.* He was turning into my father more every day, prying into my sexuality.

Evening came with a welcome relief as we all sponge-bathed and had campfire cuisine. Father asked me to have a seat beside him near the fire, which I reluctantly did. He appeared sedentary and stiff-necked, gazing straight into the woods from his lawn chair.

"Son, I realize that I've probably been a little hard on you at times, but someday when I'm dead and gone, you're gonna understand why I had to be as tough as I have been with you. I always thought my dad was hard on me and my brother, but after he passed away, I saw why he did things the way he did. And I regret ever causing him any sorrow."

"Your father made you boys stop bickering by forcing you to put on boxing gloves and beat one another until one of you knocked the other out cold," I hissed, stunned that he would justify his father's abusive discipline—actions that would rightfully send my grandfather back to prison.

With eyes still refusing to look at me, Father smirked as though I was an imbecile. "Mark my words, Son: you and me are gonna have our golden years someday," Father's words drifted with the smoke from the fire.

"After all these years, we'll never get along," I muttered, rather pleased at my growing lack of fear of him.

"Oh yes, we will, Son. Yes, we will."

Sure, I thought. *Someday when I see the light and become mesmerized by your primitive breed, I'll realize that the years of terror and contention I endured were entirely my fault. And that tragic day, you'll be smiling down from the clouds with your buddy, Jesus, while I'm crying over your sadistic but sanctified corpse in the coffin.*

After receiving my talking to, I grabbed my memoir and pen, and what little money I had, and decided to walk down the mountain, and then I would keep walking in hopes I'd be brave enough to leave my abductors finally. Halfway down, I spotted the white bark on the birch trees starting to pull loose. The pages of my memoir had grown scarce, but I figured the paper-thin white bark should work well enough. I peeled a sliver of the bark and on it wrote a letter to my grandmother in Jackson. I was delighted to tell her that Father's "plans had changed," and we actually had a mailing address, which I carefully wrote down. I remembered Stewart Cully, who lives on the farm across from the community mailbox. "If you ever need anything, just let me know," he had told my family. "Just let me know …."

Appealing to Grandma is better than running away and the risks involved if I do that, I concluded and walked to the farmhouse at the base of the mountain. I asked Mrs. Cully if I could buy a stamp and an envelope from her, which she agreed to. Stewart raised goats and, like a mischievous candy man, fed them confections to sweeten their milk. He said the mountain residents often parked their vehicles on his property during the long dreadful winters. With a breath of promise, I dropped the letter in the mail slot and hoped it would reach Grandma.

The six-mile mountain trudge proved difficult for my city legs, so it was dark before I made it back up and spotted Hansel a half mile from the camp.

"Milan! I thought you ran away or got lost."

Father and I still weren't talking much the next day while sitting around the campsite. All seemed calm until two large dogs charged toward us within a heart-stopping moment. Janis Joplin and a David Lee Roth clone came running over the hill next, franticly chasing after the bloodthirsty mutts.

After managing to restrain the beasts, they introduced themselves as the Hedgpeths and said they lived in the mobile home beside us. Father acknowledged that our real estate agent had mentioned them. It didn't take long to learn the middle-aged couple was Bob Dylan-loving hippies from California. They embellished every other sentence with an annoying whistle before adding, "Primo, man!"

"I'd better warn you guys," said Mrs. Hedgpeth with a mischievous grin. "Be careful while walking through the woods. My husband occasionally goes down to the base of the mountain in the nude. He loves to bathe in a waterhole he dug at the bottom of our property."

Father's face shriveled in several deep ridges. I'm sure he knew I had every intention of accidentally wandering near the valley where garments thrived not, though I never saw Mr. Hedgpeth or any naked man. Hansel and I did sneak onto their property to see what the couple had spent so much time building. We expected a large structure of a home after their many trips and the endless hammering, but all they had built was a tiny outhouse on the edge of the mountain cliff. A charming cedar-shingled outhouse lined with silver Asian wallpaper. They had embellished the walls and toilet with incense bottles, chimes, and a little Buddha statute. This brought back a memory of Father grabbing a hammer and smashing a red Buddha statue to bits in the garage. It had taken him a while to learn it was the image of a god in India, but the smashing of the plaster absolved him of the mistake he imagined.

"Man, Milan, do you suppose they sit in here to meditate?" asked Hansel. In the narrow outhouse that afternoon, his body rubbed against me, making me weak. I quickly stepped outside and blamed the incense for making me nauseous.

The next time I saw Mrs. Hedgpeth, she began asking me personal questions while singing the praises of Bob Dylan. Strangely she felt a need to warn me about trusting gay people.

"They'll lead you down some very dark paths," she said. I felt sure my parents had encouraged her to fill my head with vicious nonsense.

CHAPTER 11

A FTER being on the mountain for just two weeks, we annihilated all the trees and underbrush, including their large roots, around the area the size of a football field where Father planned to build the cabin. My family had also uprooted me but hadn't succeeded at annihilating my sexuality.

About this time, a mountain resident named Alan Rogers came to see who the newest refugees were. A clean-cut married man in his early forties, he had two adorable little girls around the age of nine. The Rogers claimed they were home-schooling the girls, and though they had not lived on Whiteraven long, they were planning to move to Alaska to get even more remote.

More remote than this? Secretly I already resented Alan. He and his wife might choose to throw away their lives by hiding in the wilderness, but his daughters were too young and voiceless to have a decent future snatched from them. The fullness of how my parents had done the same to me flooded my awareness. *Some parents refuse to see their children as individuals with unique personalities and screw it if their kids have their own preferences and belief systems.* Father shook Alan's hand as though he was digging another foundation hole.

"Nice to meet you, Alan. Do you know where I can find any hardwood trees in this area? I need to get the cabin built before winter. All of the trees I see on this here mountain are dadburn softwood." Father folded his arms with that returning expression of defeat.

"I'm not sure if you know this," said Alan, wrinkling his forehead. "But you can't use a freshly cut tree to build anything. You'll have to wait at least six months for the logs to season, and winter will be here before your logs will be through drying."

"I'll be dern." Father ripped off his baseball cap with a snort. He didn't have the money to buy seasoned logs at this point, and his plans for living in a hole had fallen through as well as permanently hiding his weird son in the wilderness. I knew I would have to keep at a safe distance even more now.

"There's a way around it if you don't mind the looks," said Alan.

Father straightened his slumped posture, and Hansel's eyes stopped blinking. "What's that?"

"It's called 'The Burn.'" Alan smiled reluctantly.

"The Burn?" asked Father.

"Most residents on Whiteraven pay a small fee and cut their own trees from a mountain site called The Burn just thirty miles from here." Alan leaned forward and pointed westward. "The trees there caught fire years earlier, and all the bark was burned off. Now the trees are dead, and they're softwood, but the low humidity here has preserved them. If you want to, you can take a look at my cabin and see the logs I'm talking about. They're not pretty, but I saved a whole lot of time and money using the burned logs."

Father definitely found an interest in saving money and didn't need to consult God first. Soon we arrived back from viewing Alan's small one-room cabin built with hideously cracked and knotty logs turned upright, so the silver-gray logs were vertical instead of in the usual horizontal position. Father and Hansel announced that we would build our cabin with the same ugly timber.

We leveled about fifteen hundred square feet of dirt and rock and then dug thirty deep foundation holes, which we filled with concrete. To ensure the foundation was perfectly level, Father bought pre-cured foundation beams to build the floor framing. To haul logs and supplies, he purchased a used truck but wouldn't allow me to drive it in case I might use it to escape.

Drawing of me holding on for dear life.

Daybreak was beginning to expand on the mountain horizon when we reached The Burn, as Alan had called it. We scoped out the seared wood with sleepy eyes, searching for the best trees to cut on the steep incline. Father and Hansel chainsawed the timber in eight-foot lengths, and I was responsible for heaving them on my shoulder and up the mountainside to dump them on the truck. Some of the logs were so large in diameter that I couldn't reach my long arms around them. Fallen trees littered the steep mountainside and occasionally, I became trapped under a pile of logs after losing my footing. I felt like the proverbial needle in the haystack.

By the time I piled as many logs onto the back of the truck as it would carry, I had the duty of riding on top of the massive stack that was higher than the cab roof. After many trips to The Burn, I overcame my fear of deadly heights, holding on tightly atop the log pyramid as the truck teetered along the steep mountain. Though I was only eighteen, I realized I would never put a son of mine in this sort of danger. But with Father's "beliefs," a dead virgin son was better than a living gay son. In fact, Hansel had almost killed me after driving off the mountain cliff his first time behind the wheel. When I managed to crawl out the driver's window, a man passing through eventually found us. After a trip for the right equipment, the man lifted the truck from the first ledge it had landed upon. If the trees had not been in the way, I would've fallen to my death. But I was inside the truck cab at that time. I'd be dead if I were clinging to the tall pyramid of logs as I was at The Burn.

As the air grew thinner on those repeat trips, so did my respect for my father. I was sure I had enough experience to try champion bull riding after I survived the long ride back to camp. We dumped the logs near the building site, had a campfire dinner, and crawled into dusty sleeping bags.

During the next few days of the timber excursions, Mother and Karen remained at the campsite chatting and hand washing the laundry. While we had been wandering across the country, huge black ants nested in our clothes at some point and had chewed holes through most of my garments.

Ants were a nuisance in northern Idaho. One day, while I was working near the cabin site, the faint hissing of dried grass made my nerves crawl. I glanced up the cliff to see a foot-wide path snaking for yards through the tall grass. A menacing army of ants marched by, carrying little sticks to add to their mound. Having no insecticide available and fearing for my remaining clothes, I set fire to their nest.

Father couldn't wait until we finished the cabin before he went hunting. After he killed his first bear, we had the enormous challenge of dragging it back to the camp. He skinned and gutted the bear while Mother cooked large portions of the animal over the campfire. The meat was heavy and difficult to chew. Unfortunately, they could not eat that much beef before it ruined in the warm weather. I was growing sick of red meat by then, and after Father's last tantrum, I was determined to eat less than my equal share at mealtime. However, I found that even this infuriated my dad.

"Your mother worked hard preparing this meal, and you act so damn finicky, Milan. I don't know why you can't be gracious and eat like the rest of us!"

On one of his many quests for food sources, Father learned of a local man who only ate a natural organic cereal recipe that he believed was the fountain of youth and spiritual power. Father thought he would try the new diet that required him to quit coffee and cigarettes cold turkey. Without his nerve tranquilizers, I feared his wrath even more and kept my distance from him. However, he only lasted a few hours until withdrawal symptoms set in. Yet this was only the beginning of our new dietary practices. One afternoon, on the open fire, Father was boiling a wicked lather that smelled like rancid shoe polish and resembled shriveled lizards. He had spent the entire morning breaking the tops off the fiddle-neck fern that grew wild on the mountain to eat for lunch, but it tasted so awful even he couldn't stand it—a man who once ate hog brains and eggs for breakfast. His first near-death experience in his wilderness escape was when he consumed poisonous mushrooms by mistake. I was glad this was the first time he didn't force me to prove my manhood and eat them as well. He started foaming at the mouth, and his heart stopped beating dangerously too long, but it curbed his plans to eat tree bark and live off the land—at least for a day or so.

The soil was not conducive for any type of garden, and with the wolves, coyotes, and other wild beasts all over the place, Father gave up on keeping livestock on the mountain. I was always relieved some beast hadn't made a meal of me every time I trudged the three miles to and from the mailbox. Death was worth the risk of hearing back from my grandmother. It was like Christmas and my birthday combined when I opened the door to the mailbox and found a package from her. She had mailed me a year's supply of stamps, writing paper, and envelopes, along with a twelve-page letter I read as I walked back to the campsite, trying not to trip over stones and holes in the dirt road. Her heart was aflame, knowing she could trace us to a physical address.

"Dear Grandson, I'm so thrilled. I did not expect to hear from you all again. I thought I had said my last goodbyes back in April."

America's Independence Day had arrived but not mine. I awoke to a commotion in the camp. Rancid odor permeated the thin air as I overheard chatter outside the utility van.

Father had caught a skunk.

He had set primitive traps, hoping to ensnare the monster pilfering around the camp at night, seeking food. I leaped into my outworn shoes, flung the van door open, and ran up the dirt road as far as possible before taking my next breath. Everyone else had adjusted to the stench and was sitting around the campfire, feasting on a haunch of venison. They laughed at me until tears were in their eyes, but the tears may have been from the foul skunk scent.

That same morning a cold front blew in, and a few snowflakes fell. We were in for a brutal and binding winter since it was snowing on the Fourth of July. With the same realization, Father had a greater urgency to finish the cabin's construction.

That afternoon the wind continued to ripple as the pageantry of the birch trees whipped at the mosquitoes. Between the trees, the lumpy figure of a man came limping up the road toward our camp.

"Hi-ya, I'm Mike Busby, and I live on the property just before the split in the road. I hear you guys just moved here from Missouri."

"Mississippi, yeah. I always wanted to move to the mountains and leave the rat race behind," Father repeated his cover story, resting his shovel on the ground to shake hands with the intruder, yet another person violating his "never see another human" plan.

"I became disabled after moving my family here six years ago, and now I am glad I don't have all the utility bills to pay for," Mike continued.

I had seen Mike's wife and six small children hauling food and supplies up the mountain stretch. If disability truly affected him, I found it amusing that he managed to make his rounds all over Whiteraven Creek to socialize. Mike filled us in on all the mountain folks: The Portmans, who had built the tiny cabin over the trailer on the edge of our property, home-birthed all their children and had butchered a home circumcision on one of their boys.

"Yep, they gave 'im a frilly dilly," said Mike. "Do you wanna know something else? They feed their kids canned dog food. They're very private people. I never see them leave their property, and I don't think they even homeschool their kids. Edsel Portman's wife is a nut case, so if I were you, I'd stay clear of her."

"Yeah, we sorta got that impression when we first drove up to the property," Hansel chimed in as he and Father listened intently to Mike's synopsis of the mountain residents, seeming relieved there had been no mention of any gays. Mother and Karen emerged from the van, and Mike's demeanor became more dramatic and formidable.

"Now let me warn you guys: There is a town just over these mountains called Stonevengeance. Do not drive through there, especially at night. Rumor has it that folks have come up missing or were found dead there from a ritual sacrifice." Mike shook his head as if he had chills.

Father looked on with disbelief. A tight-lipped smirk formed on the side of his face. "I assume this has been reported in the local news."

"The news? Nah. As far as I know, nobody on Whiteraven Creek gets a newspaper or has a television. The local authorities don't want to get involved. Some think it's a coven of witches," Mike said.

I couldn't believe my ears. *Could there be witches way up here in the mountains?* Mother excused herself when she heard the mention of wicked witches, followed swiftly by Karen, who needed a cigarette. Father grabbed up his shovel. *Was he ready to dig a grave?* He was a firm believer in the Bible, even the part where God's people weren't supposed to suffer a witch to live. Since America was in the middle of the Satanic Panic, I'm sure he thought over half of the country should either be put to death or isolated.

Mike focused his attention on Hansel while avoiding as much as a glance at me. I was becoming paranoid because men always seemed to have difficulty making eye contact with me, even the rare moments when I was the only one speaking.

"... Just last week, a friend of my wife's sister was driving through Stonevengeance on her way to Spokane, Washington. She made a wrong turn around ten thirty at night and wound up on a rural back road. When she turned around, several of the residents formed a line across the road, and they were carrying garden hoes, axes, and such. Then as the witches started to attack the woman's car, she hit the gas pedal, running over, and crushing one of the attackers. When she got to the next town, she called the sheriff, and after they went back to the exact spot where she ran over the attacker, the witches were gone along with the body! Oh, and if you aren't careful, the wildlife up here will attack. A man was driving up Whiteraven the other day, and a huge moose was standing in the middle of the road. He waited for the animal to move but grew impatient and honked his horn. The moose charged his car and damaged it so badly you'd think a giant can opener ripped it down the middle."

Mike wiped his glasses on his shirt, pleased to get a reaction from Father. He squinted to see if the glasses were smudge-free before placing them back on his balding head. Father's hard-life forehead formed six deep ridges. He readjusted his cap and rested his right foot on the shovel as he leaned slightly forward, wiping the sweat from his face. Mike seemed uneasy with Father's silence and soon hobbled off to the next available ear.

I read about witches existing in the olden days, but the prospect of witches wandering this far into the wilderness didn't concern me. I suppose because I had already seen so many lies and exaggerations that people had used to demonize and encourage animosity toward people they feared and hated. Never mind legends of evil broom flyers, why didn't my parents or at least one conscientious individual from my church or schools teach me to fear the people who roasted witches alive on bonfires instead—or at least fear the people who are still indifferent to the fact?

CHAPTER 12

THAT autumn, the towering mountain birch turned sunny golden yellow and crimson. Occasionally when wandering over Whiteraven, the trees parted their curtains, and the sun glistened across the rolling bluffs. The oppression eased during times such as this.

Stewart Cully's pride and joy was his granddaughter, Piper. She occasionally burned dirt on her motorcycle trips up and down Whiteraven. Her mousy brown afro offset her freckled face and razor-stubble on her chin. Her John Wayne gait evolved from an injury sustained after spinning off the cliffs of Whiteraven on her motorcycle. I knew my parents hoped that I would find a love match with the only female I had met since I left the Deep South. But there was a far greater chance I would deliberately eat poisonous mushrooms instead.

"After a few months in the mountains, Milan will make love with a grizzly bear!" Father said when the pairing attempt went nowhere. I always felt confused, defenseless, and violated when he made such comments in front of others. Bestiality jokes contradicted the Christian crusade for which he intended to isolate me, especially when he had beaten me at eight years of age for playing doctor with a girl and the innocent curiosity all children have.

After near completion of the cabin, it resembled a walled fortress, a gloomy prison, and in many ways, it was. Wherever Father became inclined to put in a window, he and Hansel carved out a square opening in the log walls with the chainsaw. Surprisingly, he didn't insist on a window facing the eastern skies. The tin roof we constructed at a steep pitch so when it snowed, it would not accumulate and put too much weight on the structure. Underneath the cabin, we collected a few cats that someone had abandoned. The terrain was deadly for humans and pets, and they were becoming more aggressive to survive. I brought out a plate of raw meat from either Hansel's or Father's recent kills, and our surviving cats raced up my legs and chest to get to the bloody flesh. I flung the meat on the deck to get the cats off me.

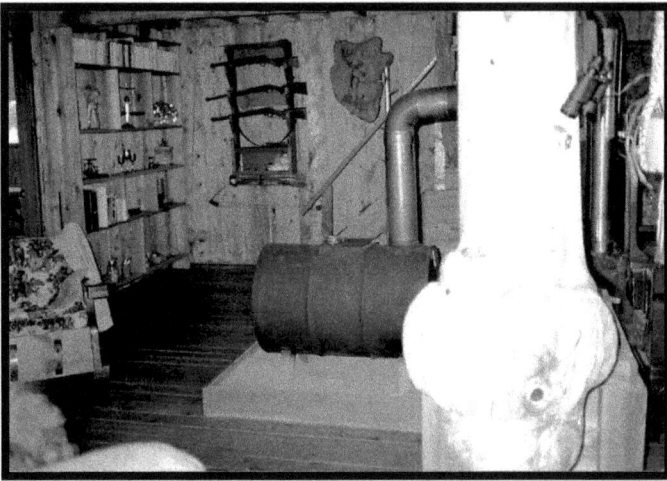

Inside the log prison.

As soon as we moved out of the van and tent, we had lived in for five months and into the cabin, we hastened any necessities. The air grew colder, signaling the coming winter. In the last fleeting weeks of October, we built a woodshed, converted a fifty-five-gallon steel drum into a wood heater, and bought an old wood-burning cook stove. We also built a cedar outhouse with a little window overlooking the mountains. One of our kittens fell into the bottom of the outhouse. Not knowing how else to rescue the little fur baby, I lowered a huge cedar board down into the sewage hole, the kitten climbed onto the end, and I pulled her to safety. The kitten started hemorrhaging, which attracted yellow jackets to the blood. The bees were torturing the poor kitten, so Father put her out of her misery.

I made a sign and nailed it to a birch tree at the entry to the property: "To heck with the dog, beware of the people!" This was my SOS, my cry for help, I suppose. No one could be trusted. The police arrested two of Whiteraven's residents that afternoon for running an amphetamine lab. According to the sparse locals, the perpetrators had manufactured enough chemical substances to blow up the entire mountain. Father nearly got the Armageddon he was most eager to have to guarantee my soul got to Heaven, but the damned police ruined his plans.

Not long after we settled in the cabin, my parents' money dwindled dangerously low. "We have supported Milan long enough. It's time he finds a job and starts supporting us," Mother said to Father as if I weren't standing there. Most of their manipulations of me were spoken in the third person. Mother was only thirty-six and fully capable of supporting herself but always acted as if she needed to prepare her lengthy obituary.

Even though I had not found a moment's rest since Father chose to settle on Whiteraven, I had a surge of expectations. Finding employment might be my only chance to get away and live a normal life.

Whenever we went into the five rooms of our newly built log prison, we automatically reached for a light switch, forgetting that we did not have electricity. This one simple gesture brought back memories of civilization. The same thing also went for the outhouse when we would occasionally try to flush, but there was no flusher or water, just yellow jackets and wasps that we hoped didn't sting our exposed bottoms before we finished doing our business. The only time I was glad we were so secluded was when high winds blew the outhouse off its foundation, and there on the toilet sat my father with his pants down to his ankles.

The beehive outhouse.

The next morning, I awoke to what I thought was fog on the ground, but it was low-lying clouds drifting through the forest clearing. Father, Hansel, and I journeyed to the unemployment agency in the town of Sandpoint to see what jobs were available.

"I want to work at one of the stores in the town mall or a bookstore," I said, wanting something that wasn't designed to prove my manhood.

Father's neck stiffened and, without acknowledging anything I had mentioned, selected a job for the two of us where he could keep me in his sight and continue his plan to make a straight man out of me. He accepted a factory job where we shoveled and bagged brown coal, also known as lignite. Hansel got a job at the local newspaper company, and Karen eventually became a waitress at a pastry shop. When I got back up the mountain in the evening, I couldn't wait to clean the coal dust from my ears and nostrils.

After the demand for work ceased at the lignite plant, Hansel and I, along with meddlesome Mike Busby, took the van to Bridgeport, Washington. An apple orchard there needed apple pickers. Along with the immigrants, we slept in the apartments on the property and spent the entire day on top of rickety three-legged ladders with large sacks strapped over our shoulders to collect the apples.

Tensions were high, and pay was low within our depressed group. As Hansel enjoyed doing, Mike played a joke by throwing freezing water on me when I was in the communal shower. When I played the prank on him, it made him furious. I never understood why there was always a double standard when I returned a favor: After growing tired of Hansel trying to snatch my pants and underwear down, he called me a pervert when I finally attempted to expose his nakedness. That night with both Hansel and Mike pissed at me, I left them in the orchard apartment while they were drinking and playing cards. I was going to get some quiet sleep in the van. An hour later, without warning (the pervert's manner, I imagined) the van door flung open, jarring me from my restful slumber.

"You came over here in *my* van, and if you don't straighten up your attitude, then you can just walk back to Idaho!"

"I don't know what you're talking about; the van belongs to my dad," I replied, puzzled as to why Hansel had become so territorial over the old child-abduction wagon.

"No, he sold it to me. It belongs to me," Hansel answered, tapping his chest smugly.

I realized at that moment that Father had given him the van for helping build the cabin and couldn't bring himself to tell me that only real men deserved compensation for it. As though I had bedded down in a rent-by-the-hour hotel near a military base, Mike then barged into the van, drunk as well.

"Hansel and Karen are still newly married, and newlyweds need privacy because they make noise when they have sex," said Mike with a huff.

I was speechless as to what in the bloody hell I had to do with Hansel's sex problems. What did he want me to do, leave the cabin so he could fully take my place as my parents' son? He and Karen chose to move to the mountains and, like a jar of earthworms on a permanent fishing trip, squeeze in a hole in the ground with my family.

"Look, dude, when you first moved into our home in Jackson, I generously shared my bedroom with you. Besides, before you got married, you and Karen left our house almost nightly to screw. So why am I in the way now?" I bitterly wanted to say.

The next day I hit bottom emotionally. Wanting to avoid Hansel and Mike, I stayed at the orchard while everyone else drove back to Sandpoint for some weekend sex with their wives. Not long after the van drove off, I walked forever down the highway, determined never to turn back. By night I was exhausted and worried about where I would sleep other than on the side of the highway. The area was so desolate. I crossed the road, and a man thought I was hitchhiking, so he offered me a ride. At that point, I didn't care if the truck driver was a serial killer, so I climbed into the passenger seat.

"Where are you headed?" he asked.

"I don't know—to the nearest tote-sum store, I guess," I responded out of hunger.

"A what?" From the man's wrinkled forehead, he seemed to regret offering me a lift. After some explanation, I assumed that only in Mississippi did people call convenience stores tote-sum stores. As fickle fate would have it, he took me to a gas station not far from the apple orchard, so I slept in the workers' apartment.

The following day, I tried to make an escape in a different direction and walked through the Washington orchards until it seemed the shadows of the fruit trees were swallowing me up. Eventually, I came to a dead end at the Bridgeport Dam, which the town had fenced off, putting a long, deep barrier in my path. The orchards ended at the dam, and it was there that I found the irony; I was damned, damned for being gay. At that moment, I was in the Garden of Eden when the serpent tempted Adam and Eve with the fruit of the knowledge of good and evil. *For when they both did eat, it opened their eyes, and God damned them for all eternity.* There I was, standing beside the most beautiful tree at the farthest point in the orchards, an isolated tree loaded with beautiful plump fruit, which I assumed were figs. The limbs hung to the ground in the shape of a weeping willow. I walked underneath the tree, totally hidden beneath its protective branches. The fruit was the most delicious I had ever eaten.

I spent the afternoon there until the sun was starting to set. I could not get across the dam, so I ambled farther through the orchards. Soon Hansel called my name in the distance; I collapsed under an apple tree to avoid detection. He had caught a view of me under the tree, and as he lifted the branch, his oily face was covered in sweat.

"Milan, you scared me! I thought you ran away or something. I feel bad for acting the way I did the other day. I don't know what came over me. I was drunk and felt like you wouldn't understand."

Perhaps the forbidden fruit had done its job. I saw through Hansel as if he were glass, and I understood completely why he had vented at me the other day. He had been afraid to confront Father, so I was the next easy target. I think he and Karen had assumed that wilderness living would be carefree, and they would never again have to work for a living. And now they were forced to seek employment back in the wicked metropolitan world that Father had promised to flee for the redemption of my soul. Father had gifted the van to Hansel out of guilt, but Hansel's drunken gripe session with meddlesome Mike had convinced him that he needed to get his independence as well. But with my stupid feelings for Hansel, especially seeing him kneeling humbly in front of me under the apple tree, I could not let him suffer.

"Hansel, it's not you. It's me. I'm … not like other guys. There is something wrong with me." I lost control of my emotions and wept. I decided to confess my secret to him but couldn't bring myself to say that I was gay.

"I know what Rowan has been trying to do with you, Milan. Karen and I have reached our limit with him," Hansel confessed, along with something from his childhood that assured me the three-letter word I couldn't say wasn't a big deal to him.

Upon returning to the cabin in Sandpoint, I gave Mother my entire paycheck from the seasonal work at the orchards. Hansel and Karen moved into town so they could be closer to their jobs and have privacy. My parents saw no need for personal privacy. Yet strangely, right after Hansel and Karen moved, Father took their bedroom upstairs, leaving Mother alone in her bedroom downstairs.

CHAPTER 13

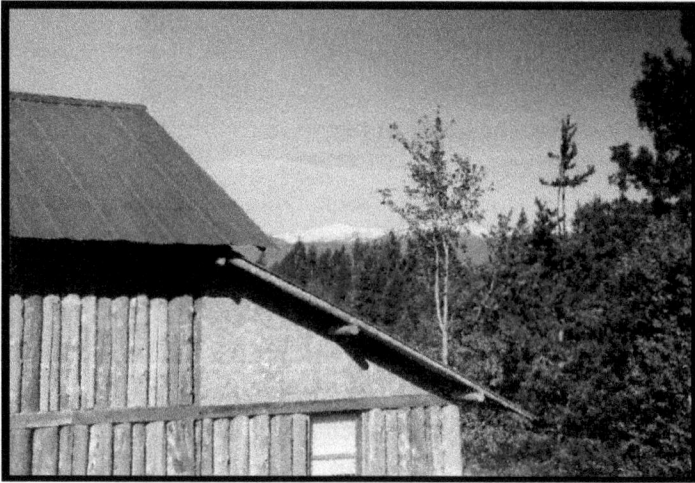

Front of cabin and distant snow-capped mountains.

THE last week of October arrived, bringing snow. Everyone gazed with enthusiasm because we had never experienced significant snow in Mississippi, and it was strange having a white Halloween. It became impossible to get to town daily, so we could not maintain employment. We stocked enough non-perishable food to hold us over for a couple of months.

One afternoon, while Father was off hunting, a curious-looking man with a long beard and a beanie cap sneaked up on Mother and me while we were outside shoveling a path through the snow to the outhouse.

"Hello, I'm Martin Pollard. I live in a tower over on the next mountain. I have a telescope in the top room, and I often see you on your property here, so I thought I'd come and introduce myself."

Mother invited him inside the cabin, but I kept thinking, *who is this pervert who has the nerve to confess he has been spying on us?* I held back my uneasiness, especially after I had a few private moments naked on a sunny mountaintop between our property and his.

"Did you build the tower yourself?" Mother asked hospitably.

"I did. And all I have to do is wave my hand in front of the doorway, and the doors automatically open." The man also said he was a Quaker and didn't say much else before excusing himself to leave.

I remembered thinking he had made a long trip for such a short and creepy greeting. Later that day, Father returned from his hunting trip earlier than expected and appeared as if he had seen a ghost.

"What came of your hunting plans? I thought you were going to be hunting all weekend?" Mother asked him.

"You ain't gonna believe what happened to me!" Father said.

"Well, are you going to tell me or not?" Mother asked, still uneasy after the peeping Quaker had left.

"I arrived about halfway around the second ridge on the mountain and walked upon this huge brown bear, so I aimed my rifle at him in case I had to defend myself. Then the bear rose up on his hind legs and put his front paws together as if he was praying, and then he started whining as if he was begging me not to shoot him."

Mother stood there with her mouth open, obviously stunned, her laughter a delayed release from the day's earlier amusement. With the animal's behavior, which Father was describing, I wondered if he hadn't encountered the legendary Bigfoot. Though I wouldn't dare suggest such a thing to a man who tolerated nothing beyond his comfort zone of beliefs, for then, it would automatically be a lie or unnatural. To him, a bear that prays was more believable than a hairy man trapped midway on the evolutionary charts.

"This beats all I've ever seen, Brigitte. It got the best of me. I lost all desire to shoot anything." Father grimaced ruefully.

He wasn't one for fantastic tales, and he wasn't afraid of bears. Mother was worried, however, especially after she ran back to the cabin and locked the door when a brown bear chased after her while she was drawing water at the well.

Father placed his gun back on the rack, but I mistrusted that he was capable of any real change of heart.

CHAPTER 14

WITH the snow accumulating daily, Father created snowshoes that resembled a set of primitive tennis rackets. Taxing it was, trudging across the mountains and sinking up to our nostrils in the snow when we least expected it. In my eagerness to receive letters from Grandmother, I tried the crude snowshoes in hopes they would ease my steps over the rugged terrain when I journeyed to the mailbox.

The trek was downy but stable at first until I reached the base of the first mountain, and I again sank deeply into the snow and became embedded under five feet of ice. About twenty yards in front of my path stood a menacing elk with antlers longer than I was tall. I froze, unable to maneuver in that much snow, and couldn't unhook my feet wedged inside the snowshoes. I tried to think of an escape plan in case it decided to attack.

The elk eyed me for a minute as if contemplating ripping my head off before darting through the woods. The noise from its antlers, tangling up in the trees, echoed beautifully across the mountainside.

The only way I could free myself was to wrench my feet out of the snowshoes, but my leather deck shoes came off in the process. Barefoot, I couldn't go far in the snow, so I trudged swiftly back up the mountain to the cabin. I feared Father's reaction when he discovered that I couldn't reach the buried snowshoes or my deck shoes under the ton of powdered ice. Other than one pair of work boots and well-worn tennis shoes, they were the only pair of shoes I

85

owned.

I soon defrosted but worried that frostbite had affected me as I nibbled a few morsels of food. The landscape was deafeningly quiet: No sounds of people or the distant humming of industry or aircraft. Nothing. It was pitiful that I missed the sounds of the antlers that nearly could've gored me to death hours earlier. I couldn't remain in seclusion until I died, and I knew it.

"Milan, get your boots on. Joan and Marty have invited us to a party at their cabin." Mother emptied her bucket of cool and murky bath water. Her enthusiasm sounded strained, as if Joan had coerced her to attend.

Had my parents sensed my growing loneliness that afternoon? They allowed me a little social reprieve because they were afraid I'd leave them as Hansel and Karen had. As long as my social interactions were limited to straight old men, a party at a wicked witch's house might work.

Joan, a large woman in her sixties, ran a natural wellness store in downtown Sandpoint. She had a frontier smile and knowledge of all things paranormal, which she spoke of proudly. Joan was well aware of her reputation as the Witch of Whiteraven Mountain and had her straw broom to prove it. I knew her props were a barrier of intimidation, which she put in the simple-minded mountain folks to keep them at bay.

"That woman is pure evil. I can tell by the look in her eyes," Mother had said upon her first glimpse of Joan. Of course, Mother silenced her judgmental opinions every time Joan brought us free bread that hadn't sold fast enough, which was part of Joan's charity. We were so starved half the time that a loaf of French bread and a few cinnamon rolls brought back memories of the Thanksgivings we had back in civilization.

Marty, her partner, had youthful skin, cold as flint eyes, and was admirably fit for his advanced age. He admitted to eluding the IRS because he thought there was nothing in the U.S. Constitution forcing him to pay taxes. He and Joan never discussed their private living arrangements. Father guessed they were lovers and probably never married so Marty could remain anonymous.

"Oh—what kind of party is it?" I asked in disbelief that the scarce residents of Whiteraven knew what a party was.

"Just a few of Joan and Marty's friends. They made some homebrew for the occasion."

"Homebrew … what is homebrew?" I asked, crazily excited. I grabbed my boots from the primitive closet made of thin plywood.

"It's a type of moonshine, some sort of homemade alcohol," Mother said, not appearing the least bit concerned that it might be illegal in Idaho.

Father had many rules when I was growing up, and one was no evil alcohol was ever going to find its way into his home. Of course, a few months after Hansel and Karen first came to live with us in Mississippi, they all guzzled screwdrivers on Saturday nights while playing poker. Father allowed me only a few sips to see what grown folks had the liberty to do.

"Now, it'll just be for a couple of hours, and then we will leave," Mother said as she tried to make herself presentable with a tiny mirror and the remnants of the afternoon sun.

If I were indulging in homebrew that evening, I did not ask as we walked the frozen mile to Joan and Marty's cabin. My mind was transfixed on finding the one thing my body longed for—to escape the mountains and find a cute boy to be with. When we arrived at the cabin, a few old people were outside, watching us.

The view from Joan and Marty's cabin was equally as beautiful as ours. They had a classic two-story house constructed with brown-stained horizontal logs. Rock-walled gardens, now buried under snow, spiraled with the icy wind around their cabin. Turning my gaze away from the deck where the guests huddled, I noticed a lonely shed with a sign on the door that read Casa De Pollo, which Joan informed me, meant "Chicken House."

The pot of homebrew saw many returns as my parents accepted their loaded cups.

"This is Leslie; she's a belly dancer," Joan announced to my parents and the Hedgpeths, who lounged zenned out on the stairs deep inside the cabin.

"Hi, nice to meet you," said Mother.

"Oh my, Brigitte! Your son has such long pretty eyelashes. Oh my! Just look at his lashes, Debbie," Leslie continued to babble, insisting I take a seat beside her. Eyelashes were new on the list. I had always been told I had the prettiest smile. However, pretty wasn't an attribute that was supposed to be ascribed to boys, but I didn't mind except when my parents seemed displeased by it.

"Are you and Rowan okay with Milan having a little homebrew?" Joan asked sheepishly as she twirled the brew ladle.

"Yes, it's fine with me. The Bible says most things in moderation are a'ight," Father replied. He flip-flopped with this issue depending on who his friends were at the given moment. Usually, Father denied that Christ drank, claiming that it was merely grape juice. I suppose he thought that when the Pharisees called Christ a drunkard that He just had an allergic reaction to the grape juice.

I took my first reluctant sip, and after several more sips, I got my first buzz. I was instantly drawn to the Polaroid snapshots of various people interspersed all over their cabin. On different body parts in each photo, someone had strategically placed little transparent cubes filled with something ashy looking.

"It's crushed herbs," said Marty. "I do healings for people. I also have a secret machine in the loft that can cure people of cancer or completely disintegrate them depending on what level I set it on."

At some point during the party, someone mentioned the problems they had been having with the local busybody, Mike Busby.

"Marty and I have already had the same issue with Mike. That's why we didn't invite him," said Joan. "Rowan and Brigitte, you should join us in a group ritual one evening, and we can levitate the Busby family off the mountain."

Quoting some Bible scripture, Father did not agree to the invitation and announced it was time for us to leave.

I visited Joan and Marty a few times that winter. No, not for the homebrew. I occasionally checked on their property for them during their many trips back to California. Cutting arctic chills settled over their desolate cabin that winter, resting its icy claws upon their food pantry. The extreme cold caused her glass jars of fruit preserves and other edibles to burst. Despite the damage the blizzards caused, their exotic plants remained lush and green throughout the extreme dips in temperature. I assumed it was the effects of magic because they were deep into metaphysics. I looked through their shelves of books and saw strange and wondrous spell books for plants, one that explored the research done on the mother plant when scientists set fire to the baby plant in a separate pot. The experiment showed the psychic connection between the two separated plants, using monitors that picked up disturbances from the mother plants. Their library kept me entertained during the long heavy winter. They encouraged me to borrow any of the books I wanted, so I took books on telekinesis, Edgar Cayce, UFOs, and one titled *The Power of Positive Thinking* by Dr. Norman Vincent Peale.

I adored Joan; we often played mind-reading games with Marty.

"Oh, Milan, you are such a pill," Joan said when I beat her at the game. I'm sure they knew I was gay without having to gaze into a crystal ball, though the subject we never mentioned. They did have an outdated book on homosexuality in their library. Although the graphic illustrations of the men in the book with their scruffy beards reminded me of overly friendly *Old Testament* prophets, who greeted one another with more than the required holy kiss, it proved rather educational for my starved brain.

CHAPTER 15

So my parents wouldn't know, I stayed up late many nights with only my oil lamp for light. I searched through the UFO book to see if I could find a saucer described as cigar-shaped, similar to the one I saw when camping in Homochitto National Forest when I was fifteen. My search uncovered a listing in the book for cigar-shaped sightings in Mexico during the 1970s. The Sergents never discussed the paranormal, but I always had more than a passing interest in it. I practiced some psychic-development exercises until I was convinced I had momentarily learned to see my hand aura and swore I had moved the corner page of my memoir with my mind. My "discoveries" may have been the early symptoms of cabin fever. Still, I truly believed positive thinking was inspirational in helping me, if only to foolishly daydream of a future where I might be able to be my true self.

By the first of December, we were already weary of the snow. Darkness came as early as four o'clock and getting necessities from town was now a whole day's challenge. To carry supplies in the winter, the Sergent trinity each took a red sled and tied a large plastic garbage can to the back of each sled to store everything. Only a couple of people on Whiteraven Mountain had vehicles powerful enough to make it up and down the roads during the winter. These trucks equipped with snow chains often pulled snowplows, which would form walls of snow on both sides of the road. Thanks to the protective walls, we could sled down most of the three-mile mountain road without going over the cliff.

Rarely when the pitch leveled off, we would have to walk, pulling the sleds and garbage cans behind us. On one such occasion, we were pulling our frosty sleds when a truck plow came zooming past us. Mother stepped back into the road too soon, and her foot got in the plow's way, which tossed her in the air, and she landed flat on her back. The driver jumped out of the truck, realizing what had happened.

"I'm so sorry," he said.

"That's all right. I'm just a little sore," Mother said after landing in the soft snow.

When we finally arrived at the base of the mountain, where we had parked our truck, we attached snow chains to the tires, loaded up the sleds and garbage cans, and then drove another twenty-five miles to the nearest grocery store. We stocked up on flour, sugar, and large quantities of non-perishable food as would fit into our lovely garbage cans. Double-checking that we did not forget anything, we hoped our supplies would sustain us until our next trip back. Pulling the load three miles back up the mountain on sleds wasn't nearly as much fun as going down.

Later that afternoon, because of the relentless snow, we had to shovel the usual tunnels to the well, shed, and outhouse. The height of the snow tunnels averaged nine feet. While I was shoveling the snow, my father agreed he would take a family's offer for a big dog to keep Mother safe. He came back just before nightfall with Duke, an old black lab. His previous owners kept him inside at night, and he loved to sleep by their wood-burning heater, snoring and passing gas. He was old and slept extensively. His fur became so hot by the fire we feared he would go up in flames.

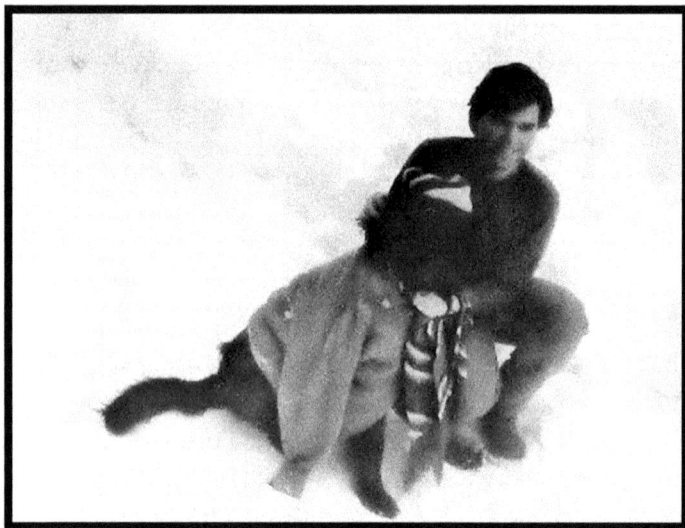

Me with Duke.
I was desperate for a friend.

Even though the sun was behind the heavy winter clouds, I was eager to take Duke for a walk to the mailbox and mail my latest memoir I had written to my grandmother. The snow fell almost daily and what had fallen months earlier remained unmelted. I had become accustomed to the primitive lifestyle and was on the verge of depression from the lack of stimulation. I was losing touch with life as I remembered it. Duke seemed used to it and led the way eagerly until we passed his old homestead that now stood vacant and vanishing under snow; he paused for a moment, and we both listened in vain for the faintest sound of humanity or industry.

"You miss your old home, don't you, Duke, old buddy?" I said to the dog.

Duke snapped his furry neck back to face the road and continued toward the mailbox.

"How about that? You like your new home better than I do."

When I reached the mailbox, a burst of joy shot through me. I received another letter from my amazing grandmother. With each step back up the mountain, I devoured every word she had written, hardly looking up from the folded pages. I paused and had to reread what I thought I was seeing.

"She wants to come and get me, Duke!" I squealed. "If the roads are drivable, she wants to bring me back to live with her in April. She's building an addition to her house and wants to help me enroll in college! In the meantime, she wants me to try and get my GED. Isn't that wonderful?"

Somewhere during my excitement on the return walk, I didn't notice until too late that the snow around Duke's furry legs had formed into several balls of ice. His walking soon became difficult, so I tried to remove the ice, but it had hardened onto his long black fur. We rested a bit, then I managed to get old Duke back to the cabin, and he spent the rest of the day defrosting by the wood heater. Unfortunately, he developed a cantaloupe-sized knot on his front leg from the ice clumps and had trouble walking. Despite my protest, Father took him out into the woods and shot him. At this point, losing pets was commonplace, and Rowan was developing quite an aim. I worried when he soon got another dog. Rocket was a Rhodesian Hound mixed with Husky. While he was just a puppy, he was already terrorizing the few mountain residents, tearing down their underwear from clotheslines and lugging them back to our cabin. Rocket became the next victim on Father's assassination list, and thankfully Rowan gave up on having more pets. To my knowledge, the meat we ate that winter was never dog meat, but I wouldn't put it past Father.

Using some of the money I made with seasonal jobs, I bought used history and math books to study in preparation for taking my GED. I needed to find out where and when I could take the test, so I walked to the only available phone in the area, at Cully farm. They graciously let me use their phone to call the local high school. When I picked up the receiver, people were talking on the other end, so, feeling like a pervert, I hung up and told Mrs. Cully.

"I'm amazed you've never heard of a party line before," she said, unaware that I had grown up in the city of Jackson where the only party line was, "Hey, babe. You wanna come back to my place and party?"

Alone in my cabin room, I sped-read through as many books as I could. The light of my oil lamp flickered when the unnerving sound of wolves surrounded our cabin. The cats under the deck clawed their way up the cracked gray logs to the eves of the roof. Wearing only his pajamas and a robe, Father slipped into a pair of leather moccasins and grabbed his rifle.

"Stay inside the cabin," he yelled to Mother.

When Father darted out of the door, the wolves slowly scurried away until he slipped on the icy porch ramp and tumbled onto his left side. When the wolves saw him hit the ground, they charged after him. The leader of the pack had a scar that ran across its right eye down to its drooling muzzle. Fearing for his life, Father quickly picked up his rifle and shot at the wild beasts from his hip, sending the whole pack fleeing up the road into the darkness. Father ran back into the cabin. Determined that he would shoot the pack's leader, he grabbed me and demanded I come with him and hold an oil lamp so he could at least see.

Father walked more carefully with his rifle as we headed out into the dark. My job was to search and follow the tiny drops of blood in the snow from where he had shot one of the wolves. I had seen slasher films that were less frightening. Though wolves were both dangerous and clever, Father ordered me to the front of the line to trail the blood and paw tracks to the edge of the woods up the road from the well-house. Realizing he had lost their trail, he gave up, and we returned to the cabin.

CHAPTER 16

The first big snow. Soon the cabin disappeared.

THE snow had accumulated up to the roofline. To amuse myself, I walked up the snowbank onto the second-story gable and hung a wreath I had made from waxy tree branches. Branches weren't the only thing I gathered while roaming Whiteraven. I also scooped up animal feces. The soil was so bad on the mountain that Father made me go around the forty wooded acres with a bucket and collect frozen moose and elk feces in the snow. He hoped to get enough to use as fertilizer for the mountain soil the following spring. I questioned if I had reached the lowest of the low, wandering around Whiteraven with a bucket, collecting frozen shit. Though I felt Father was also near senility, I was afraid to refuse.

The dawn of my mother's undoing came sooner than expected. We had endured multiple animal deaths, hunger, and a crushing average of nine feet of snow for six solid months. Father was away hunting, and she began pacing back and forth on the bottom floor of the cabin. Her usually short hair had grown unkempt to the middle of her back. Gazing out of the front picture window, her sporadic laughter choked.

"Is it ever going to stop snowing?" she asked helplessly. "If I don't see some green grass or dirt soon, I'm going to lose it, you hear me!"

Mother was not talking to me but letting God know her demands. Her frenzied laughter soon broke into convulsing sobs. She didn't even put on her coat before darting out of the cabin to the shed. She grabbed a shovel and dug manically through the snow.

"I've got to see what the ground looks like; I just can't take it anymore."

I thought I would have to slap her to bring her back to her senses. It always seemed to work in movies. I knew how she felt. We learned that what she was experiencing was the legendary experience known as cabin fever. She had spent many snowbound months looking for the northern lights, gazing out at the distant nightscape for any flicker of sky activity. The sparkle of a firefly would convince her deprived senses that a comet or UFO had landed. Across the smaller mountains stood Mt. Schweitzer, and this view was incredible from the cabin. We heard rumors of the U.S. Olympic skiers practicing there, and Mother swore she spotted them skiing down the mountain with torches at night.

When the time came to take my GED, my parents refused to discuss it. They didn't offer to drive me into town to take the test either. I was so hopeful that I didn't think twice about their refusal. Before the first light of dawn, using what I learned about the power of positive thinking, I trudged three miles down the frozen mountain and twenty-five miles along the main road.

After reaching downtown Sandpoint that late afternoon, I somehow found my way to the high school where I took my test, though almost too tired to think. Only one other teenager was there for the test, so the results were available early that evening. After holding my breath, the teacher delivered the news.

"Congratulation, Milan, you have successfully passed your GED," the teacher announced.

I cannot describe my elation and relief. I couldn't wait to tell my grandmother the news and move forward with my life. I spent the night at Hansel and Karen's apartment in Sandpoint. My soaring energy level carried me to the next day when I walked the twenty-eight miles back to the snow-covered cabin. Mother and Father forced their lips into something resembling a smile. Deep down, I knew their worst fears were coming true. Another link in the enmeshment chain had broken, and they would soon be unable to isolate me from the big bad gay world they feared was ready to ravage my soul.

March arrived, and Grandmother wrote of her pleasure that I had gotten my GED and said she would get her brother to drive her to our cabin in April. Father and I resumed working at the lignite plant, shoveling coal. He had suffered from kidney stones on and off for several years, and once again, he started having severe pain. Only this time, he was unable to pass urine. The stone was huge, and where it was located, the doctors wouldn't attempt to remove it. With no insurance or money, he returned home with a six-pack of beer to ease his pain as he waited to die.

While Mother was on her knees, crying and praying in her bedroom, Father reclined in a fetal position on the sofa under the influence of the beer and kidney-stone pain.

"Son, I need you to boil some water on the wood heater and apply a hot rag to my back to ease my pain—as hot as you can get it."

While I applied the scalding rags to his back, Mother slopped out of her room and began pacing from the front picture window to the smaller window by the kitchen cabinet.

"What are you planning on doing after you move to Mississippi in April?" Mother asked, trying to take her mind off Father's pending death. This was another trick question designed to micromanage my life. The last time we had a similar conversation, I had mentioned my fascination with hair and the whole salon environment, so I said I might go to cosmetology school.

"Oh no, Son. You can't do that. Only gay men enter that profession," Mother had protested.

I laughed to myself and wanted to scream, "That's the main reason I want to do hair, Mother dearest." But I had adapted to my parents shooting down everything I ever wanted to do—shot down like our pets when they didn't measure up. Realizing their religious enmeshment game, I tried to think of a profession they might not know about.

"I think I might go to college and become a nuclear physicist," I said, placing another hot rag on Father's back while they turned up the heat on me.

"You can't be a nuclear physicist and wear a dress," Father retorted with steam rising from his skin.

The alcohol had seared his inhibitions, so he finally confessed what I already knew he secretly thought of me. After chopping and hauling wood every day, digging a septic tank, building a cabin, a wellhouse, shed, and outhouse, and leveling a mountaintop of rocks, I couldn't have been any more manly at that point in my life. Did I have to kill a grizzly bear with my bare hands to make Father accept me as normal? I fought the urge to walk out the cabin door and never look back, but Father was so helpless. I not only had to help him, but I also had to feel sorry for him. His confession cut the last connecting thread I had to him.

"I don't know what else to do, but I'm not going to wait around. I'm going to look for Joan and Marty and see if they can help us," Mother said, zipping up her coat, drying her last tear, and heading out into the blizzard.

This was a shock. Mother was going to Joan for help—the witch—the woman she and Father judged as not just ungodly but evil. While she was gone, my time alone with Father was the most silent and awkward ever. It made me sick to look at his pink, mole-speckled backside. But part of me was rewarded with a weird sense of vindication that I now had him where he always had me, especially all of the times I had to bend my ass over my bed to receive countless lashes from his leather belt.

Two hours later, Mother and Joan pulled up to the cabin in a huge truck.

"Seattle has the best hospitals near here. Now don't you all worry about a thing; I'm paying his hospital bill, and there are no strings attached," said Joan as she and Mother helped Father inside the truck where Joan had placed several pillows for his comfort.

Alone in the cabin the next day, I was so ready to forget this misery and move back to civilization that I burned my memoir in the wood-burning heater. With no phone, I had no idea if the hospital could help Father or if he would survive. I realized then that if my parents had indeed vanished into the wilderness as they had planned, Father would have died within the first year.

The next day, Joan's truck arrived back at the cabin. Father hobbled out, appearing destitute and paler than ever.

"Were they able to remove the stone?" I asked, meeting them halfway down the path to the front deck.

"We barely got him there in time," Mother said with a sigh. "The hospital just received one of the first laser tanks in the country, and they were able to blast the stone into tiny pieces, and he was able to pass them through his kidneys."

CHAPTER 17

B Y the middle of April, after the last snowflake had fallen, we had endured a white Halloween, Thanksgiving, Christmas, New Year, Valentine's Day, Saint Patrick's Day, and Easter. The day before I was to leave, Piper Cully drove me to her grandfather's farm on the back of her motorbike. My parents must've told her I was leaving in hopes of a last-minute love interest developing.

"Before you return to the city, I need to initiate you into mountain living."

She took me to her grandfather's barn and placed two buckets on the dirt floor. One for me to sit on and one to hold the goat's milk. I suppose she thought the warm hairy teats would make me stay in the mountains. I quickly figured out that she had already milked the goat earlier that day, so all that came out was a couple of drops of blood. The goat squirmed and kicked at me, which Piper enjoyed immensely. Though I didn't even know her, she took me to her little shed of a house, and we engaged in small talk until I worried about why she had invited me there.

I was relieved to return to the cabin and get to work down in the septic tank that afternoon. I was hacking away at the boulders with a dull pickaxe when Mother leaned over the surface of the deep hole.

"Son, what am I supposed to do when you leave, and something happens to your father?" she asked.

"Well, Mother, you all chose to move to the wilderness. You don't have to stay here," I replied, glancing up at her from the bottom of the pit. I couldn't believe the guilt trip she was trying to put on me.

Mother walked away in her well-rehearsed martyred silence. I had never talked to her that way, but she could not stop me now. Something was changing with Mother. Going against Father, she confessed her regrets that she hadn't salvaged some of her sentimental possessions before the escape to the wilderness.

That evening she and Father went on a Bible-reading binge. Even after I went upstairs to bed, she read as loud as she could out of the first chapter of the book of Romans about how people at the time didn't apparently praise God enough, so God cursed them by giving them over to a reprobate mind to commit homosexuality.

A sick feeling swirled through my stomach. There, in my little section of the cabin, I began to question the logic of it. At what point in my childhood did I not worship God enough that He had stricken me with this curse of being gay? And if God caused it because of His selfish cravings to be praised, how could religious people hate me for it and think I can change?

The day before getting my freedom.
Trying not to show any excitement in front of my parents.

The final day arrived, and I packed my few belongings in the same duffle bag I had left Jackson with. Grandmother's car pulled up to the end of the dirt road like a glorious ship coming into a muddy harbor. After an overnight visit, I had a moment alone with my parents the next morning to say goodbye. Everything went smoothly until I climbed inside the big Buick and closed the door. Even Grandmother and her brother, David, could hear Mother wailing all the way down the path and through the thick walls of the cabin.

"That was a bit disturbing," said David.

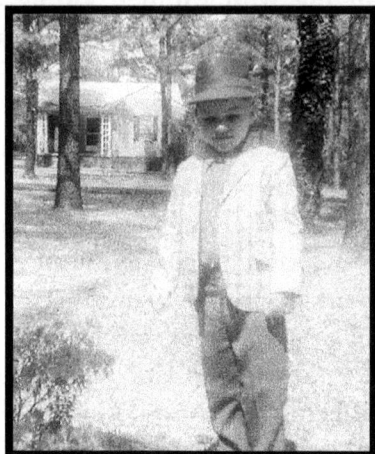

Me as the poster boy for Christianity.

I wanted to say that my whole childhood had been disturbing. Even as a toddler, it was apparent—something wasn't right. Whenever someone placed me in my crib, on the floor, or in a chair, I sat quietly like an old soul in a nursing home—alone, self-contained, and unamused with toys. Expecting me to be an adult as soon as possible, Mother potty trained me at ten months of age, and I learned to walk at twelve months. She had placed me on the front lawn and watched me from the kitchen window in passing. I never walked more than two or three steps before she realized I had vanished from the front yard. In her frantic search, she found me two streets away, holding onto a frightened cat's tail. Father worked day and night to pay expenses and was seldom home to see these events.

I knew that, back inside the log cabin, Mother was putting on her emotional theatrics, as usual, screaming as loud as she could to make Grandmother and David think that my getting free of them was a betrayal against her.

The farther David drove the dark-brown Buick out of the mountains, a warmer and warmer feeling of safety and relief came over me. I would never have to die with my captors again.

CHAPTER 18

Happy to be free and back in civilization.

I hardly blinked as soon as the car crossed the border into Jackson, Mississippi, the city of my birth. I wanted to see everything as I remembered it. The inner warmth and joy grew deeper within me. To think, my parents had planned that I would never escape isolation in the wilderness, much less see my home city again. Stepping out of the car in my grandmother's driveway, it was as if a giant water bottle had misted my body. I had forgotten what humidity and heat did to the skin.

The garage had been rebuilt into a master bedroom and bath, and she had upgraded the driveway and front walk. I had also forgotten what it was like to walk on flat ground and concrete without the hindrances of snow, rocks, and holes to trip me. I was in a whole new world again. Grandmother let me have the front guest bedroom, a palace compared to the rough cabin I had been living in. The first thing I did, of course, was to reach for a light switch. It had been a long miserable year since I had seen electricity, an actual restroom, running water, or a telephone.

The next day Grandmother bought me a small gold Toyota she saw for sale in someone's yard. She got a good deal on it because it had survived the flood that devastated Central Mississippi a year before my parents headed for the wilderness. To me, the car was pristine.

"You think you can drive a stick shift?" she asked, handing me the keys.

Before I could answer "No," and that "Father had never trusted me to drive anything," she said, "Well, you're gonna have to because you're driving it home." She got in her car and left me standing there. I figured this was part of the blossoming she said it was time for me to do. All my old classmates were now in college, yet I had never even pumped gas into a car, much less driven a stick shift. I got a couple of driving pointers from the original owner, who was holding the check in the driveway, and off I went. Most of the way home, the car jerked and made grinding noises as I learned to work the gearshift. After stalling in the middle of an intersection, I finished the route and successfully parked the car in Grandmother's driveway.

As soon as possible, I drove to Hind Community College and took the admittance test, which I passed, much to my relief. Then before the fall semester began, I got a college grant and a part-time job in the shipping department of a tool supply company. Stanly Purvis, a semi-friend since elementary school, was working there and told me they were hiring. Everyone considered Stanly a nerd throughout school because the charismatic church restricted his behavior and social activities, and he developed a stutter that became more annoying than cute with time. The worst curse word he would say was "oh, butt" when angry.

"I just w-want to take a baseball bat and b-beat homosexuals," Stanly said, swinging his arms as though he had hit a home run when he learned I was gay.

Children will be friends with anyone. There is such innocence and unbiasedness in them. I was realizing how religious dogma grooms children, and by puberty, many become paranoid clones, especially boys. How could I remain friends with someone who wanted to beat me to death with a baseball bat just for existing? Even after I had stood up for him throughout our school years. Although kudos to him for his honesty while saying such a troubling thing with an evangelical smile.

It was the middle eighties, and the fashion and music industry, with the likes of Boy George and Marilyn on every magazine cover, was at its most flamboyant for men. Father wouldn't even allow me to wear a knit shirt with a square-end knitted tie as the preppy boys had worn in high school.

"No son of mine is going to go around looking like a damned queer," he said, scowling over his plate of biscuits one morning while I removed the beige necktie as if the thing had suddenly become a set of anal beads.

It wasn't just Father; I had seen my share of girls ridiculing guys for similar fashion dares. Girls who fought for years to get the liberty to wear pants, boots, short hair, and play any male sport developed memory loss and began bullying guys for eating sushi or wearing pastel-colored shirts.

The forefathers must be so proud, I imagined bitterly. Forefathers who wore makeup and foot-high powdered wigs, who fought freedom wars adorned in gold-embroidered skirted waistcoats, billowing lace sleeves, ruffles, and collars accessorized with extravagant jewelry. When these men weren't fighting, they swanned around carrying furry muffs, tasseled walking sticks, and bejeweled snuff boxes while wearing feathered hats, silk stockings, beribboned slippers, or bright red heels higher than some of the girls in the last school beauty pageant I had seen.

If I or any current day man dressed as the ancestors and carried around a small bunch of flowers, called tussie-mussies or nosegays, and wrote every word in the most frilly cursive handwriting while enunciating every word as poshly as possible, men and women with my parents' mentality would at best torture such a man—torture the very men who gave them their freedom in the first place. I was shocked to learn the history of men's fashion from my library studies. One thing I discovered: teachers and parents are selective of the history and fiction books they want their children to focus on when neuroscientists have shown that reading fiction alone makes you a nicer and more empathetic person.

I wasn't going to remain ignorant and allow them to control me. Until I could earn enough money to wear what I wanted, I began shopping at thrift stores, making my clothes by cutting apart my shirts, mixing the fabrics, and re-sewing them. To hell that mixing fabrics was listed as an abomination in the *Old Testament*. I also started wearing plaid shorts and a jean jacket like some of the boys in college, who were also considered an abomination.

In my new bedroom back in Jackson.
Grandmother liked to photograph me in front of mirrors.

In the local mall, I ran into Samantha Fratesi, the coolest girl I had barely known from my old school. While all the other girls were still trying to be Farrah Fawcett, she was the first and only "Valley

Girl" that would ever bravely set foot inside McKenzie High dressed like one of The Go-Go's. Everyone loved to mock her manner of talking with all of her "totallys," "likes," and "fer sures" because they secretly wanted to speak the same way.

"I'm going to barbering school," she said. "You should let me give you a perm."

I agreed and let Samantha cut and curl my hair into a wedge-shaped fauxhawk at the barbering academy. I loved the whole environment there until she told me I was talking too loudly because it was hard to hear anything under the hood dryer.

When her masterpiece was completed, she got a gleam in her eyes. "Totally awesome. But you fer sure need to come to my parents' house and let me pierce your ear."

That weekend, with a Dead or Alive video playing on MTV, I let Samantha freeze my left earlobe with an ice cube to numb it. She placed a bar of soap behind my ear and shoved a wig needle into my lobe, but it only went halfway through and became stuck. After much sweating by the both of us, and an extra gold hoop from her collection, I had, in my mind, officially been transformed into the much-needed member of Culture Club they never had.

Starting college in thrift store thrills.

Grandmother seemed relieved that I finally had a friend with a vagina, though I hadn't yet told her that nothing sexual or romantic would ever come of it.

"You need to invite Samantha to that Missionary Baptist church you've been going to, Milan."

The secretary at the tool supply company was the pastor's wife at the church, so I started attending after Grandmother urged me to go. The members seemed a bit taken aback by Samantha's neon high tops, white fur Bolero jacket, platinum mohawk, and the multiple piercings jangling down each ear. Still, they welcomed her and Grandmother after the sermon. I never felt genuinely welcome and was always bored out of my mind in any church I had ever attended. Everyone became different people once they stepped under a steeple, and like me, I could tell they couldn't wait to leave and change into their shorts. What I wanted was to get off the hard pew and find other gay people where I could be myself.

Samantha invited me to her birthday party that weekend, and it was there under the golf course pavilion that I saw a cute boy with a precious voice and mannerisms, the buns of a ballet dancer, and a wedge of blond hair that flopped around his flirty eyes. His name was Griffin or "Griff" Barfield, but we didn't get a chance to talk at the party. A few days later, I confessed to Samantha that I was gay just because I was desperate for Griff's phone number.

"I, like, think I'm gonna be sick," Samantha said over the phone. "Fer sure, every guy I meet turns out to be gay."

I didn't realize Samantha wanted to be more than friends until that moment, but my eagerness to speak with Griff smothered any shock or guilt.

"Okay, I'll give you his phone number, but I'd, like, better call him first so he can be prepared. His family is total religious nuts. They control everything he does, ya know? They only let him come to my party 'cause I'm a girl."

I called Griff and told him that I didn't have any gay friends and that he seemed nice. He was in his senior year of high school and also attended a special school for students gifted in the arts. I was interested in more than friendship, but he immediately started talking about a recent sexual encounter with a dancer from South America before the boy had to return across the border.

"Mateo cornered me after performing at my school. *Ugh*, he made me feel incredible. *Mmm*, Mateo was so hot."

Feeling like an accidental voyeur, I took it as a sign that Griff only wanted friendship instead, especially when a few Spanish words rolled orgasmically off his tongue. Or, since he was barely seventeen and I was eighteen, was he trying to let me know he wasn't off limits?

"… My parents found my diary and read everything. They told me they'd rather see me lying in a coffin than have a gay son. I lived in fear that my family would poison me every time I ate dinner."

"Oh, how awful! I'm so sorry," I said, identifying with his fears.

"There's a gay and lesbian bar in downtown Jackson called The Limelight," he said at some point later, and I had difficulty concentrating on the rest of our conversation because I couldn't wait to go to this bar. The drinking age was eighteen, so I went that Saturday.

I parked my car in front of The Limelight, not knowing there was better and more private parking at the back of the club. A hunky guy in a tight sailor's uniform had done the same and was strutting up and down the sidewalk, searching for the entrance. Everything was so dark it seemed I had entered a dungeon that had opened for just me.

"Are you sure this is a gay club?" I verified again with the bartender before I might end up dead. The bartender's towel swung in his back pocket as he hustled behind the bar.

"Yes, we are," he chimed, with a wink and a twitch of his thick mustache.

"Where are all the people?" I asked, fearing Griff and I were the only gay people in my conservative Southern state.

"Oh, they'll be here. You arrived early."

I'm sure I appeared ridiculously naïve and eager. "The early bird gets the worm," as the saying goes, but I was a half-hatched chick ready to fly out of the nest.

I sipped on my first beer, which tasted a bit like urine, but it helped relax me while I tried not to seem so desperate, sitting on a barstool in the courtyard entry. I learned the trend of being fashionably late that hour. Soon the whole club filled up with young and older patrons, and the lights around the dance floor transformed the dungeon into a neon paradise. I became friends with a lumbering part-time drag queen named Richie, who had a limp from being run over by a drunk driver who targeted him and his friend because they were both in drag after leaving the bar. The hateful woman had even backed up and run over Richie again, killing his friend. I also bonded with a girl who could have been the twin of Annie Lennox. People occasionally thought Cheryl was the singer from the Eurythmics, whose music they often played in the bar.

"Sorry. I can't stop staring at you," I told her. "You look like the prettiest blond boy I've ever seen."

"I'm flattered." She pulled a pin off her jacket that read, "Why be normal?" She pinned it to my shirt. "You are one of the better-looking guys I've seen," she said out of obligation.

Before I had to be home for my midnight curfew, I had found a new world opening its doors to me. I had indeed been set free.

CHAPTER 19

SINCE Griff was underage, and I couldn't find a fake ID anywhere for him to go to the gay club with Samantha and me, we all went to the state fair instead. We had fun until a man who ran one of the booths where you toss a ball to win a prize kept yelling at us, "Step right up, ladies! Want to test your luck and win a prize?"

Mississippians were well-trained to assume and announce everyone's gender in every circumstance, especially waitstaff in restaurants. Oddly, many refused when an individual asked them to use a pronoun they identified as. If I had insisted the game attendant call me "she" or "lady," he would've flown into a rage and broken every bottle in his rigged booth.

My first day in college was both exciting and stressful. I had chosen Psychology and English as my main career goals. Students were asked to write a comparative and contrastive paper for our English essay. I decided to show the similarities and differences between Tina Turner and Nancy Reagan. Had I been aware that the Regan presidency would turn so callus and giddy in the face of the AIDS crisis, I wouldn't have chosen Nancy, but I received an A for the essay from the teacher. I had chosen psychology as a major in hopes that I would also receive help for my screwed-up childhood. I sped through my books and learned that being gay was not mental illness as society once thought.

The only issue with the career path I had chosen was that I had to take a Speech class. Feeling like a freak, my biggest fear was speaking in front of an audience. Richie from the gay club had given me some awesome little pills he called yellow jackets and black mollies, which gave me the energy to party at night and still make my daily classes. The magic little speed pills would also help keep me skinny, which seemed to be every gay boy's goal. And since I was the second boy in the history of Hinds Community College to take Modern Dance and Modeling, I needed to stay as slim and fit as possible.

"Why do we have to meet someone in the parking lot of a gas station to get the speed?" I asked Richie, who kept nervously craning his neck at every window in his black Camaro.

I had no idea amphetamines were a controlled substance, but I was going to need all the help I could get in Speech class, especially after the teacher let a male student heckle me for wearing a toxic-green-striped shirt that hung to my knees in the back. I took speed to stay mentally alert and took valium to calm myself down, which wasn't a great idea. And what the hell did I have to do? For some ungodly reason, I chose to give a speech on how to give a speech. At some point, the valium kicked in, my vision blurred, and I could barely see to write the word *eye contact* on the chalkboard. Unlike every boy in the room, I could hardly see the teacher sitting cross-legged on the edge of her desk in her top hat and miniskirt. Near the end of the speech, I turned to face the room of students, and they were all gawking at me as if I were about to keel over in an explosion of acidic rainbow glitter. Of course, they all might've been woozy from the fumes of the "poppers" I had spilled on my shirt after inhaling it on the way to class.

At the end of the semester, my Speech teacher lured me into her closet of an office.

"You passed this class with a D, Milan. But if you plan to attend senior college, you'll have to take Speech again. Only a C or higher grade will transfer to another college."

I wanted to fuss at the woman for allowing bullies to heckle students, but I was too damned polite. She let the bully coast straight into his career dreams, but mine ended at that moment.

"Well, I won't be going to senior college then," I said before walking out of her office and switching my major to Commercial Design and Advertising for the second semester.

At this point, I was becoming a pro at attracting bullies, especially when accompanied by my more obviously gay friends. Countless times I was called a "fag" by White and Black Mississippians.

"I don't understand; some people are glad they got their civil rights, but, child, they don't want others to have the same thing," my friend Richie said after he had suffered the same abuse.

One Saturday night, some guys surrounded my car at the pickup window of Krystal's.

"Are you dudes, queers?" one of the guys asked while flagging the rest of his buddies to see the freak show.

At a straight bar with my friend Nichole, a group of guys surrounded me near the pool tables, plucked the cigarette out of my mouth, and showed me how to both hold and smoke a cigarette like a real man, daring me to make one wrong move. In a Waffle House, a group of burly truckers six tables away threw waded paper napkins at Richie and me. A guy strutting past me in the mall angled his butt toward me and farted while his buddies laughed. At a stop sign on a neighborhood street, guys blocked my car with theirs. Luckily, I was able to floor the gas pedal and pass them through someone's front yard. On the college campus, students often heckled and whistled at me, and someone pelted me with a glass bottle while another guy came at me the same way defensive tackles break through the line of scrimmage. But I didn't flinch as I walked around him.

"Oh, look, everyone. The dude's wearing an earring," another cornfed bully yelled in class. That day I was wearing a white t-shirt with roses and colorful symbols like Culture Club wore at the end of their hit video "Do You Really Want to Hurt Me." They did want to hurt me, but the scariest abuse I received was from the Jackson police, especially when they habitually patrolled the gay club at night in hopes of "bagging a fag." In my hurry to get home before midnight, I made the mistake of running a red light on the empty downtown street. An invasion of blue lights came from a dark side street and swarmed my car as though a serial killer had escaped from maximum security. As one male officer approached my car, I frantically tried to remove the makeup and wig I had worn that evening, trying to mimic the style of the British New Romantics, but I only smeared the makeup.

"Step out of the car, now!" the officer yelled. "Now, walk that white line on the road there and touch your finger to your nose."

After I successfully did as commanded, the officer told me I could wait inside my car. He then crossed the street to join the other officers sniggering at me from the street corner.

With my car window down, I overheard the officer telling the others, "He's so drunk, he doesn't understand a word I'm saying." Then the officer returned to my car and yelled, "I didn't give you permission to get back in your car. Get out!"

I dared to remind the officer of everything he had said earlier, and he threatened to jump me, which he seemed desperate to do.

"Get in the back of that van over there," he said.

I climbed inside and was icily greeted by another officer who forced me to take a breath test to measure my blood alcohol content. While I was breathing into the tube, he kissed a female officer sitting in the front seat next to him. *That has to be against police protocol.*

"Well, you passed this test. But when you get to Heaven's gates, are you going to pass that test too?" The officer in the driver's seat asked.

"What? I'm suddenly bound for Hell because I accidentally ran my first red light?" I wanted to ask, but I knew it was a Christian-love dig at me being gay. At that point, I dare not contradict one more expression of their egotistical control trip.

"I'm going to pray hard about it, sir," I said before getting a ticket for running a red light. The officers resembled a bunch of hunters slopping empty-handed away from deer camp. They were all disappointed that they didn't get to haul me in as a treat for the inmates.

Not long after I recovered from the ticket and abuse, I got all groomed and dressed to go to the club, and Grandmother frowned at me from her recliner while watching "Murder, She Wrote," her favorite TV show.

"What does that pin on your jacket say?" she asked, gaping over the top of the dark-tinted glasses she wore to hide that she was cross-eyed.

"It says, 'Why be normal?' A girl from the club gave it to me."

"Well, I don't like it," she said with a huff. "It hints that you're gay."

After all of this time, I was so shocked that she would lash out in anger over a simple pin, but I knew she, too, had wandered into the

Gaydar Guessing Game that everyone spends their whole lives playing. I wondered if I had worn a pin with the King James Bible scripture in 1 Peter 2:9, where Christians are praised as "a peculiar people," if that would have angered her.

"Well, I am gay, Grandmother," I blurted out of frustration.

As she exhaled, the recliner seemed to swallow another inch of her. Her head collapsed back into the cloth-covered headrest, squishing her white hair.

"Oh, nooo," she said. "Are you sure?"

"I've been sure of it for a few years now," I said as gently as possible.

"We can get you treatment, Milan. A coworker has a nephew who thought he was gay, and his family sent him off to some clinic, and they gave him testosterone injections. That might work to cure you."

"Okay," I said, though I was saddened and worried about what it might do to me. I was perfectly content with the way I was, but I was learning that other people's beliefs mattered most, no matter how uneducated or hateful. I retreated to my bedroom, plopped in my swivel lounge chair, called my friend Griff, and told him of the injections Grandmother wanted me to get.

"*Ugh*! That makes me so mad," huffed Griff. "Listen, Milan, that clinic your grandmother wants to send you to is a gay-conversion camp. They have transportation teams who barge into small children's bedrooms while they're sleeping. They handcuff the kids, throw them in the back of their vans, and haul 'em out of state or country. The parents okay this because they'll allow those evil goons to try anything to scare their children straight. They don't care that their kids are crying and begging their parents not to let the strangers take them away."

"I don't know if this is the same thing. I think the boy my grandmother's coworker was talking about was sent to a medical clinic," I said, feeling like a guinea pig.

"It's not! I'm telling you; those camps and farms are where they do the testosterone injections. They're legal in nearly every state in the country. They force gay kids to take all sorts of experimental drugs and treatments. They force boys into fistfights to make men out of them. They isolate and torture gay people with electroshock therapy on their genitals, hoping it'll traumatize 'em so they won't find the same-sex attractive. You cannot let her send you there."

A sickening dread crept over me. "What do I tell her?"

"You tell Grandma the only thing those injections are going to do is make you so horny you'll want to screw every man you see."

"I can't tell her that," I said, lowering my voice in case she overheard me in the quiet house. She would often lift the phone in another room and overhear my conversations. "She might keel over from a heart attack."

"If you end up in a gay-conversion camp, you might not be able to get out unless you can pass a lie detector test and convince them the aversion therapy and all worked. It is religious pseudoscience straight out of Hitler's playbook is what it is, and it has caused gay kids to kill themselves. We have to educate ourselves because they don't care about us. Christians used to think being gay was linked to boys' testicles, and they forced them to undergo castrations and transplants. Then they thought it was a psychological disorder and tried lobotomies and shocking children's brains instead of their balls. The British government even arrested and castrated Alan Turing, the codebreaker who saved their asses from Nazi Germany just because they found out he was gay. Instead of being their hero, they drove the man to suicide."

"Oh, my God! They used to cut off their balls?" I asked, thinking these people were demons of Hell instead of Saints concerned about my salvation. What made them think they had the right to torture people's bodies over deeply held religious beliefs?

"Oh, that's nothing," said Griff. "For hundreds of years, the Catholic church encouraged people to chop the balls off thousands of unwilling pre-pubescent boys."

"You're kidding me. Why?" I said, feeling even more nauseated.

"They wouldn't let women sing in their choirs. The high-pitched voices of castrated boys sounded angelic—got the Christians all chill-bumpy. About eighty percent of the boys died from it, and many of the children who survived forced castration weren't even good enough to make the choir."

"After having their entire lives ruined. Thanks for warning me. I don't think I wanna lose my balls anytime soon," I said before hanging up the phone and wasting no time in pleading with Grandmother's sensibilities as she sat in her recliner with her large-print book now in her lap and her gnarly feet hanging over the footrest. I stood at the far end of the paneled living room.

"… Griff said all those injections are going to do is make me so horny I'll want to screw every man I see."

"Oh!" Grandmother blushed and took an awkward sip from her coffee cup on the end table beside her. Her head buried in the cushion, and the corners of her thin lips curled downward. "Now, I'm sorry about this, Milan, but from now on, you can't bring any male friends to your bedroom."

Relieved she had given up on sending me to a gay-conversion camp, I still felt as though I was being treated like a dangerous criminal. "Can I at least let Samantha in my room?" If that didn't work, I was going to suggest a neutered goldfish.

"That'll be all right, I guess. Now, I don't condemn you." Grandmother touched her fingertips to her upper chest. She was stressed, and I dreaded being the cause. "But you need to write a letter to your parents. They deserve to know the truth."

She was right. My parents had written letters and even used a pay phone while in town to call and pry into my private life and give me a guilt trip. Father never called me but once on his own, but he would usually take the phone from Mother to speak for a minute or so.

"Remember to pray to God and ask Him to keep you pure, Son," Mother usually ended her communications.

CHAPTER 20

I was running out of patience and excuses. My parents knew damned well what I was, and they were counting the seconds until their phobia manifested. It was time to confront the fundamentalist dragon that had snatched me off to its lair. I felt as though I was writing a request for a prison pardon, and in the letter, I tried to think of everything in my defense, including debunking the newest popular lie that God sent AIDS to punish gay people.

"But gay women don't get AIDS, so that's not true," I wrote. "I learned in psychology class that it's normal to be gay .... If I have to move to France to be myself, then I will."

A couple of weeks later, when I had keratin splinters left for fingernails, I got a letter from my parents. Letters are always deceiving when the white envelopes offer no clue of their contents—making postal workers think all people are nice.

"Dear, Son. If this is what you intend to do with your life, then your mother and I can have no part of it. Just know that we love you, but God plainly told me that you are no longer our son unless you repent and reject that lifestyle."

No part of it? I kept thinking bitterly as I shut myself in my room and cried. Father had never been a part of my life. He had been ashamed of my masculinity for years and had chosen other sons and friends. After I emerged from a whole day of sobbing my heart out in my bedroom, Grandmother was in her long flowy housedress, straddling the floor furnace in the hall outside my bedroom. The heat popped, activating her grandmotherly fragrance.

"Milan, I made you write that coming-out letter to your parents. They are blaming your college psychological studies for warping you into thinking you are gay. I don't approve of them disowning you."

"It seems it's the only commandment Christians can keep," I said bitterly.

"Well, I love you unconditionally and think they'll eventually come to terms with it. In the meantime, your mother's birthday is coming up, and I have a jade necklace that I want you to mail her and tell her it's from you. Jewelry is the way to a woman's heart," she concluded with a smile that always comforted me.

"Okay. I hope it works," I said.

A sheepish grin broadened on Grandmother's face as the heat caused her dress to balloon out. "You might smell me. Old women get what I call rotten-ing of the flesh."

Her comment didn't help with her gay-conversion hopes for me, but in such a brief time living with Grandmother, I developed a stronger connection with her than I ever had with my parents.

After I sent many donated gifts and greeting cards, I never heard back from my parents, who kept the peace offerings anyway. Part of me was glad they were so far away in the mountains because I dreaded what they would do to me now that I had voiced their biggest fear, now that I had put a boundary up against their religious manipulations and disciplines. I still had nightmares of escaping Father's swinging arms and rages. I couldn't tell Grandmother about any of the abuse I had endured. Rowan and Brigitte were still her children, and I didn't want her to feel as though she had to choose sides. Also, she had confessed her doubts about the existence of God because she couldn't understand why He would allow countless defenseless children to be horribly abused.

CHAPTER 21

I began to drink more in the clubs to numb the rejection and sadness. I had my first sexual encounter with an older German guy who grabbed my crotch with pinpoint accuracy near the dance floor, getting me embarrassingly excited.

"I can't believe it's you," I said in the passenger's seat of his car parked in the dark lot behind the club. "I remember you at the salon where I used to get my hair cut in high school. We both loved Blondie. I loved how you pulled my head against your chest while cutting my hair."

"That's the way we were instructed to steady our clients' heads," he said, disappointing me slightly.

"Well, I started to call you one day after school and see if you would be my first—you know—sex partner, but I chickened out."

"Man, I sure wish you had called," he said between breaths as we leaned in opposite directions over the intrusive gear shift.

What a coincidence. Out of the hundred or more boys in the club, I thought. For a minute, I convinced myself I had an extraordinary power to get what I wanted. Life had just taken a strange detour to get me there.

After a few other brief sexual encounters, I wasn't getting what I needed. I wanted love the way straight women got it in the old romantic movies. Love and commitment until death do you part. Sex was great, but I was discontent with boys opening my pants like another Christmas present and then discarding me when a new and bigger package came within a mile. There weren't any first or second bases in the gay bar world. Once the bat came out, it was for a home run.

Although I disliked church, I kept going to make everyone happy or perhaps to ease the guilt Christians had imposed on me. I tried returning to the Southern Baptist church of my childhood. The youth group called their Sunday school teacher "the swinger," and they skipped the preaching to smoke and talk trash in the parking lot.

I returned to the smaller Missionary Baptist church instead. They could handle punky White Samantha, but when I took my Black friend with a big afro, only two members greeted her after the service was over, if one could call it a greeting. My welcome there was on its last ruby slipper when cute little Griff popped into the sanctuary while everyone was singing. I hadn't invited him and had no idea he could even find the church as he slid into the pew right beside me and dutifully shared my hymnal.

"Please, God, let everyone think we are brothers—super-close brothers," I prayed the whole time.

During the boring sermon, Griff took my Bible and flipped the pages to 1 Samuel 17-31 and put his finger on the story longer than any other love story in the Bible with its glowing descriptions of King David and Jonathan stripping naked and exchanging clothes, embracing and kissing each other, how they wept together. Griff's glistening eyes cut at me with a special look that put me in a trance when his finger slid to the scriptures where David declared that his love for Jonathan surpassed his love for his hundreds of wives. And ultimately, the two biblical heroes made a covenant of the Lord together, sacrificing family and rulership for their shared passion. I was taken aback by how this beautiful little boy had the guts to make such a scene in an unseemly place despite what everyone else thought. If he felt the same for me, why wouldn't he just say it? Or was he just trying to out me publicly to prove that the church wouldn't accept me?

Though there were scarce young people in the church, no one greeted Griff after the service. And the next evening service I attended, the deacons made sure the Lord's Supper plate went over my head to the row of people behind me, bypassing unworthy me. Why was I subjecting myself to constant ostracizing? It was time to stop any fantasy I had of being saved. During the prayer, while everyone held their bloody cups and transubstantiation crackers, ready to eat them, I slipped out of the church and headed straight downtown to the gay bar, where I had a far better time. It was such a comfort not to worry if my hand bent a little too limply or I didn't walk or talk manly enough. Here I could be myself and not worry about getting beaten up, killed, or receiving fake hugs and handshakes from cruel people who supported, by their silence, such heartless actions against gay people.

The following week, my boss from the tool company fired me. For certain, Griff had succeeded. He proved I had been wasting my time courting religion. He knew sharing that hymnal with me would guarantee everyone would know I was gay. It all made sense why the pastor's wife and company secretary had started distancing herself from me. My old schoolmate and coworker, Stanly Purvis, never got to use his baseball bat on me, but I got beaten down anyway. Never mind what my coworkers or most people do in their private lives: they can have their fiftieth baby daddy, been a drug dealer, rapist, or killed a bunch of people, but God forbid if they are male and love another male. Apparently, the detailed chapter in my Bible where Jesus ranked sinners from "congratulate them" to "oust them until they starve to death" had been ripped out of every Bible I had ever touched.

I later learned that the pastor of that Missionary Baptist church had been caught using illegal street drugs, abusing his wife, and had left the church in shambles before getting a d-i-v-o-r-c-e. Pastor Erickson had the image of a successful preacher—a pompadour, pressed suit, winning smile, and tinted glasses. The congregation could look at him and know he was worthy of eating the Lord's flesh and drinking Christ's blood, for he didn't appear homo or have colorful friends. I tried to appear respectful in church. I would remove my earing and makeup and wear the most modest thrift store clothes I could afford. Perhaps it was the blond streak in my bangs or the sparkly skinny necktie that had shut me out of the kingdom of Heaven, a place built with gold, pearls, and precious stones—just don't wear them on your body if you're a man in the twentieth century.

Wondering if strap-on angel wings might help.

At the end of the Fall semester, the girls in my Modern Dance and Modeling course voted me the best in the class. The instructor used me to demonstrate many of the dance moves, namely the run and leap, similar to a dance from the TV series "Fame." It was a little awkward dancing to "Sugar Walls" by Sheena Easton, especially when someone allowed the football boys inside the girls' gym to watch us dance to a song about the invitation to spend a night in one's vagina. I also didn't realize I would have to do Hi-Steppers' routines, but I swallowed my pride and kicked second highest in the line.

Christmas had just passed with no contact from my parents. I spent much of the holidays in the bar, drinking and dancing away the pain of rejection. I had grown up in a fog of cigarette smoke at home, and everyone smoked in the bars, so I began craving them one night on a long drive to a college gay club in Monroe, Louisiana, which had much cooler music and smoke bombs that the DJ threw on the dance floor.

"… Child, please. I don't trust anyone who doesn't smoke," my friend Richie said, which might've been a factor in me smoking the long Saratoga cigarettes he did. Still afraid to eat much after Father had shamed me, I was six foot tall and weighed a mere one hundred and forty-five pounds. My ribs stuck out in the front and back, but I was getting attention as I never had before. Even married men, straight couples, and single women made unwanted advances on me. I politely drew the line and refused. Occasionally people were too kind or drunk and told me that I looked like George Michael, the fantastic lead singer of Wham!

After my freshmen year of college ended, I realized that I didn't want to pursue Commercial Design and Advertising further. My instructor had been honest about the starving artist scenario, and he wasn't impressed with my "freaky" artwork and clothes.

"Commercial art is the quickest way to an early heart attack," he told the students soon after he saw my neon green portrait of Pete Burns with his eye patch and lion's mane of curls.

I wanted to get a faster career and not be a burden on my grandmother, so I enrolled in Coastal Training Institute, a cosmetology school not far from where I lived. Since my parents had disowned me, they couldn't stop me from doing hair, I realized. I was the only guy in my class of about thirty girls and was shocked to learn by the end of the year that I was only one of three students to graduate from that class, with my scores being the highest. Immediately I got accepted to work at the Glemby full-service salon in Metrocenter Mall, which caused jealousy from my friend Samantha and other stylists who had to start in the Super Saver salon downstairs. I moved out of Grandmother's house and began renting a cheap bedroom from a middle-aged woman named Marlene, who had worked much of her life as a prostitute. She had a constant phlegmy cough, a gross mole near her nose, four inches of black roots, and a chihuahua with a nasty temper. A friend named Carl Allred rented her other available bedroom.

Not long after I moved in with my scarce belongings, Carl and I panicked when the doorbell rang one night. I peeped out the window, and at least fifteen college-aged guys wearing various hats were standing like soldiers ten feet apart across the front yard. My heart quaked under my protruding ribs. I feared my parents had sent the gay-conversion camp collectors to abduct me.

"What is this? *Invasion of the Homo Snatchers*," asked Carl, stepping away from the window. I couldn't tell if any of the boys were gay, but neither Carl nor I recognized a face in the crowd. Marlene foolishly opened the door.

"We're having a hat party in the house four doors down from here and wanted to invite you two to join us," their leader said to Carl and me.

"We don't have a hat." My heart still pounded in my throat.

"Of course, you do. Everybody has a hat," the leader said.

Carl, who had served in the Navy, laughed nervously as we both continued to refuse the invitation. We couldn't understand why a crowd of half-disguised boys insisted that two strangers join them at a remote location in the middle of the night. With the increasing attacks, tortures, and murders of gay men in the news, we had no intention of becoming another hate crime statistic and having Westboro Baptist Church scream "GOD HATES FAGS" throughout our funerals and then having our gravestones vandalized for all of eternity. Even two of my lesbian friends weren't safe. For starters, their crazy neighbor set off bombs in their backyard and aimed high-powered cameras into their children's bedroom windows.

That Saturday night at The Limelight, I tossed my nearly finished beer in the trash and began making a beeline to the dance floor when "Boy" by Book of Love started its magical opening beats, bells, and sighs. Richie limped through the crowd like Herman Munster in a corset and thinning mullet. He dug his long nails into my arm, stopping me.

"Child, someone's looking for you. He's cute, but I swear he doesn't look old enough to be out this late," he yelled in my ear over the music before pointing to the wall. The someone was Griff, standing like a little boy lost in tight jeans and a generic white t-shirt with his sleeves rolled up the way many gay men wore in the 70s. I wondered if he had completed the kitsch with a color-coded hanky dangling from his back pocket, but I didn't look for fear of being labeled a child molester.

"Griff! How did you get in?" I asked, giving him a high-armed hug.

"Today's my birthday. I'm finally legal. I saw your car here, so—"

"Oh, that's great! We'll have to—"

"Anyway, I have to go. I'm leaving for New York tomorrow—for school. So, I only came to say goodbye."

CHAPTER 22

NOW that Griff had shipped himself off to art school in New York, my hopes for a romantic relationship with him had ended. He had made such an effort to find me the minute he turned eighteen. Had I missed a potential signal he might have intended? Our timing was always off. I was a numbskull, a horse with blinders. Always blind to romantic clues, I never could accept that anyone might be interested in me. I fantasized about moving to New York to be with Griff, but I didn't have the money or guts to get re-established.

Months later, Griff called me from New York to tell me how much fun he was having. Before I could open up and finally tell him my feelings, he interrupted to say that he had gone to a sex club. I didn't want to believe he had been involved in an orgy.

"Let's just say I have been vi-o-lated," he practically moaned with ecstasy.

After a minute of silence, I said, "Oh, Griff. What do you mean you were violated? You weren't raped, were you?"

When I realized he had no intention of explaining what had happened, I became jealous and gave up playing his game. *Perhaps he is trying to let me know he only wants to be friends,* I concluded before we ended the conversation.

Brooding long enough, I later realized how vulnerable and lonely I was. Going by the drag name Katrina Fontaine, I sent "I'm available" signals to the gay community by lip-syncing in a gold lame dress to the song "Looking for a New Love" by Jody Watley. In another club, I performed "Let's Do It (Let's Fall in Love)" by Eartha Kitt. I didn't find love or any fans, but I developed a respect for the pains many women endured to make themselves beautiful. Though crossdressing temporarily liberated my personality, I always felt like a crumbling ruin in a wig, makeup, bra, and high heels, and I decided drag wasn't for me. I needed to be myself. For the first time in my shy life, I resolved to make the initial move and approach another guy.

At The Limelight, Richie told me that a boy named Darrin Harris secretly had the hots for me, so I had a little more confidence that he wouldn't reject me. Plus, I took Darrin being shy to mean he wasn't into one-night stands. I had seen him alone in the club many times; he resembled a young Jason Priestly, which was cute enough for me. Darrin was working the coat check and puffing on a cigarette when I approached him.

"Richie told me that you thought I was hot. Is that true?" I asked, biting my bottom lip in a hopeful smile.

He nodded sheepishly while sitting on his stool with his back against the wall.

"Good, because I think you are, too," I said.

Darrin's eyes darted around the bar as though searching for listeners. "Are you blowing smoke up my ass?"

I leaned closer to him. "No. I'm serious."

We quickly exchanged mini-bios. He worked at a mall shoe store and lived with his parents. Soon I was standing between his spread thighs, and we kissed. He would giggle so adorably, so shyly whenever I embraced him. Between his joy, it didn't take long for the lost puppy expression to return on his face. Both of these sides endeared me to him more.

The next night he showed up at the house where I rented a bedroom. His plaid shirt and faded jeans were all pressed and perfect. He smelled like Heaven.

"I got you something. I hope it doesn't offend you." He handed me a shoebox with a fabulous pair of sneakers with blue stripes on the sides. I tried them on; they were the best-fitting shoes I had ever worn.

"They're women's tennis shoes." He bit down on his bottom lip with a sneeze of a laugh.

"How did you know my size?" I didn't want him to know that I was in dire need of new shoes.

"It's what I do."

The night went so fast I had nearly forgotten that it was New Year's Eve because we were making our own fireworks. The next morning, with Darrin beside me in bed, Marlene knocked on my door, probably in a tiff because Darrin wasn't paying her rent by the hour.

"Milan, I hate to bother you. But can you go pick up my paycheck?"

"Okay," I said bitterly, hating to leave my bedded bliss and head out into the cold and rainy weather.

"I'll wait on you if that's all right?" Darrin asked, finally releasing my hand.

Still groggy from little sleep, I made it down wet Old Canton Road, and the last thing I remember was a car slamming on its brakes for no reason. I woke up about twelve hours later in the emergency room of St. Dominic Hospital. My little gold Toyota had been crushed between two cars, but all I suffered was a concussion. I couldn't believe my eyes when I glanced up and saw Darrin waiting for me in the hall with a look of worry etched on his face. Back at the room I rented from Marlene, he stayed with me through the night to ensure I was okay.

I expected to receive a response from my parents after my near-death experience, but nothing ever came. My dependable car had been demolished, so with little insurance settlements, I ended up having to get a clunker Omega to replace it.

For a few months, I shared Darrin's bedroom at his parents' house, which was a surreal but promising experience for me. Mr. and Mrs. Harris knew we were a couple and never disturbed us. Everything was fine as long as we didn't talk about our love or personal business. For Valentine's Day, I bought Darrin a giant silk Valentine's corsage with exquisite beadwork. At the time, it was the only seasonal store prop at McRae's, where I got employee discounts.

The female cashier wearing a fog of perfume said, "Oh my! Some lucky girl is going to love this."

"He is," I wanted to say to her stupid assumption while she gift-wrapped it as though it was sweet baby Jesus.

Darrin met me in his garage when I got home and gave him the valentine. He giggled and kept peeking at the corsage he placed back in the box on his car hood. "We shouldn't let my dad see this. It might upset him."

I was bewildered over hearts and flowers being an issue for Mr. Harris but not the tub of vegetable shortening on his son's nightstand, the two-foot stack of gay porn on the floor of his closet, or me in his bed.

My year living with Darrin had been the best of my life. To spend more time with him, I went on his long bank courier trips and would huddle on the floorboard to avoid bank cameras from detecting me. We loved to sing along with the car radio and change the lyrics to something naughty, especially Madonna songs. Going on a public date was impossible without people staring at us with amusement or angered suspicion. Even when we left the mall together several feet apart, a security guard stalked us all the way to our car.

"What are you boys doing?" he asked me after tapping on my car window.

"We're waiting on our friend Lisa to get off work! Do you want me to take you to the salon she works at and prove it to you?" I said with an offhand excuse, wanting to cuss him for everything he wasn't worth. He was one of many bigoted punks with a badge, keeping the community safe from the light-footed walk I tended to endanger society with every step.

"No, that's okay," he said before walking away to use his authority to abuse someone else who dinged his gaydar.

Finding an apartment complex that would allow two men to rent a one-bedroom together proved impossible, so Darrin and I had to pay more for a two-bedroom dwelling.

"Too bad we aren't straight guys; we could shack up with our fifteenth girlfriend or baby momma," I said.

"We should go to New Orleans and get married," Darrin said for the second time.

"Gay men can't get married, though, can they?" I asked. I had never known of any same-sex couples getting married. I couldn't begin to imagine the possibility, but I wanted to be with him forever. Having love and a sense of security was magical. I had never felt more complete.

"We can at least have a civil ceremony there, I think."

By summer, we decided to brave the swimming pool at the

apartment complex. I wanted to go at night to avoid people harassing us. Darrin preferred the sunshine but thought we were too pale, so we went through an entire bottle of self-tanning oil in two days. When we peeled off our wet speedos later that evening, our privates and asses looked alien gray juxtaposed to the copper orange on the rest of us.

"*Eww*, gross." Darrin laughed and strutted in front of the bed as though his middle region was coated in sticky lead paint. It didn't kill the mood for long.

While contemplating a possible civil ceremony weeks later, I came home from work and found an unrecognizable pair of underwear on the floor of the guest bedroom, which his dog used. Something was wrong. I might as well have stumbled upon a severed hand.

Darrin grabbed the underwear and hid it behind his back. His face turned red, and every tooth in his grin glistened with guilt.

"These belong to a guy I met on my delivery route. We came here while you were at work and had sex."

At first, I thought he was joking, but this was so unlike Darrin. "Are you serious? Why?"

"I get tired of waiting on you. I have to wait on you to bathe and powder and primp."

"Yeah, maybe I do," I said in disbelief at how unsympathetic and blunt he was being. "I try to look my best after you complained that my face gets oily, and my haircut made my head look too long, and then you acted grossed out when I was trying to turn you on by posing naked."

It suddenly occurred to me how much Darrin had criticized me during our time together. He sat on the edge of the bed with his head down. His remorse didn't feel genuine; it seemed a response that his better reasoning knew he should offer.

"I don't love you anymore, Milan, but my psychologist thinks I still do."

I wanted to ask when or why he had been seeing a psychologist, but I ran to the restroom and turned on the radio to drown out my sobs. Instead of a sad song I needed at such a devastating time, "Mony Mony" by Billy Idol was blasting instead. I felt foolish and desperate. Days earlier, I had cried on the couch beside Darrin when he confessed about being knocked unconscious and anally assaulted during high school band practice.

"... His name was George. He was a big guy. Hit me over the head with his tuba. I told him this other guy in the band, Franklin, needed to get his cherry popped."

"Why would you do that?"

"Because Franklin was always annoying the hell out of us. I didn't think George would pop my cherry instead. The janitor found me bleeding in the locker room with my pants down. I had to get stitched back up."

He laughed when I began to sob at his retelling of this awful story—tears for someone I deeply loved. Instead, I should have found his lack of emotion shocking, but I was blinded by my affection for him.

Not long after I moved out of our shared apartment, I learned that Darrin was going around the gay bar, telling people I had AIDS. I was stunned at how people could go from loving someone to being so hateful, from wanting to get married to spreading vicious lies. Perhaps he was saying such awful things because I had moved in with my friend Carl Allred, who had recently been diagnosed with the dreadful disease. AIDS was a death sentence to so many gay men at the time, including Ricky Wilson, my favorite guitarist from The B-52's. Vehicles were now sporting bumper stickers that read, "Stop AIDS. Gag a fag."

"It's nothing. You'll be all right," said my straight friend Patty, insisting we have lunch inside a South Jackson restaurant where the owner had that ominous bumper sticker on his truck parked out front to drum up the right business.

"Easy for you to say. I'll have to worry about what they might put in my food," I replied, wondering if I could get to the hospital in time if needed.

I had far too many shady experiences with doctors. I developed tonsilitis and mono, which made me ill and skeleton thin. The emergency room doctor stared at me suspiciously before refusing to give me a tonsillectomy, which he admitted I desperately needed.

"Um, go home and drink some Ensure," he said before mumbling about blood transfusions and the threat of AIDS.

With a hospital band around my wrist, I staggered through the aisles of a grocery store, searching for the Ensure. A small group of young boys walked way around me with contorted faces of horror. My experiences with doctors for anything below the belt were by far the most questionable.

"Say, Milan, how many prostate exams have you had exactly?" another doctor said with a smirk while he maneuvered his finger up my ass during a checkup. Doctors know the psychological trauma this causes many men. One of my straight male clients, a judge, admitted he would never get his prostate examined.

"It doesn't hurt," I said, trying to ease his mind while blending his gray hair carefully with the thinning scissors.

"I'm not afraid it'll hurt. I'm afraid I'll enjoy it," he said out of the corner of his mouth and with wonky eyes.

A music director customer, who resembled a twinkish Clark Kent, admitted he ejaculated during his prostate manipulation from the doctor while his young son looked on curiously. "But I didn't enjoy it," he added with a sheepish grin that failed to convince me. It was always a fragile line with these male clients. I suppose being in a hair salon made their thoughts go anal, and they needed to establish their straightness by any means necessary.

I soon reached the lowest point in my life. I had lost my job, sold all my furniture to pay rent, and spent Christmas night alone on a Native American burial mound on the Natchez Trace. Desperate for money, I tried to donate plasma, and the blood bank workers vanished from the office, refusing to take my paperwork. If only I had the magic ability to make the bullies disappear throughout my school days. I realized my vanishing powers were growing. The rest of my gay friends made a pact to shun me.

"Sooo, fancy seeing you here, Milan. Richie has been going around telling everyone that you're into girls now," Ben said, over-arching his back and blowing smoke rings at the nightclub ceiling before taking a triumphant sip of his beer.

"That's not true," I said, stunned that my friend would do such a thing. I ignored Ben's warning about their resentment of my alleged sexuality change and began moving through the dark bar to seek reassurance. Rounding a corner to the girls' side of the club, I bumped into another friend with whom I had once kissed and cuddled, but nothing came of our attempt at a relationship.

"Hey, Blake! How have you been?" I asked.

"Who the fuck are youuu?" he shouted with a snarl that left me feeling decapitated.

After being ghosted left and right, I walked out of the club and sat in my car in the dark parking lot. Even the insects swarming under the streetlights seemed to be at odds. It was so not true that I was into girls. I had been raped by a drunken female cocaine addict named Nichole. My friend Richie had been sitting in a chair against the right wall of the house I was living in, and Nichole pinned me to the sofa with her body and unzipped my pants. I protested and tried to fight her off without physically hurting her. Boys aren't allowed to hit girls, and Nichole wasn't afraid of anything. She had threatened to shove the salon manager's face into a utility box, and she would squat in the middle of the parking lot and have a piss to avoid using the nasty restroom in the bar.

Somewhere in the thrashing and arm tangle, she had gotten her prize and began performing oral sex on me. I was honored that she wanted me but also embarrassed and angry that she thought she could just take what she wanted. Seeing this, Richie hobbled out of the house as if I had betrayed the gay community. Even though I had never been attracted to a girl, I gave up resisting and thought, *if I allow her to continue, I might like sex with a female, and I'll know for certain if I might be a little bit straight after all. God works in mysterious ways, they say.*

I worked with Nichole at the mall salon, and she tended to latch onto gay men. Next to Samantha, she was one of the coolest and most daringly stylish Southern girls I had ever known. Most guys would love to have Nichole, but every sense organ I had was disgusted by the entire experience with her, and I knew without a doubt that I could never be straight.

"Broken Wings" by Mr. Mister was playing on my car radio as I gazed up at the friendless overhead moon. I felt just as broken and abandoned. Richie had told everyone that I had switched teams as if I had betrayed the entire gay universe and its blood-soaked history for survival. In my mind, I was no longer welcome in the world that I had waited so long to find. I had nothing left except an endless struggle to pay rent and avoid attacks.

I had even given up on having a romantic relationship with my friend Cheryl, who looked like a blond Annie Lennox. Sure, her boyish face mesmerized me, but I could never bring myself to look at the rest of her body she hid under baggy clothes or a unisex jacket. She even walked like a cute boy. I fumbled out of the club after another girl pulled Cheryl away from me and onto the dance floor the second Salt-N-Pepa's "Push It" hit the turntable. The following morning Cheryl found me dazed and confused at my grandmother's house. I admitted I left the club out of jealousy. She took me to meet her mother in Meridian, Mississippi. From Cheryl's beautiful lips and facial features, I correctly guessed that she had Black ancestors.

"My grandmother was Black. And when we get married, we'll have Black drag queen children," she teased, adding to our ridiculous dreams.

We went on a couple of dates just so I could show her off, but we both knew any real relationship was doomed. "I prefer a woman who takes care of herself—a woman like Cybill Shepherd," she admitted. Soon Cheryl became a military cop overseas but left me one of her most androgynous photos as a keepsake.

That weekend I went home to my apartment and overdosed on amphetamines with the full intention of killing myself.

Before swallowing the pills, I asked God to forgive me for my sins one last time. Waiting to die, I reclined on the single mattress on the floor and soon began to hyperventilate. My chest threatened to burst open, and my heart raced for what seemed hours. While sweat formed over my entire body, my limbs convulsed. At some point, I wasn't sure if I had died and was traveling to the commonly reported light or was only sleeping. The light turned out to be a UFO, and I began playing cat and mouse with the craft as it morphed into a flying car. Meditating on this vivid dream the next day, after I had recovered, I thought the UFO somehow represented Satan trying to get me.

CHAPTER 23

I had always believed there was more to life than what people in authority were hammering over our heads. My fascination with the paranormal never left, and there were still so many unanswered questions. When I saw a newspaper ad about a Psychic Fair at the School of Metaphysics in an old house in downtown Jackson, I told my friend Samantha, and we had to go. I also invited my high school friend Mitch Odom to meet us there, but my stuttering semi-friend, Stanly Purvis, told Mitch I was gay before we all left for the school in separate cars.

"So?" said Mitch, shrugging his shoulders, much to my relief.

"Mitch, m-man, you don't s-see anything wrong with th-that?"

"No," said Mitch, but as soon as we arrived at the School of Metaphysics, Stanley had convinced Mitch to drive away without saying goodbye. I knew Mitch had mourned my year-long absence in the wilderness; his father confessed it to me. But now he was pulling away.

"I'm nervous," I said, walking up to the spooky old house and standing in front of the door.

"Why?" asked Samantha, a warped-mirrored image of Cyndi Lauper, while I had dressed down in faded jeans and a navy-blue crop top.

"They're psychics; they'll know I'm gay—right?"

"Not with me beside you," Samantha said, finger-teasing her

spiky "mall hair."

Once inside, the atmosphere was strained, and the wooden floors sounded like firecrackers as I walked around, looking over the shelves of metaphysical books. Samantha expected to find a pentagram on the floor but instead found a menu of the services offered at the Psychic Fair. I chose to have a dream interpreted instead of a psychic reading. After I gave a small donation, the unfriendly woman instructed me to go into a bedroom converted into an office and sit in a chair. Behind the desk sat a blond man so handsome I was sure I had already found the secrets of the universe. Like most straight men, he seemed uneasy with my presence and hardly even glanced at me.

"What dream do you want me to interpret?" he asked mechanically as if he were about to be subjected to juicy details about me being ravaged by the entire U.S. Army.

"When my parents moved to the wilderness, I had a dream about an old book with dead people on each page—mummified bodies I didn't recognize. Then I realized the pages and cover were made of human skin. I got the impression it was some sort of yearbook."

"I have no idea what that could mean," he said without five seconds passing.

Something was off. Metaphysically in dreams, books, skin, death, everything has some meaning. Even the Bible mentioned the gift of dream interpretation. After my effort to get to the school, losing my last straight male friend, and my financial donation, his response was as much of a letdown as when I discovered the pink and playful Sea-Monkey family I once ordered from a comic book was actually microscopic brine shrimp. And not one of the monkeys had a blond flip or pink hairbow.

I met a slim, middle-aged Black woman with thick glasses and a cool afro among the crowd of fair visitors. A smoky but sweet smell of incense poured off her the minute she greeted me with a deep and careful voice. "Hello there, my name is Irene."

After a brief exchange, she opened up in ways I never expected, while Samantha had her palms read in another room.

"... My husband molested my niece, and now he's in prison. I saw it coming, though. Every time I did the Tarot cards on him, I always pulled the Devil card. My son saw a demon on his back; he sees demons on people's shoulders, you know. They cling to people like monkeys. When you get the power, you can see into the spirit world."

The demon comment was a rhetorical question, but I nodded anyway. I attracted brutal honesty as a wounded animal attracts vultures. "How did you get this power? Did the School of Metaphysics teach you how to see into the spirit world?"

"I had been praying for it," said Irene.

And here we go again, I sighed inwardly. Were even the wicked psychics religious in the state of Mississippi? Did witches require baptisms when they sold crystal balls in this state?

"One night, I awoke to several spirits standing at the foot of my bed, and they said, 'We're gonna teach you how to handle power!' The voices told me to go to room number 119 at a hotel in Jackson. I finally found it, but no one was there. It didn't matter. God gave me his power because of my obedience; I just know it. I awoke weeks later, and my voice changed, and I was speaking in tongues. The power helps me intercede when I pray for people and spirits. The doctors diagnosed it as schizophrenia and hospitalized me for a month—can you believe that? My son, he didn't recognize my voice on the phone when I called the hospital. He said I sounded seductive. Now I get burdens for people. I don't get any sleep until the Lord releases me from intercession." Irene fished a notepad from her simple brown purse. "You are being oppressed by something. You know what? I keep a list, and I'm gonna pray for you also." She leaned forward, smiling sheepishly. "Jesus can help you through this, Milan," Irene said adamantly.

"What is speaking in tongues?" I asked, having never heard the Baptist churches mention it. It sounded paranormal, which was definitely of interest to me. I was desperate to see some tangible evidence that Christianity was real. If only to ease my fears after being endlessly told that gay people were going to the hottest part of Hell.

"You need to find a Pentecostal church for that, Milan. They believe in the power of the Holy Ghost."

CHAPTER 24

GRANDMOTHER occasionally received letters from my parents, but they never did try to contact me. I couldn't believe they didn't acknowledge that I had attempted suicide. This cut me so deep that I would never get over it.

"Your father got a job at the local newspaper company. He and Brigitte have taken up bird watching," Grandmother told me. "They are happy to have their first grandchild."

"Their first grandchild?" My head tilted forward. "I'm their only child."

"I didn't want to tell you this because I knew it would hurt you, Milan. Your parents have been calling Hansel and Karen their children for a while now, so they have their first grandchild also. They gave Hansel and Karen some of their mountain property and built them a house right beside their cabin."

I was so hurt and shocked that I became lightheaded, so I sat on the sofa across from Grandmother. "Did they at least ask about me?"

She offered a regretful smile that assured they hadn't.

"They've had problems with Hansel. He started doing drugs and cursed your mother."

"Are you serious? I would never have done any of that living under their roof. I take it God never told them to disown Hansel, huh?" I smiled weakly at Grandmother, trying not to upset her.

"Your mother said Karen went to a bookstore in Idaho and

bought a huge book about homosexuality. They gave it to Brigitte in hopes she would come to terms with having a gay son."

"I'm sure Hansel was too inhibited to buy the book. They must've felt a little guilty for becoming my replacement."

Oh great! No telling how much disinformation it contained.

"Your mother said the book had graphic illustrations and descriptions of every manner of gay sex, which made her want to vomit."

I'm sure Karen and Hansel devoured the contents in private before giving the book to my parents, I reasoned. Mother probably mistook needing to vomit as a sign from God that being gay was indeed an abomination.

"I want to vomit when I see menstrual pad commercials or people eating liver or cottage cheese, but that doesn't mean it's wrong." I laughed bitterly, feeling as if my whole life had been exploited by a book that had only made things worse. "And why would Mother bother to look at gay porn after they claimed God already had that final discussion with them—had already instructed them to abandon me?"

Mother wasn't a complete prude when it came to sex. I sneaked a peek at one of her romance novels and was stunned at the sex scenes with all of the nipple nibbling, throbbing shafts, and moist mounds. *Had Karen and Hansel planned it this way to place a bigger divide between us?* Either way, I tried not to judge my family as harshly as they had done me, and I didn't need to see graphic photos and details to decide if I should show them love.

CHAPTER 25

WANTING to get away from the mall salon and its limitations, I took a job at a salon called Cutters and Shakers in South Jackson. Their business was struggling after the owner died of AIDS. Conservative groups began advocating that everyone should start wearing face masks to prevent the spread of the virus. Much of the clientele had fled after this misinformation, afraid they would catch it in the air though the virus proved to be non-aerosolized.

Perhaps my childhood obsession with Cher and her long dark hair was a motivating factor, but I became quite skilled at perming extra-long hair. Old-fashioned Pentecostal girls with their floor-length hair, no makeup, and long skirts began filing into Cutters and Shakers. The regular clients loved to deride the Pentecostal girls, which amazed me; I thought they would've welcomed the extra femininity when time after time, the same women would sit in my chair and say, "I don't care what you do to my hair, Milan; just don't make me look like a lesbian."

I became frustrated with the rude comments, so I made a laminated printout of over eighty famous lesbians who resembled any other bombshell actress their husbands would drool over but realized people secretly wanted and needed their stereotypes to remain.

"We have the reputation for swinging from the chandeliers. We throw down when we have church!" a Pentecostal girl named Dana said between pops of her bubblegum while sitting with crisscrossed legs. Her broomstick skirt spilled down the edges of the hydraulic salon chair as I quadruple piggybacked the perm rods in her waist-length hair.

"What's 'throwing down'?" I asked, stunned at the boldness these girls displayed, compared to the Baptist youth I grew up with.

"We call it 'shouting.' When the glory cloud of God comes into the sanctuary, sometimes we run laps around the pews or dance. You've heard the term 'holy rollers,' right?"

"Yes," I said, noticing a few clients' powdered eyes cutting toward Dana, who grinned with clean-skinned satisfaction.

"We roll around on the floor, too. It helps loosen the shackles the Devil tries to put on people. You need to come visit us. But don't say I didn't warn ya."

This business of shouting and throwing down fascinated me. I couldn't imagine people behaving in such an irreverent manner in a formal setting. I was already wondering if I needed to get the Holy Ghost as I had been hearing more and more about—the guaranteed missing ingredient for deliverance from the gay spirit that was possessing me as I had been taught. Surely, if there was a God and this church was the most apostolic in its faith and teachings, then I would find deliverance. However, all the talk of ghosts from Christians was new in my world. Being possessed by the Holy Ghost, was that what I wanted after watching "The Exorcist" and being terrified by heads spinning around and unlearned languages spewing uncontrollably? Would I feel a need for such a thing if I hadn't had so many people manipulating me? I had heard the spiritual research that claimed eighty-five percent of gay people were possessed by ghosts of the opposite sex. Apparently, they didn't think a woman could turn into a lesbian as long as the male spirit possessing her was a capital Him. Had I, at some point in my childhood, given some female spirit permission to walk inside me?

Wondering when a female ghost had taken possession of me, as the Christian research experts had concluded, I began tracing my thoughts as far back to my early childhood as I could remember. At first, I wondered if one of the ghosts of my dead sisters might've taken possession of me.

No, that's doubtful; they died when they were babies, but it could've explained my late social development, I reasoned.

Then I recalled my mother telling me about her alcoholic mother, Lorna, who lived in the French Quarter of New Orleans. According to Mother, Lorna didn't spend much time raising her and had even left her in a bar when she was still in diapers. On my mother's fourteenth birthday, Lorna called her from the Big Easy.

"Brigitte, you know I am so proud of you!" she said, sounding surprisingly buoyant and sober. "I always have been. I am coming up to see you for your birthday party tomorrow, and, well, I've put off telling you something for a long time—until you were old enough to handle it. But I am going to wait and tell you in person. You be good, sweetie, and tell Mom I want one of her famous butterscotch pies when I get there."

Mother's heart surely must have sunk with this news, as she had no fond memories of former times when her mother wanted to talk in person. What did Lorna possibly need to tell her after all those years? This would prove to be a secret my mother would never learn.

The next day my mother got a phone call from the hospital in New Orleans: A passing car had run over Lorna while she was crossing Bourbon Street. She died in the hospital hours later. In my mother's mind, Lorna had passed away years earlier, so she kept the remnants of her heart behind walls of stone.

A black hearse had carried Lorna's body to Jackson, Mississippi, for the graveside service. The funeral had been insincere and boring, and even though there were few people there, except for immediate family, the tension had been grim. Perhaps the others knew the dismal secret that my mother would never learn; if they did, it remained under their funeral veils, along with their emotions. After the pallbearers had lowered Lorna into the ground, Mother and her friends and family crept back to their cars like pensive monks.

Immediately after the graveside service, Mother's friends took her to lunch in a pale-blue Nash Ambassador Rendezvous. Hardly a cloud hovered in the sky that early afternoon. But the soured atmosphere overtook them the moment the car stopped in the parking lot of the Terry Road diner beside Battlefield Park. Out of nowhere, an ominous black cloud swarmed over the car, engulfing them in complete blackness for about thirty seconds.

"Oh my God, is that smoke covering the car?" Mother's friend, Jane, had yelled.

"I don't know, unlock the door. Hurry!"

"It's too dark. I can't find the latch, Brigitte."

They completely lost time as they sat there speechless about what had just happened. When the black cloud dissipated, they were too upset to get out of the car, so they drove home instead.

After sandwiches and leftover butterscotch pie, Jane spent the night to comfort my young mother. They both shared the twin bed in her room, trying to keep as quiet as possible not to disturb the adults. My mother's dolls sat quietly upon a marble-top table at the foot of her bed while her Jesus statue rested on her dresser. Mother left the lamp on as they lay on the bed, sharing family stories.

"… It's as if someone hexed all the men in my family, Jane. Impotence, sterility, infidelity." Just as my mother was naming off the family curses, that same black cloud that had engulfed them earlier at the diner came through the eastern wall of her bedroom and hovered just inches above Mother's reclining body. They both saw the dark shadow and let out blood-curdling screams until the mystical specter exited through the western wall.

I'm sure my mother forced Jane to get on her knees and pray— plead the blood of Jesus, as she often said. As a staunch Southern Baptist woman, she had never talked about ghosts or the paranormal except for this story.

Was the dark cloud that kept trying to reach my mother the ghost of my maternal grandmother, Lorna? Had she passed through my young mother's bedroom wall and waited to possess me when I was born five years later?

"Where fear doesn't exist, there is always a concerned soul ready to instill it," my genius friend Griff had assured me.

Trying to keep my sanity, I could hardly look in the mirror. I tried to shut out any thoughts of being possessed by my dead grandmother or baby sisters. Still, all I could hear in my daily thoughts at this point was, *"God has cursed you since childhood, Milan, and you're going to Hell!"*

I couldn't stand it; I had to visit the Pentecostal church.

"Barry is paying for us all tickets to attend the hair show in New Orleans. If you don't go, don't you think you are disrespecting his generosity?" asked a female coworker.

"I feel I need to go to church instead," I apologized, not wanting to be around my mean boss anyway.

The staff at the salon didn't understand, especially a coworker named Douglas, who nearly looked like a thirteen-year-old boy if it weren't for the crow's feet around his eyes and his ridiculously thick mustache coated in nicotine. He decorated the salon Christmas tree with ugly black ribbons while listening to an ancient cassette tape of Hank Williams singing "Your Cheatin' Heart."

"I once went for a job interview at a salon where they played Christian music," said Douglas. "They made the staff go to the prayer room each morning before starting work. The owner went to one of those churches and wouldn't hire me because she said I was devil possessed. She wanted to lay hands on me and pray it out of me." Douglas whipped his head to the side sassily. "I told her, 'I ain't *got* no demon,' and I walked out."

That weekend, trying to shake Douglas's terrible experience out of my head as just the product of him being "a bitter old queen," as they say in the gay world, I arrived late to the Pentecostal church. I slipped nervously into a pew near the right back section while the music pounded soulfully. A sea of young people scattered among the two thousand members lifting their hands in the air. Some were crying, and others were trembling. The young men could've been male models, but the women and girls looked older, like homely Victorians in their teased-up mounds of hair and long dresses. No one had on wedding rings, much less any other jewelry except gold watches. I had on a silver tie tack and feared I was standing out worse than a male Jezebel.

"Men, I wanna see you lean back and pull out your wallets. And, women, lean forward and pick up your purses, and I'd better not see any men leaning forward. *A-man, a-man!*" the pastor said, followed by a bit of praise to God while gripping the pulpit's edges as though he had to sneeze violently.

Barely able to pay my studio apartment rent, I had no money to put in the offering plate while the ushers began to pass it around. But it was probably a good thing in case I didn't retrieve my wallet manly enough. I was even more afraid someone would sense that I was gay and drag me out of the building or worse. *If these people operated in the spiritual gifts of Word of Knowledge and Discerning of Spirits as they claimed, surely, they would know as soon as I had entered the building,* I rationalized.

"This church and this doctrine are the only way you can be saved!" Pastor Whittington blasted over the pulpit.

In the middle of the sermon, a woman began screaming for help in the vestibule, and she or something made a sound that resembled a bunch of pigeons cooing in a manic flutter. The congregation mostly ignored the occurrence. But why? Were they used to such strange outbursts? Had the woman been delivered from demons? At least the attention wasn't on me as I had feared.

Upon returning from the hair show in New Orleans, instead of my boss, Barry, being angry at me, he gave me a two-foot stack of his old gay porn magazines, which I binged upon until guilt sank in. From what I had been taught, I assumed it was the Devil trying to keep me in bondage, so I lugged the magazines down the hall from the studio apartment I was renting and dropped the treasures I could never have afforded down the garbage chute. The next thing to go down the garbage chute was a brand-new television a rich fling had bought me for my sadly empty apartment. Sleeping with him was the only time I felt guilty about having gay sex. I found out he had a lover away on business, and he thought he could buy me.

"Every successful man needs a mistress," he said with his damned nose in the air while driving me home.

Boy, was he mistaken. I was done being another pebble in someone's path of stepping stones.

I had many weak moments in my quest for salvation, but in preparation for my return to church the following Wednesday night, ditching television was one of the significant holiness steps the church believed and taught. I wrote a letter to God and fasted from food and cigarettes in case they were polluting my holy temple and hindering my deliverance. It wasn't difficult to fast from food. About all I could afford to eat at the time was a bowl of instant grits every day or a few saltine crackers with mustard on them. I stopped coloring my hair, cut it short and boring, and threw away my evil tie tack. The Pentecostal men only used safety pins to keep their neckties from flopping around while they shouted in the church aisles. Church members met almost every night of the week, and some services lasted until late in the evening. They encouraged all the male children in that organization to become ministers, so I also began entertaining that thought. The Bible became my television.

That evening the choir sang a song about returning to the old landmarks. The song also scolded churches that used projectors to project hymns on the church walls instead of the traditional hymn books delivered straight from Heaven's dumbwaiter. The gelled-haired men and pale-faced women, with their piled-up angel hair, gazed heavenward with expressions of righteous hunger. Their worship and singing seemed spontaneous as they broke up midway to testify accordingly, or they burst out in tongues and tears as the choir scattered out of the loft, shouting. The worship was similar to the snake-handling churches, where, as in the pagan religions of old, they charmed serpents with their sensational chanting, music, and dancing.

Shawn Whittington, the boyfriend of my perm client Gina Ford, came to the back of the church where I was worshipping with my hands raised toward Heaven, hoping God was making as much effort to reach down toward me.

"Do you want to receive the Holy Ghost?" Shawn asked in a gentlemanly voice.

"Yes!" I nodded my head as he placed his left hand on my back. I felt as though I had floated down the long aisle to the altar under a trance of eagerness. A group of men and women soon surrounded me, laying hands all over my back, head, and raised arms as they spoke in tongues echoing the language Irene, with her Tarot cards and Ouija board, had spoken at my apartment. I had never experienced a church service anywhere close to this. The chaotic prayers and worshipful noise resounded fervently between the balcony and lower ground. The crowd "rocked and rolled" me as if they were trying to push me to the floor. After what seemed an hour, the chanters grew tired, and their voices became hoarse as the group dwindled to three men.

"He is so close to receiving the Holy Ghost," one of the men said to the others while I strained with closed eyes. It had to happen. If it were a devil or a ghost, it had to leave me, especially with all that had just happened.

"Lord, forgive me—change me!" I kept praying.

"Yes, he is—I can see it all over him," the other man replied as he stepped back from my swaying, entranced body to evaluate me. I wondered if these people could see an aura of God radiating from me when it happened; I wasn't sure.

"Do you have any sin in your life that might be holding you back from receiving the Holy Ghost?" the second oldest man asked me after they wanted to know my name. They maneuvered me to my knees, where they knelt around me.

I knew enough about the Bible and the early church's practice of confessing their sins before the entire congregation. Although growing up, I never saw the members of the Baptist churches confessing their sins openly. As humiliating and terrifying as it was, I was convinced I had no option but to obey scripture and confess.

"I'm a homosexual; that's the only thing I can think of."

The youngest man's lips compressed into a frown, and he lowered his head. The older men seemed to deflate a few inches as if they had just heard from the doctor that their babies had terminal cancer.

"But I believe God can change me," I added.

"Marty, go see if Pastor Whittington would be willing to go ahead and baptize Brother Sergent here in Jesus's name," the oldest man asked, and I took this as a sign that everything wasn't as grim as I had thought since they didn't order an exorcism.

Immediately I went up some hidden stairs into this small room, then behind a changing room with a saloon-style door and dressed in a white baptismal robe.

"Are you a student, or do you work?" Pastor Whittington asked, filling out my baptism certificate just before I stepped into the baptismal booth.

"I work."

"What do you do?"

I thought it odd that the pastor needed these details when I was trying my best to stay prayerful in my eagerness to receive the Holy Ghost. Plus, I dreaded telling the pastor my occupation. I knew what most people secretly thought of male hairdressers. Most straight men, in particular, would rather rush off and clean out their gutters with broken fingers.

"I am a hairstylist."

"Uh-huh, and do you make good money as a hairstylist, Milan?"

"No, sir," I said. "I'm still paying for my student loan, actually."

I realized that my earlier sin confession had not yet reached his ears and that he was only baptizing me because his nephew had led me to the altar to get saved.

Pastor Whittington made sure he submerged every inch of my body under the cool chlorinated water. I was glad he did, especially after a distant uncle requested the church re-baptize him because he recalled his pinky finger sticking out of the water while holding the pastor's hand. I, too, didn't want to risk an eternal roasting in Hell because of two inches of unredeemed flesh.

After my baptism, I returned to my studio apartment on State Street in downtown Jackson and changed out of my wet clothes. There in solitude, I prayed further, hoping to start speaking in tongues; however, all that escaped my lips was a dull thud of air. Growing tired, I went to sleep. During the night, I dreamed that Pastor Whittington had died, but the church did not mourn his death, and while the church was socializing, he resurrected from the casket, and nobody celebrated. I awoke with a start, wondering what it meant, but I could not figure out the dream. The church loved to preach that people would have prophetic dreams and visions in the last days, so they were always looking for signs.

Between clients at the hair salon the next week, I went to Metrocenter Mall to buy proper clothes to wear to church when a familiar voice spoke out behind me. It was Griff Barfield, but I almost didn't recognize him; his cute wedge haircut had grown down to his shoulders. It was the beginning of the Grunge movement, and Griff could now be its poster boy for all I knew.

"Griff, hey! How did you find me here? I thought you were still in New York."

"I came home for the weekend. I called the salon where you work, and they said you were here. What's this I hear about you going off on a *Pentecostal* binge." His voice was bitter, and he stayed behind a display table of folded pants as if he wasn't sure it was me.

"Who told you that?" I asked, hanging a jacket I couldn't afford back on the rack.

"Oh, I have my sources," he bragged with a sneer.

"I am Pentecostal now, Griff."

"WHY? You have no idea of what they'll do to you." He folded his arms and rolled his blue eyes. I thought if anyone would understand—would consider not laying into me so viciously, he would. He had returned home to visit his religious family, who said they would rather see him dead than for him to be gay—a family he feared would put him in a coffin every time they served him a meal.

"I'm a new person now, Griff," I said, holding out for a glimmer of real change, for some heavenly revelation where miracles were real, and prayers were truly answered. Griff was nearly shaking with rage now. After we began to argue, I did what any seasoned Christian had been taught to get the upper hand. "I'll be praying for you, my friend."

"*Humph!* I'll be praying for you, too," he said with a snarling whine before spinning around and walking out of the department store.

I feared Griff misunderstood me. I wanted to pray that he would lose his rage toward me, not because he was gay. But at this point, he had vanished from the store, and I didn't have his address or phone number. I was impressed with his efforts to find and stop me from what he considered to be my certain ruin. I convinced myself that the Devil was just working through him to rob my victory. I was beginning to learn the teaching that nearly everyone and everything outside the church walls is evil—out to devour our souls, which starts by leading us away from the only denominational truth.

CHAPTER 26

AFTER a few weeks as a regular member of the Pentecostal church, I was still searching for deliverance from my homosexual yearnings. I was confused. The youth pastor announced to the entire youth group that the change in me was profound. *What the heck did I look like beforehand,* I wondered. Was I glowing now, or was his assessment a form of brainwashing? The church considers infirmities and addictions to sin, especially homosexuality, as demons that need to be cast out or "dug out" if the prayers don't work.

"... If any of you are gay and sneaking around this church, I'll dig you out with a posthole digger," Pastor Whittington said with a growl so fierce his jowls shook over the pulpit microphone. "If you're a young person and going to have premarital sex, it's better to have it with the opposite sex than the same sex."

I stiffened in the pew where I was sitting, worried that my sin confession had finally reached his ears. Later I learned that two boys from the ministerial college, which the church owned, had been kicked out. The other student ministers suspected they were having gay sex, so they broke into the dorm room and caught them in the "sixty-nine" sex position. I imagine they got the eyeful they were hoping for in the process. Around this time, the choral was returning home from a singing tour, and on the bus in mixed company, the holiness boys stripped the pants and underwear off one of the boys and tossed the garments out the window and onto the highway, leaving him to run to his dorm room naked. God led other student ministers to journey down Bourbon Street in New Orleans—to witness to the sinners and nothing more, they swore with blushes bright as cherries. Another student from the college admitted to me that he and his new bride watched porn on their honeymoon and tried to duplicate what the couple was doing with the whipped topping. This same student preached against watching television. I was stunned at the hypocrisy I saw all around me, but I shut my eyes to it and tried to focus on getting saved. Unlike the other boys, I was always shutting my eyes.

"… The Holy Ghost is a gentleman. He doesn't force you to speak in tongues. He doesn't make you become a robot. You have to do the speaking," the assistant pastor informed the congregation.

This was a relief to know; the ministry wanted the congregation to read between the lines. So, subconsciously mimicking the other members, I began making one and two-syllable noises they called our prayer language. With the fire and damnation sermons, the emotional music, and the ecstatic worship displays, I, too, was convinced I had begun speaking in tongues. I was certain the chills I felt were from the Holy Ghost now in me. But in my moments of doubt, I wondered if the chills came from the fact that I was allowing myself to behave unseemly in a formal environment, violating the rules of public behavior—a naughty child kicking his legs out of his diaper and running free at daycare.

For my third visit to the church, I arrived over an hour early. The church was already decorated for Christmas, with a beautifully lit tree in the lobby. The pastor's nephew, Shawn Whittington, had said he wanted to have a Bible study with me before the evening service. But after the empty sanctuary began filling up with members, I realized he didn't keep his word.

Paranoia filled my head. *Shawn found out you're gay and stood you up, Milan.*

As I sat there by myself, as usual, a girl slipped between the pews behind me. She had a flawless peaches-and-cream complexion and light-brown curls that danced around her shoulder blades. For an overweight girl, she glided in high heels more gracefully than any I had ever seen.

"Hi. I'm Holly Ross. I'm the official door greeter for the youth group. I noticed you sitting by yourself. You're welcome to come and sit with me and my friends."

I was delighted someone finally included me, so I moved about fifteen pews back and greeted her friends after she introduced me. The sermon was about taking new territory, and I was beginning to feel I had found mine, especially when Holly and her friends showed up at my apartment uninvited a few nights later.

"Who are these old men on your walls," one of her friends asked while the others checked out the view from the top-floor window.

"They're the founding fathers of the Pentecostal movement," I replied. I had torn out pictures of William J. Seymour, Charles F. Parham, and others from a book I had bought from the local Christian bookstore. I was determined to keep my living environment as holy as possible. If that weren't enough, I threw away old clothes that didn't look Christian enough. I got rid of old photos, music records, and more gay friends that might be a gateway for Satan to rob me of my miracle.

And then doubt would set in on occasion: Why should you need a miracle, Milan? If God didn't want anyone to be gay, and He helps millionaire football players score touchdowns, He'd surely be willing to change you, deliver you, or whatever was needed the minute you prayed about it.

For laughs, my new friends imitated various church members' methods of worship. Some members mooed like cows; one clucked like a chicken. One short stubby man the members coined "Jumping Jack," another man they nicknamed "Whirly Bird."

I felt compassion for the members they were mocking, and it became apparent I was uncomfortable with their game. "And what do I look like when I worship?"

The room grew awkwardly quiet. Blushing, Doug closed his eyes, lifted his stiff arms, and stood serenely. This was probably an exact imitation because I had to make darned sure I never gave them what they expected by bending my wrists too limply.

After the conversation began to drag, we all piled into my car and rode around downtown Jackson to admire the Christmas lights in the park. A group of girls in skin-tight jeans was swishing across the street.

"*Whoa!* Those girls would make good Pentecostals," said Doug, nearly panting with lust. He was just out of high school and shaved his sideburns an inch higher than his hairline in his overkill attempt to out-clean-cut the other guys.

Another boy named Hunter lowered his voice so the girls couldn't hear. "Talking about hot girls. I love to help Pastor Whittington with the female baptisms. This one girl, she had the cutest little booty."

I slowed the car and shot Hunter a scolding glance.

"Well," he squeaked defensively, "you can see straight through their white baptismal robes when they step out of the water."

After I turned the corner down the long side of the park, another of Holly's church friends made a disturbing confession.

"The young people from our church come here all the time and throw eggs and stuff at the gay men who hang out in the park."

My heart was troubled upon hearing this news. Hearing them all laugh, except for Holly, was more painful. The lone man walking around the park in his thick coat could be me. His family could've abandoned him, leaving him homeless. At that moment, I relived all of the things that had been thrown at me in public and the times I feared for my safety. I couldn't believe the church wasn't stopping their Christian members from assaulting gay people who might be on the verge of suicide. Because many parents in Mississippi cut off their gay children before they're even of legal age, many of these children are sadly under-educated. They're forced to take low-paying jobs if they don't end up homeless or on drugs. I should've asked Holly's friends to get out of the car and walk home, but I had to forgive, forgive, forgive, and show that I, too, was a new man so my miracle would happen.

I often broke out in gut-wrenching tears at the altar and many times on the pews, begging God to forgive me for the gay thoughts I still kept having. Usually, a male church brother prayed over me but at a safe distance. This culminated in a few attempts to deliver me from the Devil. One elder resorted to an exorcism attempt in Latin behind me.

"Brother Milan, you need to be at the altar jumping up and down if you are going to loosen the shackles of bondage that Satan is using to keep you bound," a ministerial student said to me.

A boot-scooting preacher from Texas stopped the sermon and, with a scowl, pointed his finger at me. "Young man, good God! You have walls built up around you that you need to tear down. If you don't tear them down, then Jesus will. God doesn't make any man's wrists limp. *Argh!* We have some gay men who've started coming to our church in Texas and got the Holy Ghost an' all, but I wanna blowtorch my hands after I hafta shake their clammy palms. We had real men in the good old days; they could wipe out an entire army by lifting their smelly armpits."

The church members laughed, and a burning sensation rose from my stomach into my throat. I kept walls for protection, no doubt. I was trying my best to act naïve during these endless public humiliations to keep my sanity, to avoid the danger of exposure. The boot-scooting preacher later got arrested for harboring stolen goods in his home and even in his church after his daughter's boyfriend was killed from his involvement with a drug gang. The pastor took his socks, light bulbs, and anything he could unscrew from that boy's home, but the congregation quickly reinstated him to his pastor's position with no disapproving frowns to restore.

"I have a feeling that God just wants you to be happy," said Ted Gibson as he leaned over the pew while I lingered in a bitter mood during the next church service. This was news to me. Everything that had ever made me happy had been called evil, as in the song "It's a Sin" by Pet Shop Boys, which they often played in the gay clubs I used to attend.

"Are you sure about that?" I asked him defeatedly.

Ted's forehead wrinkled and his beautiful smile noticeably wilted. He nodded his head apprehensively.

The next week, while I was at a low point again, the phone rang in my apartment.

"Hey, it's Holly. My office Christmas party is tonight at seven, and there's going to be people there drinking. I need another Pentecostal friend for backup. I was wondering if you'd be willing to come with me."

Holly's charm was infectious, but I was becoming concerned by the intentions of her persistence and wondered how she had gotten my phone number. She had tons of friends; why did she need *me* to go to the party at her workplace? I didn't want to go to the event. Perhaps it was from never being allowed to have boundaries, but I couldn't say "no." She had been so nice to bring me into her circle of friends.

An hour later, she called me again. "My cousin Delyn is coming with me to the party. I just thought I should let you know."

"Oh, okay," I said, assuming she had found a replacement and was letting me off the hook.

The following Sunday morning, I sat near the front of the sanctuary, waiting for the sermon to begin, when Holly came through the door leading into the back hall.

"I cannot believe you stood me up for the Christmas party!" she said so everyone around could hear.

I didn't think it was supposed to be a date, so I was stunned. After she kept showing up with friends at my apartment and salon, I knew I needed to tell her the truth. That was the only way to get her to back off. I took her to a low-budget pizza restaurant near the mall, and we both ate pizza, drank cola, and knotted the paper straw covers into tiny balls. I needed to place a boundary and drive away any romantic intentions.

"In ninth grade, my school voted me 'Most Mysterious,'" I said, working up the nerve to tell her why that was so, and I had to do it carefully.

"I was voted 'Most Friendly' in school," she interrupted. I learned that she was five months older than me, and the only time she had ever been in a hair salon was when she had come to visit me. In eighth grade, she cut her hair for the first time and begged her dad to spank her since, according to the Pentecostals, the Bible says it's a sin for women to cut their hair.

"I refused to be mysterious. I always volunteered to be the cootie on the playground to get kids to be my friend," she continued, and her rosy-cheek grin wilted into long-suffering regret, perhaps.

"I need to tell you something, Holly. You see, I've only ever lived a gay lifestyle." I awaited her reaction, fully expecting her to recoil in horror or run out of the pizza place as every other straight person would.

"Oh, that's no big deal. Lots of people experiment, especially in college," she said. I could tell that she didn't want to talk about the matter. Perhaps it was her quirkiness and beautiful spirit, but I felt as though I had known her in a past life, a spiritual connection more than just sympathy between us.

After I drove her home, we sat in my car in the driveway and talked further. "As soon as my mother saw you, she said, 'That's the man you're gonna marry,'" Holly said.

I assumed in my naïve youth that the elders in the church, including Holly's mother, were prophets of God.

"She's looking out the window now, waiting for you to kiss me," Holly continued.

The darkness hid any bashfulness she might have expressed. I couldn't see anyone standing in the window of the darkened house. This was her signaling me to kiss her. Endlessly abandoned and desperate for unconditional love, I wanted to weep. I assumed the feelings I was experiencing were the Holy Ghost indicating approval. Maybe God had led us together as a test to receive deliverance from homosexuality—a test of faith like He gave Abraham to see if he was willing to slaughter his only innocent son. The definition of faith in Hebrews 11:1 had been taught to me in the Baptist church: "Now faith is the substance of things hoped for, the evidence of things not seen." I also learned that to activate faith, you have to declare things that weren't as though they were. For this reason, for keeping in faith, many prayerful Christians struggle to relay negative health reports on their hospitalized loved ones until their loved ones die, leaving everyone stunned by the news.

For faith, for my miracle to work, I had to claim victory already. In other words, I had to fake it until I made it. But then I was taught that dishonesty and deception were at the heart of most sins. I don't think I would've been attracted to Holly even if I were straight, but I had never been attracted to any woman. As a Christian, I was forbidden from having sex before marriage or even entertaining any sexual thoughts.

"You need to test drive a car before you buy it," a lot of Christians confessed when it came to sex before marriage. I was learning increasingly that young straight people were having oral and anal sex before marriage because they didn't consider it "sex." More and more, husbands were letting their wives use strap-on dildos and anal stimulators on them in acts they called "pegging." But if gay people were doing the same things—the same sex acts straight people stole from gays—then straight people want them to be severely punished or executed. As long as the sacred vagina remained unpenetrated by a penis, they were still holy virgins. I was becoming increasingly bitter about the hypocrisy and evil double standards. The young people in the church who chose not to have sex before marriage often confessed that they married as soon as possible to experience sex before the Rapture and the end of the world, which was a constant and fearful topic of religious discussion.

My resentment led me to do some research. I learned that oral and anal sex, even among straight people, once violated the Colonial Era sodomy laws when the anti-crimes against nature and anti-nonprocreative sex generations also murdered children suspected of being witches who flew over the moon on brooms. Until the churches, with their claws on the lawmakers, realized sodomy and masturbation were far more common among straight people than the old puritans had envisioned. Any sex act that didn't lead to pregnancy was considered wicked and could lead to ten years in prison in many U.S. states who still refuse to take these outdated laws off their books in case they can one day reuse them on just gay people. Once this glaring double standard became known, it took a lot of mental gymnastics, but the lawmakers and police could no longer bring themselves to kick down the doors of homes and arrest Adams and Eves on their kinky wedding nights.

I relayed this information to a Christian client who was complaining about homosexuals in my salon.

"I had no idea that sodomy laws once included straight people. Where did you hear that?" she said, appearing suddenly ghostly under the hairdryer. The woman never rescheduled another appointment even though she loved her hair. I imagine she never sought out a male stylist again and probably screened the female hairdressers so she could still orally pleasure her hubby without the risk of guilt from learning further uncomfortable history.

I discovered that the more you know only depresses you—makes you bitter and judgmental. It all made sense to me as to why so many are ill-informed. Modern men especially want this part of history forgotten in case their Bible-toting girlfriends experience guilt for giving them head, their favorite form of sex. I found several online Christian blogs dogmatically arguing whether believers can have oral or anal sex with their wives or even masturbate. However, the arguments were usually with less colorful language.

"Chicks can't get pregnant in the first and third holes, but I always like to complete a three-hole par, fellahs," the other bros always say before bragging they "Fucked the shit out of her."

Over the weekend, several members of the church accused and reported a sweet young girl named Tracy of being a lesbian. The only reason I could gather is that she occasionally played the drums during church services. Sharing God's love even more, some of the youth group beat up an atheist for holding a sign at an out-of-state youth rally. Pastor Whittington once again showed his hypocrisy after he scolded the young people in the church because someone carved obscene words on a balcony pew.

"… Hollywood is to blame for all of this. Elisabeth Taylor is the B word, and Magic Johnson couldn't've slept with as many women as he claims. He'd be numb on one end and dumb on the other."

The assistant pastor nearly slid out of his chair, trying to suppress his red-faced laughter. They despised Liz Taylor after she became one of the leading activists to help stop the AIDS epidemic. "The most awful thing of all is to be numb," Liz said about fighting for the cause, yet the members of my church were not only numb to human suffering, they were gleeful that AIDS was killing people they hated.

Heterosexual couples finally being allowed by the government to engage in "sodomy" and non-procreative sex didn't transform their love-hate obsessions of gay people, not in my world. Nevertheless, I sincerely believed that if I stepped out in great faith and did as God instructed, as He demanded, then He'd surely take care of my lack of sexual attraction to females.

Within six months, Holly and I set a wedding date. I privately struggled to quench any homosexual urges and thoughts as I had been taught, convincing myself they were an illusion of the Devil trying to destroy my miracle. It wasn't an illusion to some church members, however, especially on the night of the church's annual foot-washing ceremony, where they emulated Jesus when He humbly washed His disciples' feet. The men, stiff as boards, made their way to the prayer room while the women headed to the fellowship hall. As I reluctantly walked to the prayer room for the ceremony, a group of men behind me said, "Is this the door where the fags go in?"

I wanted to disappear at that moment, but I had to ignore the comments and actions of others and keep my eyes on Jesus in hopes He would perform a miracle, at least by my wedding night. Once inside, I found a boy named Sawyer, who was also rumored to be gay, sitting on a pew against the far wall of the prayer room. While the men began pairing off with a trusted buddy, looking like they'd rather have root canals than touch another man's feet, Sawyer appeared as lost as I felt. It became clear that no other man in the room was going to get within ten yards of us, so we both were drawn together to get through the ordeal. Even though it would make my sexuality more obvious, I sat beside him, and we washed each other's feet. Down the hall, the women prayed and spoke in tongues loudly while the men sat virtually silent, except for a few perturbed grunts as they sloshed water on cringing feet as if they'd catch a testicle-shrinking germ from touching another man's foot.

And what about men who had foot fetishes? How could they always tell the difference between a woman's and a man's foot? No one ever discussed that. It was the bit of flesh in the middle of the body that needed regulating.

CHAPTER 27

PASTOR Whittington's wife, Martha, was teaching Sunday school that morning. She abruptly stopped the singing and raised one sharp eyebrow at the members.

"There are some of you in this congregation who are not singing, and I can point you out right now." She was notorious for spying into her neighbor's windows at night with high-powered binoculars to see if they were skipping church, and she had better not catch them on their computer while missing. Apparently, being clothed in righteousness was not sufficient. She also was known for snaking around the church with a pair of white gloves and swiping her fingers across the Pentecostal women's faces, doing a surprise inspection to see if they were wearing makeup.

"Go to the restroom and wash your face now. We are the holy body of Christ, and paint belongs on a barn," she would say.

The girls made daily trips to tanning salons to pass the makeup inspections. They would also rub toothpaste on their cheeks to redden them. If a girl wore her long hair pulled to one side of her head, Martha called it the "Wicked Tilt" and frowned upon it. The boys were discouraged from using sissified hairspray, mousse, or gel. Instead, they would dip into their wives' and sisters' petroleum jelly they used to thicken their eyelashes since they couldn't wear mascara. But I had to bite my tongue when Martha stopped her morning lesson and raised her eyebrow at Benjamin, another skinny boy the members labeled a "fag." Almost every time the boy came to church, he wore a bright green jacket.

"Benjamin, you need to go to the store and buy a brown, gray, or black jacket that is more masculine."

The boy sank in his chair and lowered his head. I assumed the green jacket was all he could afford, but it was a beautiful coat that fit him well. The biblical Joseph, with his coat of many colors, would be considered the son of Sodom by this church's superior standards.

"It's so twisted. The entire congregation embraced Eric Steersmen at the altar—prayed for the flasher like he was the prodigal son after he got caught flashing his erect penis at little schoolgirls. But poor Benjamin needed to be shamed for his color choice. I wonder if the church would accept him if he had worn a camouflage hunting jacket?" I asked Holly, who shrugged with a weary smile.

The members would never dare disobey the ministry, but the next time Martha taught a class I couldn't forgive her for her mistreatment of Benjamin, and I refused to give in to her sadistic intimidations.

"Raise your hands if you believe God is going to fill this classroom so full of people that we will need a larger building," Martha commanded.

Oddly for a church against the doctrine of easy believism, everyone did as she instructed, except me. I sat quietly and debated whether I truly believed; after all, I had not yet seen any tangible evidence of rewarded faith.

"You mean you don't believe, Milan!" asked Martha.

The young people stiffened. I shrugged my shoulders in a gesture of uncertainty. I could have lied and pretended I believed like the trembling throng, just going through the expected motions like the others. *Behold it is written, and the people are smitten*, but not my damned soul. No, I had to think and question—two things held in contempt under a steeple.

I prayed harder to keep my heart from becoming bitter, but I was now extra self-conscious of everything I said, wore, or did. I immediately stopped wearing my turquoise-blue jacket and threw it in the trash. I became utterly perplexed, especially with how God's servants targeted some people, passing select souls through fire while they swept others' multiple indiscretions under the wall-to-wall carpet. The Christian church formally considered divorce and masturbation evil sins. Yet nearly half the church members had divorced and remarried multiple times. Those two deadly sins the ministry strangely omitted and replaced with condemnation of skinny boys in colorful coats instead. With this as my motivating factor, I met with Martha Whittington in her office the following Sunday.

"I want to ensure I have these holiness standards down correctly, but I have a question. Can you please explain why the women in this organization can wear their skirts up to their kneecaps, but the men and boys have to wear their pants to their ankles, even when playing football in a hundred-degree heat?" The only conclusion I could make was that the church men liked to see women's legs walking across the church platform, so they made allowances for female legs. Unless they feared boys might become gay if they saw another boy's bare legs.

Martha's eyes mischievously squinted, offsetting her cancerous smile. Ignoring her reaction, I continued my questioning.

"And why can't married couples wear wedding rings as proof of their bond in holy matrimony when you allow them to wear gold wristwatches? Pastor Whittington's mother even wears a cameo brooch, and I see several women wearing jeweled barrettes in their hair?"

"That's just the way it is here," Martha said through half-pursed lips. "Besides, you don't go to another church."

I was stunned, but why did I expect a reasonable answer? Reason and faith constantly contradicted one another. Her pitiful response would never have held up in a court of law, which I realized these types of religious leaders needed, especially if they were going to crush people with their double standards and dogma.

My faith received a boost when that same week, my last remaining gay friend, Carl Allred, called me at the salon and claimed he, too, had been attending a Holy Ghost church near Tupelo, Mississippi, where he had recently moved.

"I believe a miracle happened, Milan. I believe God cured me of AIDS!"

"Oh, that's great, Carl," I said, feeling as though my prayers for him had worked wonders. I would finally have an understanding friend on my lonely spiritual path. "You should come to Jackson and go to church with me, and that way, you can meet Holly."

Not long after Carl arrived, I didn't see much, if any, difference in his effeminate behavior. He slapped my knee limply and giggled with delight over something I said in front of a group of my new friends. I tensed when he came close to saying, "Oh, girl! No, you didn't," like he used to do. When his usual "screaming queen" behavior continued, I led him out of the church and into my car so nobody could overhear our conversation.

"I'm a new person now, Carl, and I'll be married soon. It wouldn't be fair to rub my wife's nose in my old lifestyle. We can't turn back. You've heard the warnings of Sodom and Gomorrah."

"Like a billion times," Carl said. His head collapsed against the headrest. "Christians are obsessed with that ancient story. But it was only two desert cities, Milan. For some reason, they ignore the story about God demolishing the entire planet with a flood because everyone was evil. Think about it. The whole planet! That's a blockbuster I'd think they'd be preaching to oppress everyone. They have the nerve to call people like us Sodomites and abominations. If the Sodomites were so awful, it's because they were rapists who'd assault anything with a pulse. Gay men wouldn't have been interested in Lot's daughters he offered them. And preachers never mention that after righteous Lot left Sodom, he had drunken sex with his own daughters. Incest! Why, Milan? Why do they always twist everything out of context? I'll tell you why: because it would take away from their anti-gay agenda."

Normally Carl would've snapped his fingers fiercely after making such a comment, "reading someone" queens called it. He was right, but this discussion was too raw, and I wondered what his intentions were—if he was faking his new walk with God. Most of all, I feared he would mess up my faith.

"But that's just it. I'm not gay anymore, Carl. Look, I wish you the best; I do. But I think it's time we should go our separate ways."

Carl's face lost its usual animation. With his mouth ajar, he nodded numbly and stared straight ahead into the parking lot. He fumbled for the door handle and soon vanished between the maze of cars.

Faith required denying everything about myself—dying to myself—crucifying my wants and desires as the *New Testament* commanded. By doing so, I was essentially lying or pretending at best. I pretended I now preferred Christian music instead of high-energy gay club music. I had to claim that I believed women shouldn't wear makeup or cut and color their hair, though secretly, my favorite look for women was blood-red bobs and cabaret makeup like Columbia wore in "The Rocky Horror Picture Show." I couldn't bring myself to be truthful about any of this, especially to confess to Carl that I was still fighting an intense attraction to men, especially preppy-type boys with a swimmer's build. And no more shorts or speedos for me in the long sweltering summers; from now on, I would be a fully covered beacon of holiness.

CHAPTER 28

DESPERATELY missing my parents, I wrote them a letter informing them that I had abandoned the gay lifestyle and was attending church. I sent them a photo of Holly and told them that I was going to marry her. The abandoned boy in me healed somewhat when they—when Mother—responded for the first time in five years. She wrote of her joy at the new state of my soul and for God answering their prayers. But my eyes crossed when I came to the next paragraph in the folded letter.

"Oh, Son, we are worried about Holly. She doesn't look healthy."

I thought that was harsh since my parents had always struggled with obesity. Mother sent a plastic trashcan and tissue dispenser for a wedding gift. It arrived as cracked as we were.

Holly and I started receiving strange and threatening phone calls at odd hours. "Angie boy," one guy said in his Southern twang over the phone after a menacing silence. An older man called me at work. "I wouldn't touch your ass with a ten-foot pole. No, sir," he mumbled insidiously. As if I wanted him to touch my ass.

It became evident that a few people in the church were trying to stop our wedding. One bridesmaid and two of my groomsmen backed out, and even Doug, my best man, tried to back out of the ceremony at the last minute with a word salad of excuses. He was more concerned about his future ministry than being aligned with a suspected homosexual. During a two-week revival, Pastor Davidson, a guest minister who had barely survived a forty-day food fast and claimed to communicate with angels, prophesied that my friend Doug would be the most prolific evangelist the church had ever seen. Unfortunately, Ted Gibson, the only man who told me God wanted me to be happy, died from a church-ordained fast. It was challenging to work as laboriously as he did and not get adequate nourishment. By the time his fast was up, he was so hungry that he choked on his food and had a brain aneurism. Of course, the church members kept this under tight lips.

Before Doug even began to be the prophesied greatest soul winner, he got an underaged girl pregnant out of wedlock. This would get a man arrested outside the protective walls of a church, but the brothers in Christ patted him on the back and let him attend the school of ministry anyway. I didn't get any back pats. After having what I thought was a friendly conversation, a preacher shoved me against the sanctuary wall in front of everyone during the revival.

"I know all about you and the other fags in this church. You need to be at the altar praying," he said to me with a snarl. I wasn't prepared for this and was more stunned that nobody questioned the assault or tried to stop it.

Holly's wedding shower opened my eyes to the secretive behavior of the church women. The host of the party, like many in the church, kept the family televisions hidden in closed armoires. The women looked prudish in their Old Mother Hubbard uniforms, but once together, they weren't much different from the worldly women they felt superior to.

"Milan said he wanted you to have this special gift for your shower tonight," a group of girls said, handing Holly a massive gift box containing a crude jar of petroleum jelly. The women got a laugh from their gag.

"Oh, that's kinky," said another girl when Holly received a steel wool scrub pad. Almost every gift she received had sadomasochistic potential for their starved imaginations. Another girl asked if Holly used my sperm to make her hair grow.

The day of our wedding arrived, and a couple of church members stared at Holly in a smirking intimidation game and left before the vows began. A kindly woman attached my groom's flower to my lapel, and I peeped through the sanctuary door, searching the seated guests for my parents or Hansel and Karen. When the organ music began, I realized they had made no effort to attend the wedding. I felt as though I was gazing down on myself from outer space, and I was a lone speck on the planet. After all the years that my parents had disowned me and after all of the dramatic moves I had made to please them—nothing.

"If any man knows of any lawful impediment why Milan Sergent and Holly Ross may not be joined in holy matrimony, let him now *confess it*," Pastor Whittington declared forcefully as we stood at the altar. With all eyes watching my every move, I was afraid I wouldn't be able to say my vows. For the first time in my twenty-four-year life, I did lose my voice. I couldn't get a sound to escape my throat until Holly made her way down the long, carpeted aisle and stood beside me.

The wedding went off without any further dents, except my groomsmen tied large fruit cans all across the back of my car, which they also covered in shaving cream. The cans popped and pounded against my bumper and trunk as I drove off with my new bride until

I pulled over at a gas station to cut them off, and there I discovered little dents and scratches across the back of the car. Despite my displeasure, I was more concerned about why they had used fruit cans. *Were my groomsmen implying that I was fruity?*

The drive back to the apartment was tense for me. The traffic flowed too smoothly. Every red light changed too fast. After entering our new apartment, I prayed that I would find her sexy while I dimmed the lights in the bedroom. Holly eased from the bathroom in a red-lace negligee the youth minister's wife had bought her as a wedding gift. I was expecting her to come out in a floor-length curtain as the holiness women wore in public, a "Little House on the Prairie" gown. Either way, I would soon be expected to see her naked and consummate our marriage to orgasm.

My much prayed-for miracle never happened.

In the past, I had always been more concerned about my partner's pleasure. The only way I could describe sex with a woman was that it felt as if I were being raped, like when Nichole had violated me on the couch, except I loved Holly, so it shouldn't feel this way, so unnatural. To avoid being crasser, I hated every aspect of it. With Holly being a virgin, I hoped she couldn't detect that I had to fake my pleasure. But by morning, she awoke in tears.

"Oh, God!" she said. "I dreamed you died for some reason, so I rushed to the bathroom to take a pregnancy test, and it was negative. I realized I wouldn't even have a baby who looked like you."

Her dream only added to my guilt, and I wondered if it were somehow prophetic.

After several attempts at making love with my new bride, I tried not to panic and held onto the go-to saying that Christians fall upon when all else fails: "God's timing isn't always our timing." So, I was going to have to pray and believe harder, double the tithes and offerings, fast more, and search every remaining crevice in my life for any speck that was unchristian.

For our honeymoon, I bought two plane tickets to Idaho. It wasn't the typical desire for brides to spend their honeymoon with the groom's parents, but it was important to me for everyone to meet and get along.

"I'm nervous. I've never flown before. And the only time I've traveled out of the state of Mississippi was for my senior trip to Disney

World," said Holly as we drove to the airport.

"I thought Pentecostals weren't supposed to attend worldly amusements. I thought it was against their moral standards and bylaws," I said, stunned that Holly, of all people, had been violating church rules without any qualms.

"Oh, they all do stuff in secret," she replied. Again, I was starting to feel as if I were the only one who had been duped into trusting my newfound faith, just a little too late. There was no looking back now. I didn't want to end up similar to Lot's wife in the Bible and turn into a pillar of salt. My parents had made plans for us to spend the whole week with them, and I was hoping things would go smoothly.

After the plane landed at the airport in Spokane, Washington, my body charged with excitement at seeing my parents after so long. Father was his usual self in socks, sandals, and khaki shorts, exposing his pale hairy legs. Mother was waiting beside him in a frumpy red housedress. Her hair had grown long and stringy, making it seem like an eternity had passed since I had last seen her.

As we drove to the border of Idaho, I noticed the gray hair that had increased on the backs of their heads. Father kept the music on a gospel station instead of the country or oldies music he used to listen to. Occasionally, he would raise a clenched and trembling fist toward the car roof. I had never seen him do this before and realized this was his attempt at lifting holy hands, which the Pentecostals did during worship.

"Mom thought you guys would want to sleep in separate beds?" Father said out of nowhere.

"No, sir," Holly and I responded, wondering why they would assume such a thing, especially on our honeymoon. They still slept in separate bedrooms, but I had no idea why they would want us to sleep apart on our honeymoon.

It was mid-August, and the mountain roads to the cabin on Whiteraven Road were dusty. Mother became icily silent while Father filled the awkwardness with his version of "He's Still Working on Me" in the voice of a six-year-old, nonetheless. Instead of "Handel," he later claimed his favorite song was "Hamlet's Messiah." Bless his heart, as they say in the South. I had to give him credit for his sudden displays of spirituality and realized they probably felt a need to amp up their own spiritual life after claiming God had instructed them to abandon their only child.

First thing the next morning at the cabin, I took Holly for a stroll around the mountain property. A new house sat a few yards away from my old log prison.

"It belongs to my replacements," I whispered to Holly.

"Your parents gave Hansel and Karen part of their land and built them a house. And all they gave us is a cracked trashcan."

Her words jarred me. I didn't want to be materialistic or ungrateful, but the more I thought about it, it wasn't reassuring. I would continue to pray away any bitterness.

During breakfast, Holly found a soggy gray mop string in her food.

"You could've been gracious and not said anything. Brigitte worked hard to prepare this breakfast," Father huffed at her.

I had forgotten to warn Holly about my parents' tendency to scold others; it was sort of a secret spice they added to nearly every meal. Holly was so germophobic that she wouldn't even brush her teeth in the bathroom. After a tense breakfast, Mother strapped a new camera around her neck while Father preoccupied himself with some bird watching out the window with his new binoculars.

"Come outside, Son," she said with a devious smirk. "I want to take some family photos together."

I obediently hopped up from the secondhand sofa beside Holly, where we had been gazing at the ugly black barrel serving as a wood heater. By the time I followed Mother outside the cabin, I realized she did not invite Holly until much later after she already hurt her feelings. So far, this was not a typical honeymoon to Hawaii or the Virgin Islands; this was misery.

With a flimsy Mexican blanket nailed up as a door in the deathly quiet cabin, it was a good excuse to avoid having intimacy with Holly. After three days and nights with my parents, Holly wanted us to spend a little intimate time together.

"Since we're going through downtown Sandpoint again, we were wondering if you could drop us off at a hotel on the way back," I asked my parents as gently as possible. We had been going as a group on excursions every day that week, so Holly and I thought it wouldn't inconvenience them in the least. I thought my parents would've wanted their son to do his honeymoon duty with his new bride. After shunning me for so long, I thought they would've groveled at my feet and been ecstatic that I had married any girl—an extremely Christian girl at that.

"I will never take my vacation time to spend with Milan ever again!" Mother said to Father as if we were not standing right in front of her. "If he has one ounce of love left for me, then he'd better make these last few days we have together tolerable!" she snorted as she stomped off to her bedroom.

My parents canceled their planned excursion for the day, and the farther out of Sandpoint we drove, I realized Mother had forced Father to drop us off at the most isolated hotel he could find, where he left us for two whole days and nights. The Gulf War had started two weeks earlier, and now we were into the Sergent war.

There was nothing to do within miles, and after I didn't pounce on Holly under the sheets, she grabbed the remote control out of boredom. "I don't suppose it'll be a sin to watch the news and see what's going on with the war. I mean, nobody will see us; we're twenty-five hundred miles away from Mississippi." She aimed the remote at the television.

"No," I said, stopping her. "We're not supposed to watch anything on television. Remember? Pastor Whittington called it that lumpy vomit from Hollywood."

Now was the time for it to happen. Faking romantic passion took great concentration. With my continued prayers and obedience, I kept hoping the attraction to Holly's body—the urge any straight man would have for a female—would soon happen. But all I experienced was secret revulsion and unfulfillment.

The last two days we spent back at the cabin were edgy. I emptied Holly's bedpan, so she wouldn't have to walk to the outhouse at night to pee.

"You're just a disrespectful gal, and Milan is emotionally disturbed," Father said to Holly after she mentioned her favorite Bible verses, which seemed to contradict the ones they had just quoted aloud.

I didn't deny that I was emotionally disturbed, especially at this point, but Holly was the sweetest person I knew. Yet to my parents, she was a monster. I could only imagine their reaction if I had taken some of my former gay friends to Idaho to meet them. "Stone the

Abominations" would be the anthem.

Holly and I wanted to leave at once, but we were trapped miles up a mountain with no phone to call a cab to get back to the airport. We struggled to be as amicable as possible as we rode with my parents to see Glacier National Forest. While on a ferryboat into Canada, I whispered to Holly, "I'm sorry, my dear. We'll never return to Idaho. I'll take you on a real honeymoon someday."

What had I done? I questioned during the drive back to the airport. Part of the reason I had upended my whole life and married a woman was to win my parents back. And everything was turning out to be a disaster. I began to question if inheriting eternal life was a fair exchange for eternal misery.

CHAPTER 29

SEPTEMBER the second was the first Sunday service Holly and I attended after getting married. It seemed as though everyone was examining me to see if I had successfully consummated the marriage—if I were somehow straighter and the sanctuary was safer. Pastor Whittington did his usual rambling after promising to preach an actual sermon finally. He, too, seemed to be inspecting me.

"Aren't you all glad you didn't jump off the Tallahatchie Bridge back in August?" he asked the congregation as he peered at them over the pulpit. I couldn't help but believe he was referencing my situation and wedding day or perhaps the people who had objected to our engagement. I was also keenly aware of the movie "Ode to Billy Joe" and how Billy jumped to his death off the Tallahatchie Bridge a hundred miles from where I was sitting because Billy's homosexuality prevented him from consummating his relationship with the girl he loved.

After the service, Pastor Whittington called me into his office and instructed me to have a seat. Without the stage and pulpit elevating him, he appeared so small and vulnerable. His small, twisted nose, pitted with rosaceous scars, wrinkled up under his bifocals. In his burgundy leather office chair, he steepled his hands under his chin, fingertips touching.

"I wouldn't have married you and Holly if I had known you were a fag. Are you, Milan? Is Satan still tempting you with homosexuality?"

He leaned forward, ready to feast upon my every deviation, his beady eyes disrobed me over the tops of his black-rimmed glasses. I couldn't believe how straightforward he was finally being, especially after all the passive-aggressive ramblings from the pulpit. My sin confession at the altar from my first visit had finally come to his attention. Now he was trying to trap me. I could almost see angelic ears pressed against the stained-glass window, their platinum hearts pulsing for the sordid details of my sex life.

"He would try," I said, leaving it at that. I resented having to blame such a natural part of me on an invisible fallen angel often depicted with horns, a tail, and a pitchfork. On the day the pastor had baptized me, I could've shouted from the top of the steeple and claimed that God had taken away my homosexual yearnings and none of the men in the church would honestly believe it. *The churchmen know some things are incurable and that every man secretly lusts after strange flesh. They just can't admit it,* my thoughts could only conclude.

Something between a repressed laugh and a cry escaped Pastor Whittington's mouth. I couldn't tell which. He leaned back in his chair and smoothed his pompadoured gray hair on his large head.

"I can send you to a gay-conversion camp in Florida. They have people there who are trained to help young people struggling with … these things."

A jolt of pain shot through my testicles. Every barbaric detail Griff had warned me concerning those gay concentration camps replayed in my head. I suddenly realized how off something was about miracles and all. The church ran a yellow page ad that touted *"Dynamic Gifts of the Spirit! Deliverance! Miracles! Healings!"* Yet when it came to gay people, church prayer for healing didn't work; they had to send the individual off to a horrific gay-conversion camp.

"I can't afford to go," I quickly said while my heart pounded under my coat and tie. "I'll, um, lose all of my hair clients. They won't wait on me. And Holly—she won't be able to pay the apartment rent by herself."

Pastor Whittington stared uncomfortably long and coldly at me. It seemed as if he were chewing on a devious plan. "About that beauty salon biz. For starts, you need to get a manly job."

"I don't have any training to work in anything else, unfortunately."

"I have a lot of connections. I'll help you get another job. In the meantime, stop cringing every time I talk about faggots."

Cringing? What a shitty and ridiculous stereotype to use against gay people. Was this supposed to be another poker-faced showdown at the O.K. Corral? I was surprised he didn't add "lisping." Either way, there it was—proof that I wasn't being paranoid, I realized as I left his purgatory office, feeling as if I needed a bleach bath. Pastor Whittington just admitted that he had been using the pulpit to sexually interrogate me, to test my breaking point. For some reason, I was more upset that he had succeeded in seeing me cringe.

In the bustling hall outside the pastor's office, three preachers in training from the college of ministries were walking behind a fourteen-year-old girl named Ladina Rials. Months earlier Ladina had spent three hours getting her waist-length hair permed in my salon chair. During that time, she taught me the tongue-twisting lyrics for the Pentecostal mantra by Lance Appleton: "I'm A One God, Apostolic, Tongue-Talking, Holy Rolling, Born Again, Heaven Bound Believer in the Liberating Power of Jesus Name." One of the young ministers grabbed Ladina by the back of her long ponytail. She frowned, and the tallest of the three sang, "Ladina is a monster ...," an altered lyric from Tone Loc's "Funky Cold Medina."

Here were grown men who were probably already preaching about the evils of drugs and secular music. And they were taunting a child using a hip-hop song about a man who gives a potent aphrodisiac to a sex hookup only to discover she was a man and then bragging that he wasn't into penis. A fleeting time later, after leaving the evening service, Ladina was put on life support when a truck plowed into the car in which she was a passenger. Because of her traumatic head injury, the nurses had to shave off her long hair, further devastating her family. Sadly, the around-the-clock prayer vigils couldn't save the sweetest and most gifted girl in the church. I was beginning to wonder what prayers could do except serve as the self-convincing objective for the "Pray Away the Gay" movement that was growing in popularity.

CHAPTER 30

TUESDAY, it was hard to concentrate on my scheduled hair appointments, and my fellow stylists could tell I wasn't my usual self. The church was forcing me to quit my job as a hairstylist, yet I had to smile and pretend that I had found my Christian utopia. I was expected to convert the lost to the fullness of the truth, but deep down, I was still worrying if my church would send collectors to handcuff me and force me to some isolated gay-conversion camp. I began having bad dreams where I suddenly found myself standing naked and susceptible in front of the church sanctuary, and all I wanted to do was find a way to escape undetected. I knew if I walked out the church door my car would be stuck in mud or wouldn't even crank.

After lunch, my friend Irene came to the salon. Fearing for my soul and even my safety, I wasn't as happy to see her as I used to be. Christianity taught that what she was practicing with her spirit board and fortune-telling cards was considered witchcraft. The people of God were commanded to put witches to death along with disobedient children and an extensive list of other people. But all I heard Christians calling for was the death of gay people like myself. And these were the same people who disliked scriptures being taken out of context—the context they preferred.

Just recently, Martha Whittington, the pastor's wife, preached a sermon and mentioned Irene's non-denominational church in Jackson—a multi-racial house of worship that had broken away from their church years earlier.

"… That church is controlled by so many demons that I can see them clinging to the building. I hate to even drive past it. They have lowered their standards and allowed women to cut their hair."

When Martha said this, all I could remember was the pastor of that so-called "demonic" church preaching against Martha's church: "You can have your hair piled up to the ceiling and still have lust in your heart."

Pentecostal women prided themselves on their years of hair-martyred submission, claiming they had worked too hard for their holiness to use wicked scissors on their hair. They loved the teachings of Apostle Paul, who claimed long hair was a sign of authority on a woman, and long hair on men was a disgrace. The church members became furious when I put this teaching on the spot with the story of Samson retaining his God-given power only through his uncut hair.

"That's *Old Testament*," they said, even though they preached primarily from the *Old Testament*.

They considered long uncut hair on a woman a requirement to enter Heaven, yet if they wore it too pridefully, they would err on the other side of the holiness tightrope. To make examples of these women, preachers were known to dishevel women's hairdos if they were too elaborate or pristine.

Even I had learned that one must never contest the man of God and that if God has a problem with his chosen servants and prophets, then only He alone can reprimand them.

"Milan, I just had to drop by and see you. Have you recently met a blond-haired, blue-eyed male who is a Pisces?" Irene asked when I met her in the salon waiting room. The only new friend I had made who might match her description was a boy named Jay, and I didn't want her to bother him. He was struggling with lusting for his blood sister, but I didn't judge him for it.

"No, not that I know of. Why?" I asked, hoping no one had overheard her.

"I got an image of him when I was praying, and the Holy Ghost gave me a strong burden. He's going through some things, but Jesus can help him."

After Irene left the salon, I was more perplexed. I had never seen anyone spend every waking second praying for people. How could she be evil, as they claimed? I asked a preachy salon client who attended a charismatic church, wanting her opinion about Irene's strange mix of Jesus and occult practices.

"She isn't operating under the power of the Holy Ghost. It sounds more like necromancy," the woman said. "For reasons such as that, the staff at my church never lets anyone testify until they screen their testimony first."

Screen their testimonies? I thought. I was led to believe that the movement of God was supposed to flow freely and spontaneously. I was amazed at how different every church was and even more how opposed they often stood against each other. Christians trying to distance themselves from Evangelicals and vice versa. I looked up the word necromancy in a dictionary and learned that it is considered a form of witchcraft involving ghosts. A thought leaped into my brain: *Never mind Irene. Was my church operating under necromancy instead of the Holy Ghost?* Then I worried that the Devil was trying to make me doubt, so I thought it was best to stop thinking.

The following Sunday was "Biker Sunday." A film crew came to document the service as Pastor Whittington rode down the church aisle on a motorcycle. The congregation praised God as if the pastor had just split the eastern skies right beside Jesus upon His return. I styled Holly's long hair into a large bowtie at the nape, and the motorcycle headlight shone through her crown of curls as the engine roared down the aisle. I wondered if the organization would be willing to have a male florist or male ballerina Sunday. The congregation, full of rough-looking bikers dressed in their leather chaps and vests covered with rebel flags and badges, put on quite a show as the choir belted out a song declaring war upon the Devil. Sister Wellington, an elderly blind woman, believed to have the Gift of Prophesy, began shouting in the aisles when a young ministerial student started bucking like a mule and trampled her under his flailing limbs.

Instead of inching past rows of seated observers, several churchmen skillfully leaped out of the choir loft. Then they walked on the backs of the wooden pews to quickly reach any souls they judged as needing prayer, which were usually female visitors who wore the most jewelry and makeup or "good old boys" who'd make potentially good Pentecostals.

I searched the right section of the sanctuary and spotted Irene.

THIRTY-SEVEN-YEAR ABDUCTION

She was sitting on a pew near the front. And, sure enough, of the over two thousand members, she had found Jay, the one I had kept from her. She grabbed his hands and swayed as she prayed defiantly for him. His pale cheeks turned crimson, and he kept his eyes closed.

This worried me further. *Was Irene, the witch, more aware spiritually than the church members?* If the Pentecostals worked in prophecy, the word of knowledge, and the other gifts of the Holy Ghost, then surely someone would know that Jay was sexually soliciting his sister in his lust for her. Still, he hadn't received any condemnation from the church as I continually did over a past sin confession.

My thoughts began to evolve: If Irene had been hospitalized for schizophrenia, a mental disorder, then was she genuinely responsible for any moral lapses? Should they stone her to death, and should she spend an eternity suffering in Hell for something she had no control over? Christ and the early Christians considered infirmities and mental illness as demonic possessions, which can now often be cured or helped thanks to the advances in the medical field. Was it also a mistake that I was struggling against my sexuality? Had I become a delusional Christian turning wine into water?

"You have received the purest apostolic truth, the way God intended!" preached Pastor Whittington. "Therefore, brethren, God has brought you out of darkness into his marvelous light, and if you ever leave this church and this truth—you are in danger, my friend— in danger of the very gates of Hell!"

The roar of the worship scene was deafening until someone silenced the church with tongues and interpretation. They were good at this, and many got chill bumps because it seemed like Jehovah spoke directly to them. A few members fell to the ground in what they called being slain in the spirit. During the interpretation of the tongues, I saw a cute boy sitting in the row in front of me. He turned his head and stared at me many times during the service. I tried not to meet his gaze, so I locked my eyes on Pastor Whittington. The boy had an asymmetrical haircut with platinum fringe, reminding me of the haircuts a few of my former gay friends had worn in the clubs. When I thought I would crack under the exposure, he darted to the front vestibule and ran maddeningly back and forth. Two deacons escorted him to the altar for prayer, where he remained curled in a ball for over an hour, refusing to pray aloud.

"He has a gay demon," Holly's friend Matthew said with a goofy grin. A week earlier, Matthew had almost shot me at his parents' house while showing off some Barney Fife moves with his pistol. Thankfully, only the living room ceiling now had a hole. He told everyone he was going to go to ministerial school and preach, perhaps to mask his rage. He bashed up his house with a baseball bat when he got mad at his father just because the poor man had asked him to drive him to the grocery store.

"How do you know he has a gay demon?" I asked Matthew in disbelief that he would make such an accusation that could potentially cause the boy harm.

"I saw the demon wink at me when I was praying for 'im. He called me by name and said, 'Leave me alone, Matthew, you're hurting me.'" Again, Matthew blushed with a toothy grin.

He had to be lying. I had experienced this attitude so many times I wanted to barf: So many straight men seemed to think every woman or gay man wanted them. And in Matthew's case, a gay demon that just couldn't resist his two-hundred-pound ass.

"He needs an exorcism," one of the deacons said while he looked down at the boy like an amateur chef does a half-cooked casserole in the oven.

An exorcism? I questioned with disbelief. The boy is acting weird because he's full of booze and drugs. Not devils.

The church overseers were ready to lock up the sanctuary, which wasn't difficult because most members had already headed to the fellowship hall for the special potluck dinner. The men began dragging the boy to the prayer room. Wanting to see where fate was leading the boy who was suspected of being gay, my inquisitive nature would not let me abandon the scene for a plate of fatty food. In the hall outside the prayer room, the boy stretched his arms and legs across the doorway, blocking the men from pushing him inside. I worried about him and wondered if the deacons' rough control of him was necessary or legal.

Weeks earlier, a woman, who attended a Pentecostal church in the area, came running into the sanctuary during a baptism. "Please, you have to help me," she cried. "My church—they have my son in a cage, and they're starving 'im and beating him with a whip, trying to cast the Devil out of 'im."

"Where?" A burly elder stood up and blocked her from moving farther down the church aisle.

"Down the street from you. They're gonna kill him. Please, you have to help me."

"Have you contacted the police?"

"Yeah, but they won't do nothing."

The elder began questioning what medications she was taking as he wrangled her out of the sanctuary. To my disappointment, no one took her seriously, and no investigation came of it. From the spiritual nature of the matter and my experience with local law enforcement, I was inclined to believe they were washing their hands from all manner of abuse. I had been passive and amicable in allowing the church to manipulate me, but there was no way I wouldn't see for myself what the deacons were planning for the boy they currently had under their firm grips.

When the deacons managed to maneuver the boy inside the prayer room, he broke away momentarily and ran toward one wall and then another, searching for an exit. The deacons subdued him on a prayer bench, where they pinned his arms behind his back. To my observation, the boy began gnawing at anything his limbs couldn't reach, like a frightened animal trying to free itself. When that didn't work, he began to bang his head against the floor.

"Jesus! He's gnawing on the prayer bench."

"Satan hates prayer."

"Put a Bible under his head in case he cracks his skull open."

In disbelief at what the churchmen felt they had the authority to do, I stepped back into the hall and watched through the door window in case they questioned me or worse.

"Identify yourself, demon," one of the deacons commanded while the boy writhed on the floor.

"Spiratos!" the boy hissed, and I suspected he was giving the old farts the show they expected. Possibly the boy had a video game with a character by that sinister name.

"Well, Brother Billy, I don't know what else to do; I think he's close to deliverance from that demon."

"Yeah, *haaa*, I believe he is," Billy panted and dabbed at the sweat on his forehead with a white handkerchief. "I think we should go ahead and baptize him, Brother."

While they baptized the boy and praised Jesus, assuming they had set the captive free, I headed to the packed fellowship hall for dinner. The women cooked and brought their best recipes, which were all spread out on long tables on one side of the enormous room. Still worried about what the pastor planned to do to that boy and me, now that he wanted to send me to a gay-conversion camp, I was extra careful with every move I made. It reminded me of a time in the first week of ninth grade when I ate fresh fruit from my lunch tray in the school cafeteria. I wasn't eating a banana manly enough for the boys in the lunchroom. I learned that guys were super paranoid about how they held their silverware, drinking glasses, even how they ate bananas, corndogs, popsicles, suckers, or anything penis shaped. But these Pentecostal men were extra toxic in their masculinity. They showed me how to bite from the side of the banana and not a tender or deep mouth-inserted bite—it should be more of a deadly werewolf sort of chomp.

The waiting staff in restaurants hated when Pentecostals came in after the Baptists. They often complained that the members would take up whole banquet tables only to split one or two dinner orders without tipping. I quickly learned the slang "Pentecostal lemonade" and why store clerks and waitstaff called us "penny-cost-als." To make the thrifty citrus drink, after a loud prayer, the worthiest at the table for ten would collect the sliced lemons from everyone's free ice water, and they'd squeeze them into their glass along with the free packets of sugar.

I was a novelty with my blend of manners and insecurities. My cousin's husband once hid a camera to record me eating my entire Thanksgiving meal at my grandmother's house and gave a copy of it to the whole family except for me. It wasn't just unspoken rules for eating; the men in the congregation made fun of me for letting Holly drive me to church once when I had an ingrown toenail cut out.

The next time I saw the boy that the deacons had performed the exorcism on, they had taken him under their wing and dressed him in a secondhand suit and a comb-over. An immaculate Christian doll— a little poppa. They tried to force him (a boy with acute drug withdrawal symptoms) to eat, but he flung the spoonful of potato salad in their faces. The church stationed watchers to monitor his every move in the congregation, while women grabbed their children away from him if he glanced at them.

"Oh dear, I just had a vision of that possessed boy throwing that child over the balcony. Someone needs to get that child away from him." A sister's hand brushed the ringlets near her temples as her bare lips whispered into an available ear of a woman in a tight French twist. A few days later, the boy had vanished. I often wondered if the church had disposed of the boy in a gay-conversion camp in some undisclosed location.

CHAPTER 31

O N August 21, 1992, after fasting all food for a week and bowing, crying, and praying to God on the living room carpet, I allowed myself to read something that wasn't the Bible. I unrolled the daily newspaper to see the headline: "Ruby Ridge Standoff." The name stood out to me.

"That's where my parents live. Their cabin is a short distance from Ruby Ridge, Idaho."

"What happened?" asked Holly, appearing at my side to see the paper.

"It says six federal agents were in an eleven-day shootout with the property owner and self-described white separatist, Randy Weaver. An FBI sniper killed his wife and fourteen-year-old son." I got chill bumps. "God, from the news article, it sounds exactly like my parents and what they did to me. Randy Weaver was a college dropout, just like my dad. He and his wife were fundamentalist Christians who distrusted the government, so they started hoarding guns and took their children to the wilderness to live off the grid without electricity or utilities. They even read the same end-of-the-world books as my parents and were convinced Armageddon was about to happen."

The same week I quit my job as a hairdresser, and since Pastor Whittington had not yet found me a replacement occupation, I went to a job placement center. I had no skills or training in anything other than cosmetology, so the only job available was a train-as-you-go position at an optical eyewear company. They stuck me in their office in a dangerous part of town. I had such little training that I didn't know what I was doing. When a customer called in a complaint, wanting to know what had happened to her new prescription lenses, the owner told me to "lie like hell" to the customers. I immediately quit and walked out of the warehouse.

After months of searching for another job, the bills began to go unpaid, so Holly and I were forced to move out of our townhome into a drug-infested trailer park where the neighbors kept me up many nights with their acid rock blasting and the area kids sexually assaulted a boy with a broomstick. Later the rapists' mothers surrounded the victim's trailer and threw rocks while armed with knives strapped to their legs. I tried to intervene for the victim and his family, and the women surrounded me near the community mailbox.

"I know what you are," the leader sneered through rotted teeth and a web of oily hair stringing around her face. "Yer a goddamn smart ass."

I wanted to laugh. For once, I had received a compliment from an angry straight person. But things weren't funny after this, and I began to fear for my and Holly's life when strangers kept idling their cars in front of our trailer and whistling through their dark-tinted windows for me to come out. Unsurprisingly neither God's nor Pastor Whittington's help ever came. And I returned to my wicked job at the same hair salon.

Holly's hair teased around a roll of toilet paper.

Around this time, Pastor Whittington insisted that Holly wear her hair in an updo while in church. He had a problem with women past their teens wearing their uncut hair hanging down, especially in tight curls.

"How about that, huh?" I complained to Holly. "Not only are women not supposed to cut their hair, but they're supposed to go their entire life with it wadded up on their heads. It doesn't make sense and certainly not natural."

"I don't care what he wants," said Holly.

"For church tonight, I want to tease your hair up like some of the older women and show him how ridiculous it looks. And wear that floor-length dress with the poofy sleeves. He's kidding himself if he wants younger women to look like those old-timey Holy Rollers."

"No, I don't want to look ridiculous. It won't matter to him," said Holly, looking as though she would be sick.

"I'm tired of him harassing me. You won't be the only one looking bad, I promise. I'll cut my hair in an old farmer's crewcut and wear an ugly plaid shirt. Trust me; I know it'll work." I also knew it would go over well in the trailer park.

Holly finally agreed with a frown. We got countryfied up like Holy Rollers from the seventies when women had to recline across seatbelts and leather upholstery on the way to church because their car roofs weren't high enough to prevent squashing their towering hair.

We walked into the packed sanctuary that evening and sat on the second row. As soon as Pastor Whittington looked down from the pulpit and saw us glaring up at him, he choked on his words and couldn't look straight ahead for the rest of his bumbling sermon. The assistant pastor knew what Holly and I were up to. Clenching his lips to keep from bursting with laughter, he squirmed in his chair on the platform until his face turned pink. One of the slim and popular young girls from the ministerial school paused several pews away and snarled at us. Inside I was basking in victory, for I knew I had proven my point to the older men who tried to control the women in the church and me. Perhaps they would forget about their beloved saying, "The higher the hair, the closer to God."

CHAPTER 32

A year passed, yet I still sat on the church pews seeking absolution, questioning God as to why He was still ignoring me. Holly and I moved from the trailer park into a rental home. I refused to take the anti-depressants the doctor had prescribed for me. At home, I preferred to spend my waking hours in a dark den with no windows. I also began collecting exotic finches in every color imaginable— Orange Cheeked, Gouldians, and Cordon Blues. I even built two cages for the birds, the first from bamboo. And to accommodate more finches, I connected two three-foot metal cages. I would gaze at the birds for hours, and on the rare occasion that a male finch would sing for a partner, it soothed and haunted me.

After several months I realized why the caged birds captivated me; I was trapped in a cage just as they were. Perhaps it was all of the moody isolation. I began to wonder if the winged rascals were either taunting me or were trying to lead by example because, on several occasions, every one of the finches would find a way to escape their secure cages. After work, I would spend hours with a baseball cap, rounding them up all over the house.

That winter, Holly had her gall bladder removed, and Pastor Whittington stopped by the hospital to check on and pray for her.

"You'll be all right, Sister Sergent," he said, patting her hand beside the gurney. "I've had every procedure except a hysterectomy."

After Pastor Whittington left the room in his perfectly pressed suit and a nurse had wheeled Holly into surgery, I collapsed in the cushioned guest's chair in her room. She had been so nervous about the operation that I had to act strong and full of faith to comfort her. But I couldn't believe Pastor Whittington had just confessed to having had every medical procedure a man could have, although not with enough humor in the world to soothe me. I had allowed Christians to manipulate and shame me to the point that I had sacrificed my whole life, awaiting a promised heavenly transformation. Where were the miracles and supernatural healings the pastor and congregation always bragged about? Holly quickly recovered, thanks to the skilled doctor. If it was a miracle, it was an ungodly expensive one.

The church theatrics continued unwaveringly, and that Wednesday evening, Pastor Whittington had just finished preaching a sermon titled "A Trend Is Worse than a Sin."

"I need every man in the congregation to get up out of your pew and gather up here in the choir loft. A-man, A-man!" he shouted into the microphone. "We're going to build a bigger church—a manly church—where the boys can have their own basketball court. I'd rather them play ball than with dolls. A-man! Rock music is turning our boys into sissies and making our girls want to wear pants and become sluts. None of our boys are going to be using curling irons. And while I'm on the subject of hair: I don't like these perms our girls have been getting. It looks like they stuck their finger in a light socket—like one of those African tribes that put mud in their hair. So don't go to the light socket."

Some of the congregation laughed, but not the handful of Black members in attendance. While the congregation lifted their hands in loud praise, Pastor Whittington climbed on top of the pulpit and stood as if he were Moses before the Red Sea.

"Now, the men are gonna march around this sanctuary like they did around the walls of Jericho and we're gonna defeat the enemy!"

"I can't imagine how Pastor Whittington can even preach with all the drugs he's taking," said an informant salon client who worked at the drugstore the pastor used. Nevertheless, all Pastor Whittington had to do was pass gas on the platform, and the congregation would erupt into ecstatic praise, thinking that Gabriel had sounded his trumpet. "And suddenly there came a sound from heaven as of a rushing mighty wind, and it filled all the house where they were sitting." –Acts 2:2. The congregation loved that scripture, and someone even engraved it on the stall door in the men's restroom.

Amusingly, Pastor Whittington didn't think the Pentecostal fashion shows the church hosted to drum up new members celebrated trends in the least. During another Sunday service, he made the men take off their neckties and wear them around their foreheads in another warrioristic march. Most of the women wore tennis shoes with their long dresses, so as soon as the music cranked up, they could easily run praise laps around the church. The members often ran the aisles with closed eyes, straight into the church walls like drunken bats. Men weren't allowed to make gentle or fluid movements, so much of their praise dancing or shouting resembled grandfathers stomping on roaches in a honkytonk. The women, young and old, often spun around and around and screamed as if they were in pain until they shouted their long hair down. Injuries were quite common from the delirious worship. The music director's wife fell out of the choir loft and cracked her skull on a pew. To keep from being trampled, children often dove under the pews, collecting bobby pins and matted wads of hair used to pad their mothers' enormous updos. Holly regularly shouted and danced in the aisles, even after an ecstatic worshiper smashed her toe and busted her lip. Many times, if I remained sitting during a worship service, a member would lay fingertips on my forehead and vigorously massage my lobotomy area until I became lightheaded.

"Brother Sergent, the Devil has you bound," one member told me, while another said, "I see a demon wrapped around your neck. It's like a snake choking the life out of you. You must never leave because more truth is taught here than in any other church." Another person said, "A demon affected your emotions as a child, and another demon kept it locked inside."

Fearing these godly people were correct, I swallowed my pride and jumped and shouted in the church aisles, imagining that I was jumping into the arms of Jesus as I praised Him to the relentless noise of the musicians and choir.

As the saying goes: "Absence makes the heart grow fonder," my gay urges only became more intense the longer I was removed from my former lifestyle. After a long-overdue hospital exam, I learned I had developed an aversion to noise to the point that I wished I would go deaf. I also developed an anxiety disorder along with a bleeding ulcer and hiatal hernia, bleeding inside from fear of exposure and ending up homeless. Before passing out from the anesthesia, I overheard the doctor in the hall tell the nurse, "It's all right. He's going to enjoy having the scope shoved down his throat."

Trying with all my might to exorcise any trace of gay in my being, I realized that I had only developed into a Christian doppelganger to mask my desires and temptations. I began to question God's existence, and the church's not-so-secret actions didn't help my collapsing faith. I started sleeping in another bedroom in our first home together. Not all at once, but in small increments, I would crawl into the second bed in the middle of the night.

The church began having a noticeable effect on Holly as well. She developed symptoms of Religious OCD with scrupulosity rituals. It started with worrying that she hadn't prayed as specifically as she should. And then she feared she would forget to pray for God's protection every day. Later, whenever I would back the truck out of the driveway to leave for work, she would press her face against the door window. I could see her fingers ritualistically tapping against the glass in sequence, counting every word of her prayers of protection. Eventually, it became time-consuming to leave the house when she had to lay her hands on every electrical socket, praying that nothing would catch on fire.

Her periodic fits of jealousy and paranoia had been present even before the wedding but were now also worse. I realized that I couldn't become friends with men or women. Her reactions to this became too embarrassing for me to risk.

"If you go to the store or anything on your days off, call me and let me know first," she said in tears one day.

"What if I don't find what I'm looking for at Target, and I cross the street to Walmart? You can't expect me to call you every time I change my mind," I said.

"Yes, you will," she insisted, turning red and sniffling.

Another friendless year or two passed, and I still wasn't attracted to Holly or any other woman. I started thinking I should sell everything I owned as Jesus told the rich man he needed to do to inherit eternal life.

"We can't! We'll be homeless. We can barely pay our bills as it is," she said.

One afternoon, Holly was sitting on the den floor in a terrycloth onesie when she suddenly burst into tears and grabbed my hands. "Don't you want to make love to me anymore?"

I was stunned that she finally put me on the spot with such a question. But she had every right to ask. Seeing her sobbing and trembling was a knife in my heart.

"Of course I want you, sweetie," I lied, justifying it by thinking I wanted her as a friend and not sexually. But I couldn't bring myself to answer what she was really asking me. I just wanted the questions to stop as desperately as I wanted her to stop putting moves on me sexually. *If I tell her the truth, she'll be more upset. I can't stand to break her heart*, I thought, assuming she preferred to continue in a fantasy marriage instead—a faith marriage.

"Holly, all I know is I haven't been sleeping, and the guest bedroom helps me sleep," I replied, trying to calm her fears.

To satisfy nosy family and visitors who occasionally entered our home, Holly and I made sure to dishevel my side of the bed to make it look like I slept with her. With the stares we would get in public, I don't know if anyone ever accepted us as a married couple. People were always asking if Holly was my sister or mother.

How many adult siblings hold hands on vacation or hug each other close during church services? The pain Holly concealed was becoming unbearable. Their brazen assumptions and witch hunts were sickening. For Christians who claim people choose to be gay and that such a thing is a lie from the Devil, they were the ones always assuming certain people are gay. If God didn't intend for any sexual or gender confusion, He would not allow one out of every one thousand children to be born with both sex organs in a condition known as intersex. To appear older and less gay, I gave up maintaining my appearance. I gained weight and even began to walk stoop shouldered.

CHAPTER 33

LIKE the Queen on a chessboard, Pastor Whittington showed off his lawless crown and ordered five elder men in the church to serve as his pawns.

"That's right. Get out of your seats and move to that empty pew right there—right there in the middle section," he ordered.

It wasn't a coincidence that the pew directly in front of me had been left unoccupied. Pastor Whittington had planned to use his pulpit as a shield again—a shield behind which he could fire another one of his sniper bullets in his manipulation games.

Sacrificing their firstborn thoughts, the men obeyed and filed into the pew in front of me one by one. I could smell their musky cologne heating up under their polyester suits and hear their frustrated grunts as they settled their stiff backs on the hard bench, knowing two thousand members were looking on and probably aware of what was about to happen except for me.

"These fine gentlemen don't like these permanent waves some of our women are getting, and I talked to several of the young men at the church school, and they do not like these perms either!" Pastor Whittington huffed and puffed over the pulpit.

I could almost see him saying "checkmate" to me, but I maintained unflinching eye contact with him as he remained tethered to a microphone cord like a pit bull chained to a pulpit. Others were growing tired of Pastor Whittington's ramblings. At least two members stood up during his bizarre tirades and pointed at their Bibles, signaling him to get in the word of God.

"*Ee conda-lo sha-ta-ha! Mo-mo sha-ta-ha,*" the soloist shouted in tongues over the microphone in his most martyred voice during the choir's syncopation. The orchestra learned when to pause deadpan on cue. As soon as the spiritual rodeo reached its spaced-out climax and the congregation released their pent-up frustrations, they were ready to swallow the bitter pill. For another round of grandstanding and virtue signaling, Pastor Whittington then invited Brother Perry to come up on the platform and speak against the permanent wave hair trend that Satan and I had popularized to make the women in his church resemble that "African tribe" he hated.

"Brethren, it's always been Satan's ambition to make women pretty when God has already made them beautiful," Brother Perry said, courting all the swooning women. "Homosexuals rule the fashion and beauty industry, and we all know they hate women."

I was so furious that I had to grip the pew. That was such a lie. Gay men idolized women, actually, but no one dared contradict his lies. The women in the church had been getting perms long before I arrived. Even the pastor's wife secretly got so many disastrous home perms that her hair was barely long enough to put up in a French twist. Brother Perry wouldn't even allow his daughter to use heat rollers. When she eventually found a man interested in her, her old eggs produced a child with genetic abnormalities. I found this sort of fatherly control of his daughter's hair length almost incestuous. Brother Perry's wife, however, received permission from Pastor Whittington to thin her excessively long hair because her doctor said it was causing her to have migraines. The only stipulation from Pastor Whittington was that Sister Perry had to wear her hair up so that no one could tell it had been cut. To me, and my evil trend of rationalizing belief systems, it was tricky to reconcile that thinning the hair with scissors was permissible when the church believed cutting their hair would send the women to Hell. Long hair standards had been known to send females to either end of the afterlife faster. It was particularly tragic when one of the church's best young singers had a seizure alone in the shower and her hair clogged the drain, causing her to drown.

I had given perms to over a hundred Pentecostals, some with hair that would drag the ground if they didn't bun it up or let the bottom half collect in their dress pockets. Some were the pastor's family members, and others were missionary women from as far away as Swaziland, Africa.

Feeling trapped in a martyr's prison, I sat agonizing over my decisions until I wrote a long letter to Pastor Whittington, listing all the deeds in the church that I heard he was covering up. The list included about a hundred things, mostly about him and the members of his extended family that made up the bulk of the ministry. I never named names to avoid getting anyone in trouble. A key issue on the list was that his daughter, the assistant pastor's wife, had an affair with my new converts' teacher, who was my age. She also flashed her breasts on a tractor and propositioned people for street drugs before briefly abandoning her family to pursue her fleshly desires. The most Pastor Whittington would do to punish her was make her move back a row in the choir while he crushed others under his sanctimonious thumb. Also included in my letter were the many complaints about Music Director Daryl Crabtree, who allegedly made sexual advances on several male ministerial students who complained of him groping them and his prolonged and gratuitous prayer hugs in his office. One of the students claimed to have caught evidence on camera, and another man made a YouTube video about the scandalous music director they idolized. Pastor Whittington tore up the incriminating photos and threw them in his office trashcan.

"Pastor Whittington hates gay people. He's obsessed about the subject," I mentioned to Holly before mailing the letter. "Why would he keep Daryl on staff as music director while targeting and destroying other members' lives instead?"

To avoid liability, Pastor Whittington didn't respond to my questions in writing; he caught me off guard at home with a phone call.

"I'll get him," Holly said, putting the phone on mute.

"Most of the things you mentioned are true that I'm aware of, Milan," said the pastor after Holly handed me the phone. "But I want to get with you sometime soon and share some scriptures that'll shed some light on these issues," he said in conclusion.

I was shocked that he admitted the accusations in my letter were factual. *What scriptures could he possibly share that could justify any of this*? I shouldn't have wondered; people had been using the Bible to justify or condemn nearly everything they wanted to for thousands of years.

"Oh, Holly, I think I just opened a vicious jar of leeches." I turned off the phone.

CHAPTER 34

"**D**EACONS, I want you to place Bibles on the floor in every doorway," ordered Pastor Whittington in a grandiose manner.

After the deacon did as the pastor told them, Pastor Whittington leaned over the pulpit and lowered the microphone.

"A-man, a-man. If anyone leaves this service before I'm through preaching, then you are stepping on the blood of Jesus!"

There was no need for biblical barricades. Every sermon lasted so long that I was sure the S.W.A.T. Team would send in a hostage negotiation unit.

After rambling ominously for a few minutes, Whittington lowered his eyes to his Bible. "Now, I don't think it's wrong if a man does his wife's hair or his daughter's hair. I used to brush my little girls' hair sometimes when we were running late for church, but I don't think a man should do a woman's hair! You all know that!" Making a limp-wristed gesture toward the congregation Pastor Whittington pursed his lips and added, "I'm going to hit you with my purse."

I couldn't believe it. Earlier, he had used a stereotype that gay men cringe easily, and now he was using another by flopping his hand over the pulpit limply. Why didn't he have the balls to say my name? Was he expecting me to crawl under a pew? The air was so tense I thought the sanctuary would crack, but to my surprise, only a couple of people laughed that I could see from where I was sitting. The worst part was that nobody ever dared acknowledge a single one of the ministry's attacks against me. I thought I was going crazy because of it. At least one sympathetic glance would've been so helpful, but I suppose they were afraid the ministry would shun or attack them as well. It seemed to be humanity's best talent to pretend they don't notice injustices if not in their interest.

"I hoped you wouldn't notice his attacks toward you," Holly confessed later at home.

"Wouldn't notice! That's all Christianity's been for me my whole life—constant oppression, shaming, manipulation, telling me how flawed I am and that I'm going to Hell. These people who say they got saved because of the love and liberation they felt aren't being fully honest."

"If you stop going to church, then I am too," she said.

"No, you're content with your church status. And as much as I want to leave, I don't want everyone to accuse me of causing you to go to Hell with me."

To avoid feeling the fullness of further attacks toward me from the pulpit, I learned to stare at the pastor without blinking or thinking. I could do this until it seemed as if my soul astral projected from my body. I imagined it was what children did to survive emotional trauma—something experts called "going fetal."

That week another bombing happened at a gay bar, and the reactions from members of the congregation were eye-opening.

"I admit, I'm having mixed emotions about people who bomb gay bars—and abortion clinics, too," they usually threw in the latter to avoid looking like total bigots.

Liars and manipulators, deceiving in the name of their God, I thought to myself. Even the apologists were warped by the language of love they were taught. I began wanting to surrender back to my true self in favor of its honesty compared to the righteous lies kept so well contained within the church's platinum walls. I repressed the urge to run out through the front vestibule, past the enormous white pillars of the church façade, and between the maze of parked Lincolns until I disappeared in the dimly lit parking lot. Then I imagined myself continuing to walk the dangerous streets into the city and never turning back.

But you are a married man now, Milan. You are bound to this oppression.

A female elder in the church informed me that Pastor Whittington's only son had done that very thing—had run away. Allegedly, Whittington wanted a boy to take over his ministry so desperately that he adopted a boy and named him Cole. Eventually, young Cole had all he could take of his parents, so he went to court and had himself legally unadopted and chose to live under a bridge instead.

Kerri Lyons, the girl from my childhood Baptist church, came to my salon to get her hair cut. Naturally, her conscience was so forgiven that she didn't remember kicking the hell out of me during the youth retreat. Though I now had a constant rash on my shin where her shoe had left a dent. Unlike the Pentecostals with whom I was now trapped, Kerri and I had one thing in common: we both loved jewelry, no matter how expensive or cheap, as long as it was gaudy.

"I used to cut hair, too," Kerri said, and I was beginning to connect with her. "I cut Pastor Whittington's hair and couldn't stand the man. Everyone in the salon hated to see him come in because he was so arrogant."

Kerri's admission was somewhat therapeutic. But the more I thought about it, I became angry about all the pick-and-choose principles. Pastor Whittington found it was perfectly fine for holiness men to go to female hairstylists with their miniskirts and plump breasts leaning over their bald heads, which were, of course, only filled with the mind of God while getting their three remaining hairs ritually snipped. But to Whittington, it was an apostasy for a man to do a woman's hair.

The next opportunity I found after the sermon, I cornered Martha Whittington.

"Here," I said, handing over my records book of Pentecostal hair clients. "Pastor Whittington will want this. Tell him he wins."

Martha Whittington took the book of records. With a triumphant smirk, she thumbed through it to see who all had been doing business with me.

Around this time, before the Monica Lewinsky scandal, the church was in an uproar, and some proclaimed that President Bill Clinton was gay. The men went around with two-dollar "bills" with

Clinton's picture while quipping about the "queer as a two-dollar bill" saying.

The Talibangelicals were losing their minds over the president signing the "Don't ask, don't tell" policy into law, ending the ban on gay people serving in the sacred military. Never mind the military's history of toxic bromancers and their history of spankings, floggings, and sexually sadistic weapons of terror. Never mind their track record of proudly torturing recruits and the unreported rapes. They were proud of their heterosexual institution where the mildest initiation rituals often included naked recruits being forced by their seniors to lick whipped cream off another guy's junk or munch on apples wedged in someone's ass. And to wash the forbidden fruit down, the recruits had to drink booze poured between a displayed set of butt cheeks. Gay for pay, but only for a few days. Then they could join the servicemen and advance to the trunk-stretching elephant walks and, ultimately, for some forced sodomy.

They might even receive an award in the traditional Neptunus Rex where servicemen are stripped and shaved, or they cross-dress as women before really "crossing the line" with interrogations of their sexuality followed by some much anticipated sacrificial ass penetrations for the command performance—or commander's performance one should say.

I wanted to give the hypocrites, like my old friend Mitch Odom, a piece of my mind. When the servicemen's hormones are spent, and they finally wash their gooey socks shoved under their mattresses, they eventually return to civilian lives supporting harsh anti-gay and anti-drag laws. They end up marrying girls who like to give oral and receive anal. "Don't ask, don't tell."

I secretly enjoyed watching the godly men burn their two-dollar bills as soon as President Clinton was impeached over a consensual blowjob from an ex-mistress. The Bible was correct on one point: people do swallow a camel but choke on a gnat.

During the next morning church service, Sister Wellington, the blind prophetess stood up in the middle of the sermon. She lifted her wrinkled hands toward Heaven and predicted that the church doors were about to close for good.

"Oh, my people, oh, my children!" her grandmotherly voice cracked. "Memorize my word, hide it in your hearts because, within the next four years, the government is going to take your Bibles away from you! But if you pray as you've never prayed before, seek me as you've never sought me before, I will hasten my coming within the next four years."

At the end of the prophecy, the entire congregation groaned like a herd of ill cattle. They dropped to their knees, sobbing and praying under their pews. Sister Wellington was considered the closest to God that one could find, a living Saint. So, it had to be true; we were all about to be Raptured up to Heaven before the end of the hellacious, sky-falling, bloody-oceans four years. I bought a cassette recording of the prophecy and service. I nearly wore out the tape, rewinding it, while writing down her exact words. There had been so many wall-shaking prophecies from members that came and went unaccounted for. According to the Bible, the spiritual test of a false prophet was to wait and see if what the prophet said in God's name came to pass. Or was this, yet again, more fearmongering because we had a gay rights Democrat running the country? As usual, I was going to have to obey, wait, forgive, forget, and repeat.

CHAPTER 35

AS a loyal Christian who had to defend his faith, I couldn't tell my clients that my pastor had forced me to quit doing their hair. Instead, I let them think I was unstable.

"Don't worry, I promise I won't stop doing hair again," I said to secure their trust when I opened my own hair salon in an ugly old trailer in the parking lot of a grocery store in dilapidated South Jackson. It would've been nice to enjoy starting my own business fully, but I couldn't help but worry about what measures the church ministry would take to shut the salon or me down. My anxiety disorder worsened because of this, and I ended up dehydrated in the emergency room with so many blood clots that it took the nurse a while to hook me up to a drip.

On opening day at my salon, I arrived to find an old brown Chevy Lumina parked through two of my front door spaces. The driver, a middle-aged man in a flannel shirt and baseball cap, was sprawled out over the front seat. I pounded on the driver's windshield.

"Sir, I need you to move your car. I have clients on their way."

The man didn't flinch a nostril hair, and I began to fear he was dead. Oh, great, this isn't going to be good for business. Everyone will see the newspaper headlines: God Punishes Salon Owner with Death for Unmanly Career Choice. It was silly to look for signs, but the church had taught me to take everything as a sign one way or the other. "Everything happens for a reason," was the magic answer that had long outworn its welcome with me. Then I thought of a magic word that might resurrect the dead man hindering my business.

"Sir, if you don't move your car, I'm going to call the police."

The man popped up from the front seat, put his car in neutral, and I pushed his vehicle to the middle of the parking lot as far from my salon as I had the strength to move him. This was only the beginning of my struggles to run my own business. A few weeks later, the city sent me a million-dollar water bill, and I nearly had a stroke. There had been a pipe leak where the city had been widening a nearby creek, and they had made a typo on the bill, which was still too high for something I hadn't caused. Women threw dirty underwear and baby diapers against the front entry. Men from a nearby halfway house would pee on the aluminum siding and leave their drug syringes on the front steps. Somewhere between two break-ins, a purse snatching, stalkers, and a gunman who tried to coerce me to let him inside my salon twice, I had a security system installed with a roof alarm.

Three months of being independent, I got a call from my punk friend from high school, Samantha. "I got fired, and I really need a place to work." She sounded unrecognizable: Her enunciation was slurred, and her hip, Valley-Girl accent was now a full-tilt Southern drawl. My instincts were that she had a drug or alcohol problem.

"I would love to have you work with me," I said, hoping at best that she could tell me how Griff was doing. "But first, you need to fill out an application, and there are a few things we need to discuss."

Samantha never made it to her interview nor bothered to tell me why she stood me up.

One bustling Saturday, I had a new client in my chair, and Holly was hanging out in the waiting area, reading a magazine, when an elder church member walked into my salon uninvited.

"Brother Holms, what a surprise. You mean you came here all the way from Clinton to get your haircut?" Holly asked him.

"Why, hello there, Sister Holly. I didn't know Milan worked here. The Holy Ghost sorta leads me places sometimes. I used to be a barber once."

"I didn't know that. Did you do women's hair, too," Holly asked while I foil-weaved the new client's hair.

"Yeah, I cut women's hair, too, until the Holy Ghost convicted me."

My heart collapsed in my chest. I wanted to clasp my hand over my client's ears, but thankfully Holly began escorting him out of the salon. In the doorway, Brother Holms pointed his finger in her face.

"If your husband is cuttin' women's hair, then he's touchin' other things."

"Oh, my God! Who does he think he is, some prophet on groping?" I asked Holly later that day. "Not only is the sex-obsessed church accusing me of being gay, but now they imagine me lustfully grabbing women also. Who knew male hairstylists were such studs? If I were a rich doctor probing naked women and men all day, that church would make me a deacon."

"Oh, now, Milan, the Holy Ghost didn't lead him here. Pastor Whittington put him up to it. I'll bet you anything," said Holly.

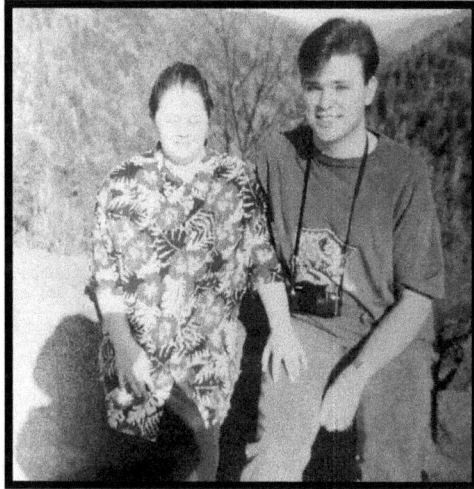

Holly and me in Gatlinburg.

Holly and I went on a much-needed vacation to Gatlinburg, Tennessee. When we returned home, the church was in an uproar. According to many in the congregation, police had arrested the church music director, Daryl Crabtree, in a men's restroom in New York while on tour with his singing group, The Crabtree Melodies. A few members were aware of Daryl's penchant for younger men. But after he propositioned another man for sex in a shopping mall restroom, he netted a police record, a situation Pastor Whittington could not cover up for once. Daryl was a Christian songwriter known worldwide, so news of the arrest traveled.

I didn't want to discuss the music director's homosexuality with Holly because I was still struggling with same-sex attraction, only I was not acting out on my needs as Daryl had made a habit of doing. I was still avoiding all occasions for sex and intimacy, even with Holly. Inside I stewed in betrayal from how the ministry had targeted and used me as a scapegoat to deflect from the corruption saturating their ranks. And God, once again, let it happen.

After Daryl and his wife divorced, Pastor Whittington forced Daryl to resign and promoted the man's wife to the position of music director, which was against the organization's rule that a divorced person could not hold a position in the ministry. Daryl's dismissal triggered a domino effect of drama and corruption in the ministry. The deacons tapped into Pastor Whittington's phone line, revealing that Tina, the music director's wife, was having an affair with Pastor Whittington. Daryl Crabtree knew about his wife's affair with Pastor Whittington, but they were all having affairs, so no one dared expose the other.

According to many in the church, Daryl and Tina Crabtree's children chose to live with their disgraced Father, who denied he was gay or had inappropriately moved on younger men, despite years of allegations.

"The police are arresting me for running through the mall; that's all," Daryl had allegedly claimed outside the restroom when his singing group saw the police handcuffing him and hauling him off to prison.

"I got a black eye because I accidentally ran into the door," Daryl had claimed on another occasion while on tour. But a young man from his singing group had claimed he gave the music director the black eye when he awoke to find him performing oral sex on him in the hotel room they had to share. When all his other excuses failed, Daryl said, "I never realized how clever the Devil was."

The board members called a private meeting with Pastor Whittington where they played the tapes of him and Tina Crabtree conversing inappropriately on their cell phones at three in the morning.

"Now, fellahs, that was all just playful teasing and nothing else. Besides, you know it's illegal to tap into someone's phone lines. Now,

I insist you give me those tapes!" Pastor Whittington allegedly sputtered, turning red in the face before faking a heart attack.

Like a soiled dove standing firm on its perch, his act gathered sympathy from those who still supported him. The deacons remained persistent in their demand for accountability.

"We also have proof that you and Tina have been parking your cars at an antique store and secretly meeting in a hotel room, so we find it hard to believe the phone recording is just playful teasing."

"I was meeting Tina at the hotel to counsel her and nothing more!" Pastor Whittington insisted.

Through all the scandals, questions went unanswered for various reasons, namely, to keep from shaking the members' faith. At the next service, Pastor Whittington stood up from his throne chair on the platform, took his place behind the podium, and loosened his tie around his pulpy throat.

"I will not publicly address any of these accusations leveled against me. If any members of this church have any questions, come directly to me and not any of these shade-tree mechanics," he said about the deacons. "I've scheduled a special service where all members can cast a vote of confidence in me. If I do not receive enough votes in favor of keeping me then I will resign. If anyone votes against me, then I will not be responsible for what might happen to you!" he said in an ominous tone. I couldn't believe he was threatening his members.

The board also discovered Pastor Whittington had been secretly dipping into the church's money. Still, he turned the tables over the pulpit and said, "I'm in control, and if anyone in this church stops paying tithes, then I will fix it where you'll no longer remain a member."

As usual, after the ushers received the tithes and offerings, Martha Whittington left the sanctuary to see who gave what in membership fees. Pastor Whittington appointed his brother-in-law as the church treasurer. His sons-in-law were assistant pastors, and he was awaiting one of his nephews to come of age to lead the congregation.

"So much for the tradition of being called by God. I suppose having Whittington blood is like blue blood and guarantees a position as a reverend," I said to Holly, who agreed.

In his campaign to remain in power, Pastor Whittington called in loyalist speakers on his behalf. The prophet, who almost died from fasting, tossed a pouch of coins into the church aisle. "Go ahead and betray this fine man of God!" he huffed, insinuating that certain members of the church were like Judas Iscariot.

As the circus ensued, more members of Pastor Whittington's inner circle publicly announced their allegiance to him. "I have complete confidence in Pastor Whittington," said Sister Richards over the microphone. "If he told me to tie a ton of bricks around my neck and jump off a ship into the ocean, then I'd do it because I know it would be God's will."

Members began questioning everyone to determine if they were voting in favor of Whittington staying in power. This, along with the ministerial misdeeds, caused families to turn against one another.

"We know y'all are against poor Pastor Whittington," a few people said to Holly and me.

"I'm voting to keep Pastor Whittington. I know he's guilty, but I'm afraid God will punish me for going against him. 'Touch not the Lord's anointed,'" some people confessed.

"… I'm voting for him to remain, but then I'm going to find another church," other people admitted.

As much as Holly and I wanted to vote against Pastor Whittington, we didn't want any more targets on my back, so we stayed home on the day of the vote. We heard that the Whittingtons called in supporting members worldwide who had not attended their church in years, but their votes were pivotal in keeping him as pastor. These events caused the church to split. Not long afterward, Martha Whittington wasted away from cancer, and Pastor Whittington soon remarried a younger and slimmer woman.

Holly and I began attending one of the churches that split off from Pastor Whittington's church. The new church struggled to find a minister willing to audition because Pastor Whittington threatened to strip them of their preaching license. Several young people from the old church threw eggs at the new church building. Holly and I joined the sparse choir, and the holiness standards seemed less hypocritical as members freely began wearing their wedding rings. I bought Holly a wedding ring with diamonds and after we showed up for rehearsal no one was there. The leaders had dissolved the choir, telling all members except us.

"There are too many people sneaking in the choir with their wedding rings—'little foxes that spoil the vines,'" the interim pastor said over the pulpit. "We should also ban men from wearing neckties because they are nothing but cloth necklaces. And we need to stop our women from wearing boots. Men wore them first! But now, I think some of you men should allow your daughters and wives to wear pants under their dresses to keep their legs warm when they go deer hunting with ya."

"I wonder if he'll have us wearing camouflage choir robes?" I asked Holly before learning that the minister thought robes on men were too effeminate.

Around this time Holly and I stopped going to church. I felt guilty because I knew deep in my heart that Holly would still be a happy member of the Sanctuary of Holiness in Christ if she had never married me and taken on my pain and tribulations. She would still be the door greeter at all the church functions, relishing the fun and fellowship no matter what atrocities permeated from the pulpit—or in public. In a craft store, a girl from the ministerial college recognized me and, without saying a word, slapped my face in passing. Soon we got a letter in the mail addressed with green ink that appeared as though a chicken had scratched out the words.

"Who's it from?" Holly asked.

"I don't know. It just has our old church address. It says we are going to catch Hell if we don't return to God." With a sick chill moving over my flesh, I tore up the letter and threw it in the trash.

"'Catch Hell'? That sounds like a threat—like on some ransom note." Holly fetched the torn envelope out of the trash to see for herself.

"I've had enough. I'm this close to never setting foot in another church again," I said, holding my fingers two inches apart. "I'm already in Hell, so I will just take my chances."

When I made the mistake of vocalizing these injustices and my spiritual disenchantments to a few clients, a networking Sunday school teacher with a big Baptist church contacted his Human Resources friend, who slyly shunned Holly in a manner to get her fired. Holly immediately applied for a new office job.

"I know I'm not supposed to ask this but are you a Christian, Holly?"

"Yes," she said before he agreed to hire her. Many times, the shareholders in the companies she worked for even hinted at the importance of whom she must support as President of the United States.

Sick of the constant manipulation and oppression, I released the insatiable hope for peace with God and a change in my sexuality that I had clung to for so long. The girlish joy and optimism that had encompassed Holly's personality were no longer there. I knew she feared my gay nature would rear its repressed head if I abandoned the idea of God altogether, so we tried returning to the Baptist church of my youth. As soon as we entered the sanctuary, Doris Trailer, an older woman who remembered me as a child, was the only person who made an effort to greet us.

"Hi, Doris. This is my wife, Holly."

"Well, Milan, I suppose all those awwwful things I heard about you aren't true after all," Doris said as soon as she saw Holly holding my hand. I was dumbfounded at the pernicious root of gossip spreading through churches and dared not ask what awful things she was referring to. *Was I supposed to have gone up in flames for stepping beneath a steeple?* I wondered.

A proxy of me hiding behind a curtain from
religious society. Acrylic on Canvas.

COMMUNAL "YOU KNOWS"

I write in riddles because of the stealth of my home
In a belt where many were hung.
A place deep, trapped — never I wanted to be.
Among the clones.
My true voice alienates me further than I already am.
Alone.
Here, the tribal unspokenness has been honed to a high level.
A knowing.
With a simple question, the phrase catchers can
Spot any dissension showing.
They secretly long for another revolution
A "cleansing."
I want to vomit on these seemingly good
Spoon-feds being humans.
Their selective judgments are considered "winning."
But the end is like the beginning,
An ism of dominion now supported by whispers.

Poem and artwork by Milan Sergent. Previously published in *Outsiders and Apparitions: Possessed Poems and Art for Family Picnics.*

That same summer, I discovered my mother and father had once again applied their nail-scared hands to the cause when they pushed for the boycott of a famous product manufacturing company.

"They are in allegiance to Satan! The whole company is an enemy of Christians," my parents said to any available ear as they passed out fliers listing all of the products they must cease using at once. Their eyes were ablaze with a vengeance they imagined gleaning as fellow soldiers in the Army of the Lord.

"My parents surely must be doing God's will, Holly. They communicate directly with Him, remember?" I said cynically, careful to select the non-satanic products in the grocery store.

After my parents and countless other prayer warriors spent years tarnishing the company's reputation, they discovered that a competing company had made up lies about the boycotted company being satanic. I couldn't believe in a "free country," these warriors for Christ had not only damaged the company but forced them to admit they were Christians all along. This made me wonder if my parents had also been mistaken when they claimed God insisted they should boycott me.

Onward Valinda Soldier by Milan Sergent.
Acrylic on canvas inspired by the above memory.
Previously published in *Martyrs and Manifeestations:
Hexed Poems and Art for Holiday Gatherings.*

CHAPTER 36

MY anxiety had reached its peak. On top of my other health problems, I developed eczema, TMJ, bruxism, and began gnawing my tongue and inner cheeks until my mouth became so swollen that I developed an underbite at times. To function, I started taking nerve medication, and Holly scheduled me for a visit with a psychologist. I didn't realize until later that, of all of the options she had to choose from, she had booked me with a Christian psychologist.

Expecting the worst, I entered Dr. Nixon's office and sat in the chair facing his desk. He leaned back in his chair with his hands behind his balding head.

"Tell me what's going on with you, Milan," he said with an easy-going smile, nearly obscured by his scraggly beard. I became hesitant. For some reason, I always found excessive facial hair to be a mask, a veil. I couldn't believe that I was about to confess things I had never revealed to a stranger in disguise.

"No one else will know what I tell you, right?"

"I assure you that everything you tell me will remain in the strictest confidence."

I took an anxious breath and explained everything I'd been going through in the churches I had attended.

"… You wouldn't believe the number of church pastors I secretly counsel, Milan. They don't want their congregations to know because they're afraid it will shake their faith."

A cloud of energized air became trapped in my abdomen. I couldn't believe the doctor had admitted such a shocking thing. I could only imagine the millions of congregational members over the years who suffered in silence because of the religious stigma of seeking treatment for mental health issues while instead waiting for God to help them. Months earlier, I had a client who was bitter over the physical abuse her husband was causing her. Her Sunday school class in the Baptist church had shamed her for mentioning the abuse during the collection of prayer requests. After that, she tried to lend me her book on why Christians shouldn't go to a psychologist and admitted she was instead trying to save me.

"Maybe I deserve everything that has happened. Maybe I should let my church send me to the gay-conversion camp," I told the psychologist. "It can't be worse than them putting me through their version of one."

"You could go if you want to. But there is no substantial evidence that gay-conversion therapy has ever worked. Your sexuality is probably never going to change, Milan." His smile under the hairy mask now read sympathetic.

"Did you know I was gay when I first entered your office?"

Dr. Nixon nodded his head "yes," and I sank into my chair. Whom was I fooling besides myself? There was the answer I somehow knew deep inside all along. I covered my eyes as I began to cry. I had trapped myself in a wishful marriage with no hope of it ever being complete.

"There is nothing I can do about it then. But I will never cheat on my wife. I don't ever want her to know. I don't want to break her heart."

After a few more sessions with the psychologist, I learned how normal parents are supposed to behave. It was painful to dig up the graves of my childhood. I battled guilt for seeing Mother and Father outside the flattering light they had presented themselves to society. I also came to understand the social psychological research of how seemingly decent groups of people have a history of conforming to commit unthinkable acts. The new findings prove that the culprit is not passive, ignorant conformists (brainwashed zombies) but a motivated followership that is full of conviction and influenced by a charismatic "us versus them" leader to commit oppression, convincing the masses that their extreme actions are justified and noble. Finally, I learned that people are often programmed to feel guilt in childhood, and guilt doesn't necessarily equal truth.

I had no choice but to write a letter to my parents and admit that God did not change me after all and that I was still the gay son they had disowned years earlier. I was perplexed that God hadn't spoken to them sooner and told them to resume shunning me, but I was hoping they would choose to have a relationship with me this time. I was beginning to think that people who claim to hear God's voice and feel His phantom flesh might be mentally unbalanced. After all, if they spoke with Medusa, Poseidon, or any of the other millions of gods, then schizophrenia would be the diagnosis.

I never received a call, visit, or letter from my parents again.

I didn't give up yet. Though I had grown leery of ministers who preached opinions as doctrine without being able to show proof, Holly and I tried a Full Gospel church next under Pastor Mason. We soon became close friends with David and Dina Regis, who ran the music ministry. David and I seemed like brothers, and a few people commented on our similarities. Despite the usual stances on homosexuality David and his friends had to establish over thousands of neglected standards, I had hoped he would become a true confidant—the brother I had lost in my youth. David's wife, however, seemed noticeably jealous. At first, I ignored it. She categorized everyone according to the four temperaments: sanguine, phlegmatic, choleric, and melancholic, as if God couldn't change one's personality.

If God can't alter anyone's personality type, why should I expect a change in sexual attraction? I realized.

At a church party, instead of sympathy for the ninety-two passengers killed in a jet crash in Colombia, I had to listen to everyone revile Rosie O'Donnell because she had recently come out of the closet as a lesbian.

"How do you like our church so far, Milan and Holly?" asked Dina after she informed us that we should be grateful they invited us to sit with the ministry at a restaurant.

"I like it," I said. "But I don't know that I agree with what Pastor Mason said. 'If any man tells you that it's not God's will that you're healed, then he is of the Devil.' Your church believes that if anyone dies before a ripe old age, it's because they have sin or unbelief in their life?"

"Yes," David and Dina said. "What's hard to understand about it?"

"I think it's monstrous to tell a sweet family after their little girl died after years of prayers, tithes, and sacrifice, 'I'm sorry, but your sin and unbelief caused your little girl to get raped and strangled to death by a crazed lunatic.' To put that kind of guilt and shame on dismayed parents without evidence is horrid beyond words to me."

Shaking, David jumped up from his chair and placed his hand on my shoulder. "You have a contentious spirit, Milan," he said before praying for me.

I allowed him to disparage and pray for me. But he could not justify that teaching, and I was shaking his shallow faith. The church attributed every unwelcome action or thought to an embodied demon causing the activity. Unless it was severe weather, which they often claimed God caused in his anger at Christians for tolerating gay people. It seemed every week I watched local weather reports where a tornado survivor thanked God for not destroying their home. As if they were holy and special. Would they dare praise a sniper for mowing down everyone else but them at a deadly concert?

Months later, Pastor Mason's "Name It, Claim It" beliefs were tested when he crashed his car in a faithless panic. He was rushing his pregnant wife to the emergency room only to discover she was only experiencing a false delivery pang. Of course, no church member held Pastor Mason's "demonic unbelief" over his head. A similar situation happened to their sister church: That Pastor refused to seek medical assistance for his chest pains, thinking it would be an act of sinful unbelief to seek man over God. He gave in too late and died on the way to the emergency room when his fat-soaked heart could no longer retain faith. According to one of my clients who attended the stunned sister church, the ministry there called in a famous pastor in the Full Gospel circles to try to raise the pastor from his deathbed. The Lazarus effect failed, and Dina denied the resurrection attempt ever happened when I asked her about it.

Dina sent me a nasty letter where, in conclusion, she claimed that God had called her and David to move their music ministry to Florida by speaking to them through the pieces of a board game.

Always to Florida and never Afghanistan or Iraq. I wonder if they were playing Monopoly, I thought bitterly.

Holly and I attended a non-denominational church next. We didn't stay long when my manliness was publicly questioned, and the pastor preached a sermon that revealed a private discussion between us to the congregation. He used me as an example without my permission. Also, after Holly suggested the members go door-knocking in the South Jackson neighborhood, the pastor's wife said they wanted quality members, not quantity.

After attending six different churches and enduring similar awful experiences, I was on the edge of a nervous breakdown. I could not stay inside a church another minute if I were going to keep my last ounce of sanity. I tried to seek help through a spiritual abuse website, where I briefly mentioned my experiences. They informed me that my story was "hardly believable" but thanked me for emailing them anyway. I tried to reply that I was not lying, only to discover that they had blocked me from accessing their website. Lucky for me, I wasn't on the verge of another suicide attempt before the rejection. If a spiritual abuse center rejects those who turn to them for help, then that is a tragedy indeed. I realized that cults and spiritual organizations were well aware that the more outlandish they behaved behind their towering white walls, the less other people would believe their victims' stories. They know it forces the victims to remain quiet or publish their horrible experiences under the category of fiction.

In February 1997, I was taking a bath when I had a vision of a man shooting people on top of the Empire State Building. Holly and I were preparing for our first trip to New York City in two weeks, and privately I was obsessing about how I could find my friend Griff who was surely finished with college in the Big Apple. *What was he doing? Had he found a lover?* It had been eight years since he became angry at me and stormed off at the news of my succumbing to religious oppression.

If only he knew of my regrets for not heeding his advice, I thought. *If only he knew how much I missed him.* But what could I do? I was chained to Holly, and as much as I wanted to leave my mistakes behind and resume the life I should've lived, I didn't want to crush her in the process.

Weeks earlier, I saw that Samantha had been arrested for drunk driving. In the police photo, it was apparent she had gained weight, abandoned her punky style, and looked dull and sad. I sent her a friend request and message on Facebook, where it encouraged me to see her actively supporting LGBT rights, but she snubbed me. *Had Griff turned her against me?*

I dried off, got dressed, and turned on the radio to hear that my horrific vision had just occurred: A gunman had just shot seven people on the observation deck of the Empire State Building before killing himself. I had many premonitions or visions before this one proved true, but they were always of such random things, never anything that would prevent my own heartaches and mistakes.

While Holly was teaching a symposium in New York, I walked all over the city: Grand Central Station, Broadway, Greenwich Village, Union Square Park, the Bowery, Chinatown, Christopher Street, and God knows where else. I foolishly hoped I would run into Griff, and somehow everything would magically reset, like the Cinderella story, only in reverse. Two months earlier, Michael Alig, the leader of the New York cultural phenomenon known as the Club Kids, had been arrested for murdering his drug dealer. The movement was flickering out, yet Griff had been in the neon spotlight of it all. I leafed through a heavy directory at a payphone in Little Italy and never found a listing for him. *Had he contracted AIDS and died?* I had to believe otherwise. It felt so liberating to walk around and not to be gawked at with suspicion like I was a disease wearing a rainbow dress. In fact, I felt wonderfully invisible.

Griff, you must've found your gay paradise here. You surely can't miss Mississippi or me anymore.

Searching for Griff in New York City,
never dreaming I would return someday.

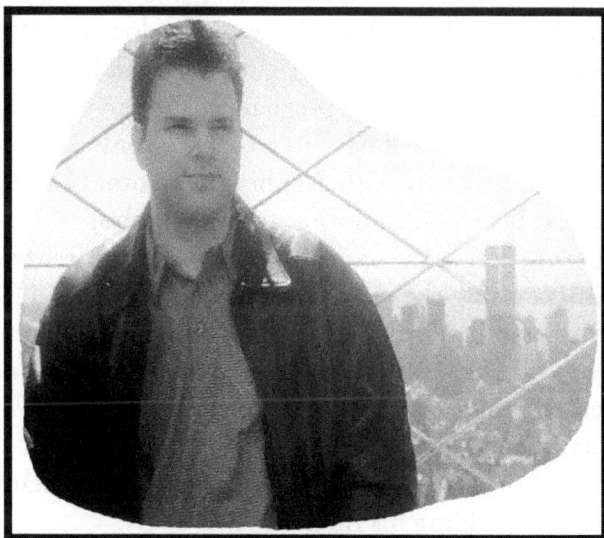

On top of the Empire State Building
with the Twin Towers behind me.

The end of my faith started after Holly suffered a tubal pregnancy. We both imagined that having a baby would add the missing ingredient to our marriage. I dreaded every time she was ovulating because it might as well have been an ominous bell chiming, "Okay, Milan, it's time to prove you are straight and go have sex with your wife." To have romantic success, I would have to dim the lights as much as possible and imagine I was making love with a man, which only brought further guilt and begging God for forgiveness.

Perhaps losing two sisters at birth had tainted me. From the earliest mention of trying to get pregnant, I fervently prayed, "God, I beg you, please don't make me have to choose between the baby's life and Holly's." I've always believed in saving the living, especially when there is no guarantee a baby will survive birth.

"If it's a boy, I want to name him Adam Alexander, and if it's a girl, we'll name her Victoria Siobhan," Holly said with sparkles in her eyes after the home pregnancy strip showed two positive lines.

"It's just a bit of spotting, sweetie. It happens. Try not to worry," I said to Holly the following week.

"If you've had a miscarriage, there's nothing I can do about it," the doctor said over the phone the afternoon of her distress.

Seven weeks later, I held Holly's hand while the doctor performed an ultrasound to see how the baby was developing. After another minute of silence, Holly's excited grip on my hand began to loosen.

"Yep, I'm afraid it's a tubal pregnancy. We can try to dissolve the pregnancy. Otherwise, we'll have to go in and remove the fetus," the doctor said inside his office with deer heads and other animal carcasses on the wall near his framed hunting and sports photos.

Seeing Holly weep was too painful to witness. After two weeks of radiation shots erasing the visions of our baby's future, Holly started hemorrhaging and had to be rushed to the emergency room. *I should've known. The things I pray for the hardest always backfire the worst.* I seethed while I paced the hospital halls. After what seemed like six hours, the doctor met me in the waiting room.

"I removed the fetus, barely saving Holly's life. That *thang* was this big," he said, holding his fingers inches apart.

That "thing" was our child, I thought in disgust at the doctor's crude demeanor.

"I feel I let you down," Holly said after I drove her home and put her to bed.

"Oh, baby, it's all right as long as I have you," I said, trying to comfort Holly, though the maternal expectations had taken hold inside her heart.

The truth was I felt like a failure, too, and was convinced God was further punishing me because I couldn't shake my gay urges, even in the fantasies I surrendered to in order to become aroused enough to have sex with Holly in the first place. It was either entertain forbidden fantasies, refuse to communicate, or lie and blame the conjugal disappointments on erectile dysfunction, which seemed convincing since my father suffered from impotence.

"You basically had an abortion," a hair client said to Holly, adding to her distress. The client taught the rhythm method at a Catholic organization, and to hell with my depression, she thought people who kept their blinds or curtains closed were perverts. She was also delighted that her son bullied a boy and called him a fag for wearing a pink shirt.

I was not amused and told her so. Like so many other of my toxic religious clients, she quit scheduling appointments with me. Once I managed to be alone, years of pent-up rage broke out of me, and I screamed every curse word I knew and gave two middle fingers to the heavens. "I'm done with you, God. I'm done!"

I gave up all hopes of being anything other than a gay man who had wasted most of his life. I'd be damned if I'd ever allow one condemning spirit or saint to pass off more opinions, lies, or myths upon me again. I discovered the spiritual brethren's love was blood-puddle shallow. A fickle love that requires those lucky to receive it to walk a thin line of similar thoughts and church-ordained beliefs and behavior, and if you fail to do so, they ostracize you from the fold.

I caught the whisper of wisdom that, eventually, the expectant seeker experiences things that they attribute as a manifestation of a higher power, a type of pareidolia. Though no missing limb ever grows back, nor has it ever. I left church and Christianity, tossing years of prayers, tears, and hopes into the garbage.

Several things I learned:

- ❖ Bigfoot is always male.
- ❖ Ghosts never ask the questions.
- ❖ The Tooth Fairy is cheap and also requires faith.
- ❖ Santa, like religion, is judgmental and was created to make nice of the naughty.
- ❖ Miracles were commonplace before the creation of recording devices. Except for successful hospital visits, those are modern miracles—expensive miracles.
- ❖ The Easter Bunny doesn't like to get wet, so he lays dusty eggs behind the fridge.
- ❖ The supernatural surges in a triangle though many shun the ones involving love.
- ❖ Jesus spoke Shakespearean and was portrayed as the first blond-haired, blue-eyed Middle Easterner.

CHAPTER 37

A FTER Holly and I left the church, people kept asking around to see if we were still married. This would infuriate me. Our differing interests became more apparent, but we had more time to focus on ourselves as individuals. After collecting many antiques, we bought a Queen Ann Victorian-era home in Hazlehurst, Mississippi, and I began restoring it after studying similar architecture from the period. We hosted a couple of neighborhood parties to get to know the locals and quickly learned that the church you attended was the only way to truly fit in. A worker in a local drugstore even gave our private phone number to her pastor without our permission.

Hiring workers to do anything needed for our house was a nightmare. When the good old boys finally showed up, they sawed through a foundation beam, and we discovered the pump organ in the parlor was leaning because of it. They replaced the subfloor with particle board and filled gaps in the floor with blue painter's tape. They didn't insulate or secure the air ducts to the vents or seal the moisture barrier under the crawl space. They shingled over old shingles and created a bedroom ceiling leak so bad I could have taken a shower when it rained. They didn't prime any bare wood, painted over a window screen, and I had to physically restrain one worker who started slathering white oil-based paint over our freshly painted blue walls. At my salon, they paved over my water meter on purpose. This was only the beginning of the issues I had to deal with. The workers always seemed more interested in what I did for a living instead of doing their jobs, and they were getting their kicks with jibes at my masculinity.

I did as much of the work as possible, including designing, sawing, and installing all of the gingerbread trim on the house, as well as putting a white picket fence around the property. I relandscaped with Spanish moss, formal hedges, azaleas, and four-season cherubim statues to look like the haunted Myrtles Plantation in St. Francisville, Louisiana. I got tired of being out in my front yard and having rednecks drive by and whistle at me, so the lush plantings gave me more privacy.

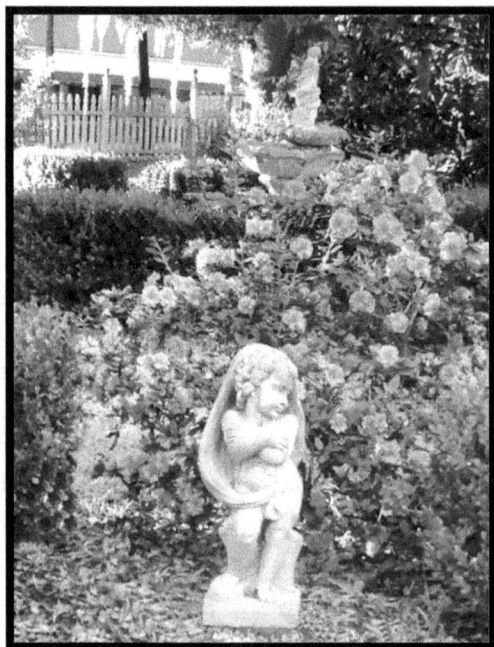

During this time, I watched Holly grow and mature into a confident business executive, honing her skills as a payroll manager for an automotive company. She made the top fifty leading businesswomen, became president of the Jackson Advertising Federation, and won one award after another.

"I think you should submit your newest position and award to the local newspaper," I suggested to Holly. "It might help you get a job closer to home if you get tired of the long drives."

Two days later, Holly came home holding a copy of the newspaper with a funny expression on her face.

"What is it?" I asked before she handed me the paper.

Underneath the news article about her accomplishments, the newspaper added a reworded Mark Twain quote without Holly's permission: "If our merits could get us to Heaven, our dogs would get there first."

"I think this podunk excuse for a town is trying to tell us something. Don't you think? I should go down to the newspaper company and fuss at them."

"What good would it do besides make things worse?" said Holly.

She was right. What good would it do?

I again picked up the reins of forbidden love and surrendered to my gay secret in my fantasies only. Hidden lust burns holes in its moral straitjacket. I learned that a married friend, Toby Neblett, had sought private counsel at Pastor Whittington's church for his struggles with homosexual urges. The minister outed Toby in front of the entire organization, even in front of the man's kids, causing him to lose his marriage. All the while, the assistant pastor bragged that they were a redneck religion.

"Disgusting! The ministry paraded Toby around as though displaying a trophy kill," I said to Holly. "If he had a fetish for various women, or if he was some limber-legged girl who got pregnant out of wedlock, the church would've taken him under their protective cloak."

Jaded reality breeds contempt. It became harder and harder for me to suppress my sadness and anger at the injustice that members of the gay community across the world had to endure. After years of social and psychological studies, I learned why many of my compatriots, salt of the earth, good old folks, oddly neglect to support or even acknowledge anti-bullying causes.

"They don't want minorities, even defenseless children, whose lifestyles they don't approve of to have any protection," I said in disgust. "They'll let the little kiddies get beat to puddles of blood and bone and call them sissies if they dare complain about it with their dying breath!"

I began to feel bitter about Holly's expectations of our marriage. I questioned whether I had made a mistake by not telling her the truth years earlier when she had asked if I wanted her sexually.

"I guess we're just roommates," Holly mumbled on occasion.

Were my love and sympathy enough reason for us to go on pretending we were a normal married couple? Should friends be locked together until death?

"You've always been insecure and jealous, Holly. I don't think you have a clue what I have sacrificed for you," I said one day when I had had enough. "Hell, you haven't allowed me to go anywhere on my own during our entire marriage. You've taken trips all over the country with friends and coworkers. You even went on a harbor cruise with a man you just met at a business meeting in San Diego. And I can only imagine how you would've reacted if I informed you on our wedding anniversary that I was going on a cruise to Cozumel with my best friend and you weren't invited. You would never let me hear the end of it."

With these realizations, I determined that if Holly questioned my attraction to her again, I would have to tell her the truth, no matter how painful or the consequences.

CHAPTER 38

O N January 1, 2000, my parents moved back to Jackson and began to mingle with society they had never wanted to see again. Father took a Sunday school teaching position at a Baptist church in Pearl, Mississippi. I was shocked to learn that he and Mother were trying to convince my family that I had abandoned them instead of the reverse.

"That's absurd!" I said to Holly. "No one knows that Mother sneaked off to the mountains without telling any of her friends or family. They have no clue that her family, every last one of them, slowly passed away while searching for her for all of those years."

"Where did y'all vanish to for sixteen years? You didn't even tell us you were leaving Mississippi," friends and family had asked upon seeing them again for the first time.

"Oh, we just wanted to get away from the rat race and enjoy nature," my parents told everyone, never revealing their real intentions.

"You know, Milan, I think your parents chose to move back during Y2K for a reason."

"Why's that?" I asked.

"Think about it," continued Holly. "During Y2K, everyone else thought the end of the world was about to happen and were stocking up on food and weapons. Churches were handing out Y2K survival pamphlets, and suddenly your parents came waltzing back from their wilderness banishment like they weren't the superstitious and extreme ones. It was perfect timing for them to save face."

CHAPTER 39

I was a pro at wearing a mask,
but it was starting to come off.

OVER time, I took up painting again, starting with watercolor before moving into acrylic, oils, and digital. I began showing my work on social media sites. Since I was still unwilling to come out of the closet and risk Holly being brokenhearted, I lived vicariously through my art. I used a lot of hidden imagery and symbolism, paralleling my life experiences. My other inspiration came from the British Blitz Kids, who turned themselves into living works of flamboyant and androgynous art, earning them a place in a movement called the New Romantics. After creating a few pictorial works for non-binary visual artist Alisson Gothz, I was thrilled when The Blitz Kids website added me and my work to their list of Blitz Artists. During this time, I got a friend request on YouTube from the pop star Marilyn, whose life had been featured in the hit musical *Taboo*. Marilyn had been an inspiration to me as well, so I was in disbelief when he publicly bragged about my art and named me as one of his top three peeps. Through Marilyn, I learned of Boy George's secret channel on YouTube along with a lot of other fun and shocking secrets.

"It's all who you know," Marilyn kept telling me about the art and entertainment industry. I didn't believe him when he told me about Andy Warhol inviting him to the Silver Factory in New York until I saw the video of Marilyn with Andy, who was another one of my inspirations. A year later, another British gender-bending pop star named DragChrist befriended me and requested that I design the cover for his biography.

"Give me some idea of what you're looking for," I asked.

"I'll use whatever you create," he insisted.

I had found my element and friendship far out of Mississippi, but for what it was worth, it was online only and soon felt as fake as a weekend spray tan. Painting was therapeutic, and I turned part of my hair salon into an art gallery. The hundred-year-old house had never seen such liveliness adorning its walls. I invited the owner of an upscale art gallery nearby to have a look and see if she would represent my work in her enormous gallery.

I held my breath as she went from room to room, examining each painting. At last, she entered the front room where I was waiting, and her nose was so high in the air that she could snort dust off the tip of the Eiffel Tower.

"Your paintings aren't the right fit for my gallery," she said.

My posture sank an inch. "What type of art do you consider my paintings as being?"

"Witches," she said with a response so sneering and quick it seemed like a sneeze.

Her curt reply spun through my head with an echo. I didn't think I had painted a single witch anywhere in my gallery—not consciously, anyway.

"Hum?" I said, trying not to appear rattled before thinking of a retort. "I thought perhaps after seeing the green alien with the big eyes near the entry to your galley that my work might fit in as well. What genre of art do you call that?"

"I know the artist and painting to which you are referring. Her work sells for hundreds of dollars," she said, raising her nose even higher before leaving.

The next fine art gallery where I sought representation called me one afternoon. "Mr. Sergent, your *stuff* is ready to be picked up," the receptionist said with a pop of snoot appeal.

By "stuff," she meant the portfolio of my work I had left with the gallery. When I pulled into the parking lot and stepped out of my car, the gallery staff hid in the back of the building. In their panic to avoid me, I was shocked to see they had left my portfolio unguarded on the front desk inches from the exit door.

The last fine art gallery I visited accepted a couple of my dullest paintings but confessed that my work was "too way out there" for further representation with them.

"Art in the Courtyard" in Highland Village.

In April 2005, I was one of six artists asked to display my artwork at the 35th Earth Day Celebration, "Relief & Rhythms," at Phillips on the Reservoir. A tree was planted at Ridgeland Elementary School in my honor.

But all was not a celebration of the "Magically Mischievous Mind of Milan Sergent." I overheard nasty comments at every event my paintings were featured—enough to make me want to use my paintbrushes for firewood for my own roasting. A collector insisted I display my art at the Tomato Festival in Crystal Springs. Since I had to work that day, I met with a few of the event coordinators to see if I could leave my paintings with them to display at the event, to which they agreed. I finished work two hours earlier than expected, only to discover that the men had hidden all of my paintings behind a truck bumper. But I had come to expect such in my state.

"You need to be positive, Milan," Holly said sweetly.

"You're right. Positive they spared my creations from rotten tomatoes flung out of righteous indignation."

I spent so much time in New Orleans that I found a better fit in the French Quarter, where I began displaying my paintings on the old fence at Jackson Square. I was always looking for Brad Pitt, who often strolled past on his way to his mansion near Decatur Street. Everything was far less bigoted there until an old carriage driver commented that his horse, Roosevelt, tucked his tail and moved faster when he pulled the carriage through the gay section of the Quarter. Lies were proving justifiable for the righteous if they worked for their cause.

The French Quarter fence spikes
complimented my gothic art.

During this time, I had been doing the hair of a few famous music artists, including Kellye Huff, Christal Noel, Fingers Taylor, and David with David and the Giants. Among my celebrity referrals was a famous actor who played a main character from one of televisions most beloved sitcoms. For this memoir I will call him George.

"What do you call the art on your walls? What type of art is it?" George asked with a wrinkled brow while I strategically snipped his graying curls into a more modern style.

"Some might call it gothic, but technically it's more pop art surreal." By the way he stiffened in the salon chair, I could tell he was growing uncomfortable, as though the paintings were monsters coming alive and closing in on him.

"Uh-huh. And where do you get your inspiration for your paintings?"

"I'm mainly inspired by people who turn themselves into living art … The B-52's, for instance. Holly and I went to see them at Party Out of Bounds, an AIDS benefit in honor of Ricky, who passed away. There were lots of fun people there—gay and straight."

I explained to George how I won the Design The B-52's Hair Contest and how Holly and I got to hang out with the band in their hometown of Athens, Georgia.

With one of the nicest people ever:
Keith Strickland of The B-52's.

Before I could finish, George jumped out of the chair as though I had stripped off a choir robe to reveal a latex bondage suit underneath.

"Man, you don't see anything wrong with homosexuality?"

"Nooo," I muttered, stunned at his reaction. But then I remembered the whole uptight straight man in the beauty salon with no boobies scenario.

"Do you mind if I pray for you so God will show you the truth of His word?"

I wanted to show him the door, but I was always such a damned pushover, so I stood there and submitted while he kept his distance, laid one stiff hand on my shoulder, and began to pray aloud as though he was casting out a gay demon.

I guess I disturbed him terribly because he never rescheduled another hair appointment even though, right after autographing his scathing biography, he wrote that I was the best stylist he had run across.

What a preference killer the G word can make. *It's a good thing air isn't gay*, I thought; *otherwise, some people would choose to asphyxiate instead.*

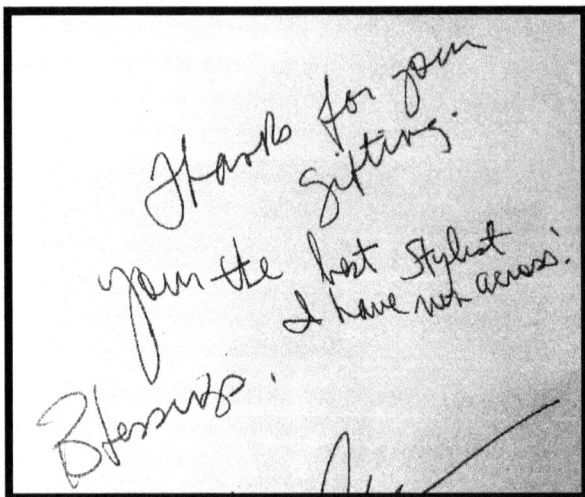

A year after surviving Hurricane Katrina and receiving further rejections by Mississippi art galleries, I began seeking representation out of the South and got accepted to have a month-long solo show at Jadite Gallery near Rockefeller Center in New York City, which I titled "Outsiders and Apparitions." The local newspaper featured a front-page article on me: "'Outsiders' in. Artist's works of prejudices, outcasts headed for N.Y. show.'"

Despite a rainstorm throughout the opening reception, guests had packed inside the gallery, and it was nearly a dream come true. Though I felt ridiculous signing my first autograph. I said "nearly" because I must've looked over my shoulder the whole night, hoping Griff had somehow heard that I was in New York—that he saw my exhibition listed in the art gallery guides and would surprise me by waltzing through the glass door. Every blond man proved to be a stranger and not Griff. It was so wrong knowing he was out there lost in the concrete jungle, and though I had returned to his turf, it had now been seventeen years since I had last seen him. The gentrification of the city had killed the culture, and the outsiders I was celebrating had moved farther on the outside. Time is such a swift and greedy thief.

My New York art exhibition.

Guests wanted to know the story behind every painting, and it was there in Manhattan that I realized I was trying to tell stories that needed to be in books and not confined to the limited parameters of a framed canvas. Once I returned home, I started writing the stories of the characters in my paintings, most of which became the cast of my young adult fantasy series *Candlewicke 13*. The five novels in the series focused on a coven of colorful young sorcerers who had to unravel the Great Deception placed over their hidden island country to defeat the Grim Warlock, who had bound the star beings of the Zodiac to use as weapons of mass destruction. For the series, I created an enchanted pet for Valor McRaven, a half-lion and half-eagle creature called an

Elusive Griffin in honor of my Griff, who was still proving elusive.

For the next twelve years, I spent every spare minute I had, up until sunrise, writing and illustrating all five books in the fantasy series before I even tried to publish the first book. I knew it was insane and a considerable risk, but that's what I did. I lived vicariously through my characters, and they carried me through over a decade of depression and isolation. I used this time to study everything I could about the craft of writing and to improve my stories. Along with burning through several expensive editors and two computer crashes, I lost months of material and constantly had to deal with people stealing my character names. For one year of this time, I spent pursuing literary agents. I started with the top agents and queried my way to the bottom before I learned that an unpublished writer without connections had a better chance of winning the lottery than landing an agent. And to land a publisher, a writer needed to secure an agent first. At this point, I had only published a few poems with *Scarlet Literary Magazine* and edited three business books, which won awards. Then I began looking into self-publishing and learned I was considered a triple threat. I could write and illustrate and also had my third weapon, Holly, who had won many awards in marketing. While I finished the writing, I turned my character illustrations into animated GIFs and then turned the GIFs into two book trailers.

I begged Holly to study as much as she could about self-publishing so that everything would roll smoothly when the time finally came to publish the first book. She was part of the reason I began writing novels in the first place. In high school, she had started a period romance novel which she had abandoned after graduating. She could dream an entire novel and still remember pages of details about it in the morning. It would frustrate me when she wouldn't finish any of the stories she started. So, I had hoped to motivate her by writing my own.

Just before I self-published the first book in the *Candlewicke 13* series over our Christmas vacation, I realized that Holly had made little effort to learn what was needed to publish. We had lost the only connecting thread our marriage had left. I became overwhelmed with the process, the wasted years, and my emotions. Why should she want to help me? I rarely performed my husbandly duty to her. We were just roommates, as she once again reminded me.

While she was napping in the middle of vacation, I wrote her a farewell suicide note and left it on the toilet lid. In a disconnected state with a rusty box cutter in hand, I climbed into the bathtub, fully clothed. I placed the blade against my wrists, ready to slice up the veins in the correct direction. The problem was that I still loved Holly too much and feared she would be traumatized and blame herself if she found me dead in a tub of blood. That afternoon, Holly knew something was wrong, so I confessed what I had nearly done and the reasons why. I acknowledged that I was still gay, but she didn't want to hear it, so we went back to pretending.

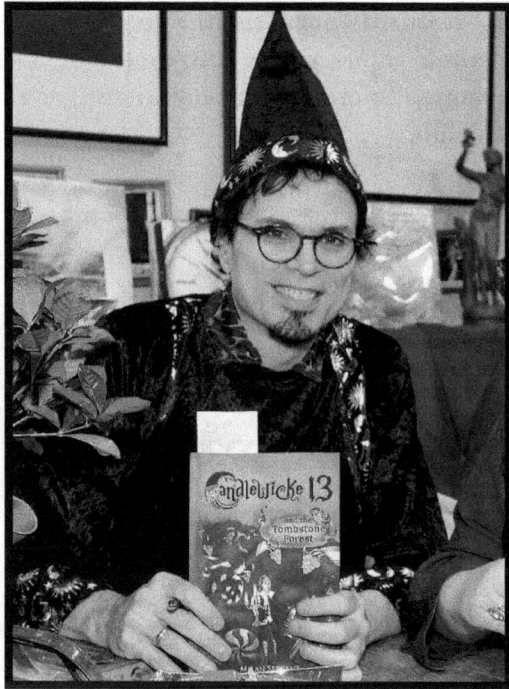

Book launch at Lemuria.

I would never have guessed how the dark cloud of hopelessness was about to lift. And thanks to Holly's long hours of work helping me, the first book of my *Candlewicke 13* series, *Candlewicke 13: Curse of the McRavens*, was featured in over two hundred and fifty news outlets and the video blog, *Around the Town in the South*. A massive book launch catapulted it to number four in Mississippi during Dr. Seuss Month. Several guests who came to the book signing, and to hear me speak, grew tired of waiting in the line that spilled out of the bookstore and into the mall, so they left. When it came time to give my speech before a packed room, I asked the audience to heckle me using the exact words I received in college Speech class. I wanted to unveil my writing career with the incident that had ended it years earlier and use my voice to speak out against bullying to show others you can overcome anything.

Months later, the second book in my series won the Book Excellence Awards as well as the Readers' Favorite international finalist award and was also featured at the Miami Book Fair, with sales going to a children's charity. Weird as I was, I was more excited that my novel was featured next to the only bookseller carrying autographed memoir copies of my longtime idol, Debbie Harry of Blondie. I had wanted to attend her book signing event but couldn't fit it into my schedule.

Milan Sergent being recognized at
The Readers' Favorite Book Awards in Miami.

After hobnobbing with other award-winning authors in Miami, I realized two things: Firstly, I had probably turned the characters in my paintings into witches as some subconscious reprisal toward the gallery owner who degraded my work as nothing but witches. I wanted to visit the gallery owner and thank her for her inspiration, but the doors to her enormous gallery had closed for good.

Secondly, somewhere during my travels to my book signings, I realized I had become a director, the profession my parents had forbidden me to pursue because it was "unchristian." Only I was directing the charters in a book instead of a play or movie. And for once, I could make the characters do whatever I wanted, and they cooperated … most of the time.

A case of life imitating art's perception.

With every attack I saw escalating against the LGBTQ community, I began writing my novels to make a statement on bullying and injustice. In a suspicious world that doesn't tolerate ambiguity, I risked exposing my suppressed sexuality.

At times I became frustrated at the long travels and rescheduling process, especially at a book signing on the Mississippi coast during Hurricane Barry. I had to outrun a tornado on the interstate.

"Nobody is going to show up during a hurricane, and I'm not going to reschedule again," I said to Holly, my eyes straining to see the road between the windshield wipers oscillating at top speed. When we finally arrived alive, I had to trudge through six inches of water in the parking lot of Southern Bound Book Shop. I downed a stout Long Island iced tea to calm my nerves and watched in surprise as guests slowly filled the bookstore. That night, I learned a valuable lesson and left humbled and ashamed of my attitude. The biggest reward was having fans of my novels and artwork brave high winds and water to be so open with their troubled lives and tell me how much my stories inspired them, if only not to feel so alone in a cruel world.

During this time, I also published two books of surreally illustrated poetry with themes of judgment, dogmatism, conformism, and marginalization. The first book I named after the New York show, *Outsiders and Apparitions*, won another international book award. I subtitled the book *Possessed Poems and Art for Family Picnics* as a return slap to the religious people who demonized me.

Thanks to the media exposure, I sold many paintings, including an abstract pen and ink drawing I had named "Hidden Kisses," which Meredith, my landlord's wife, just had to have. Later she came into my salon in a huff about the art acquisition.

"I wished I hadn't bought Hidden Kisses," she said.

"Why?" I asked, stunned at her change of heart.

"I didn't know it was homosexual men kissing," she replied.

I was positive that rumors and her bigoted suspicions of me had planted false seeds in her mind, as I in no way had drawn men touching lips with other men. But shortly after this fiasco, Meredith and her husband sneaked a monopolizing gospel-singing entrepreneur into my salon and gallery while I was away and secretly sold him the building after promising me I would have the first option to buy it when the time came. The betrayals just kept recurring. For fifteen faithful years, I had taken care of their mother and had invested money and challenging work to improve the rental property.

But things were getting worse for gay people in my state. In April 2016, the governor of Mississippi signed a controversial "religious freedom" bill allowing government and business owners to refuse service to gay people based on religious beliefs. Though Jesus commanded Christians to love their neighbors as themselves, feed the hungry, shelter the homeless, and clothe the naked, American Christians created a "but not if they're gay" exemption.

Inadvertently terrorizing the Bible Belt of the country.

Around this time, I had grown my hair to the middle of my back and dyed it and my facial hair black. I had made a habit of wearing all black ever since the Pentecostals shamed men as looking effeminate for wearing color. The wait staff in restaurants often referred to me as a lady or called me "Ma'am." Even when I informed them that I was a man, they didn't apologize. When it came time for an oil change for my truck, two young male workers at the shop, one Black and the other White, bragged loudly to the worker at the front desk that I looked like a lady.

"… When we first saw him drive his truck in the garage, we thought we were on an episode of Queer Factor," one of the boys said.

A few days later, my engine almost blew up while driving on the highway. The boys at the shop didn't change my oil as an extra insult, reminding me of the change in my sexuality I had believed God would do but only received insults for my effort. I, of course, couldn't complain to God, but I did drive to the shop and complained to the manager, telling him everything that had happened.

"Just be glad you aren't that stupid," was his only reply, and they charged me again to have my oil finally changed.

Going over the manager's head with another complaint would do no good—not with the new law allowing discrimination. This was becoming the standard treatment for gay men in my state. After many complaints from coworkers, one of my clients admitted that she had fired the best and most conscientious worker in her large company simply because the worker was gay. As always, I had to hide my rage and give her the best haircut her privileged ass expected—make her beautiful so she could land her third husband.

None of my social media friends or clients spoke out against this atrocious new law that legalized discrimination against LGBTQIA people. I was profoundly disgusted and hurt by their silence. They were content with such an evil law. I realized they could care less if every restaurant, grocer, every business in the country refused to offer services to people like me. Gay people could just die of starvation in the streets for all they cared. What hurt, even more, was that Holly had befriended the wife of the Mississippi governor behind the disturbingly anti-gay bill. Against my wishes, the First Lady attended the ribbon cutting at the new salon, which I had only a month to find and move into after my sudden eviction.

Also, against my wishes, the chamber of commerce members formed a giant prayer circle, blocking every entrance in the lobby of the new commercial center, causing other business owners to step into the halls to see what the commotion was about. Even though in the Bible Jesus condemned public prayer spectacles and told his followers to go to their prayer closet and pray in secret, time after time, His modern followers use every chance to market their faith to rub their brand and dominion in the faces of others.

During the lengthy prayer, the elevator door opened with a ding, and a woman's eyes enlarged as if she had stepped into the Twilight Zone or a gay protest by Westboro Baptist Church. The woman froze, and I didn't care if the chamber thought I was a heathen or rude; I broke through the prayer circle to help her exit the elevator and get to her destination.

Ready to cut the ribbon to my
new business and get out of there.

When it came time for newspaper photos, the First Lady offered to hold my business sign front and center for the group photo. I gripped the sign in one hand and the enormous ribbon-cutting scissors in the other and pretended I didn't hear her. A cool young man in a tweed cap seemed to understand my hesitance, so he offered to hold my sign instead, which I gladly accepted.

I also refused to do the First Lady's hair after she tried to make an appointment. Her surprise at my refusal could never come close to the rejection and hate gay people experienced when refused service because of whom they loved.

CHAPTER 40

SINCE I couldn't easily change the present, I became nostalgic and began living in the past. I often forced my brain to remember every detail of every man I had slept with. Music has a way of triggering these memories. Certain songs had played while I had been intimate with different boys. "Lovin', Touchin', Squeezin'" by Journey played the night I shared my bed with an ex-Pentecostal boy known as the "pink sheep" of his family.

"Say You, Say Me," by Lionel Richie, played the night a Madonna fan told me I was the only brunette he had ever been attracted to. Lucky me. He wasn't a top, bottom, or versatile, strictly a dull but handsome side. He made up for it by biting my lips in a death grip, keeping me his love slave. I ended up with so many hickeys that my college mates thought I had been in a car wreck with vampires.

"I wanna be a Cowboy," by Boys Don't Cry, stuck in my head because a former schoolmate known as "The White Michael Jackson" had danced to it for a talent competition. Our intimacy was cut short because he was so green that he wanted to ride his white horse straight into my closet, which I, at the time, didn't want to crawl back inside. For some people, "the closet" is literal.

With the advances of the internet, I began searching for all my old gay friends. After years of finding nothing, I learned that Carl Allred had died on Aug 15, 1994, just four years after I last told him we couldn't be friends anymore and watched him sadly vanish in the church parking lot. This was a searing punch in my selfish and superstitious gut. Poor Carl must've been wrong about God curing him of AIDS. Or, like me, he felt his faith demanded that he claim what wasn't as though it was.

I wish I could say the deaths ended with Carl, but that proved shockingly untrue. Richie, my old friend with the artificial leg, died October 23, 2007, like Carl, without as much as a mention in their parents' obituaries before them. Jerry, my gay friend from college, had reportedly died on October 24, 2014, from asphyxiation suicide. His body was discovered in the garage of his California home with the car engine still running. Douglas, a former coworker whose bitter story about the hair salon owner who wanted to cast the Devil out of him, had sadly died from AIDS in 1991. The ex-Pentecostal friend and one-time fling, known as the "pink sheep," choked to death on some soup in 2022.

Mitch Odom, my only straight friend from middle and high school, died in hospice of unlisted causes on September 16, 2017. He had retired from the Green Beret. In my lifetime, I had many intuitive dreams and visions that had proven true, and, given the nightmares about him not wanting to be publicly seen as my friend, he was no exception. Hoping I was being paranoid for once, I sent him a friend request on social media. He refused to accept my friend invitation, though he did chat with me privately a few times. I realized he had become so far right that he probably never even drove in the passing lane. Our back-alley friendship was no loss. Between the typical religious nods to his overflowing friend list, his last posts on social media were homophobic in content, the ones where he wasn't calling for President Obama's and Hillary Clinton's assassination.

I laughed bitterly. As a high-ranking member of the Special Forces, Mitch had been trained not to fear anything, yet he feared the only loyal friend he had throughout school—his gay friend—who was now locked in a doomed marriage to a straight woman. The innocents of youth—the prison of adulthood. Later I learned from a former classmate that Mitch had known where I had worked for years, yet he never stopped by in his daily commute to say hello.

Lastly, after years of searching for information on Griff Barfield, my most loyal friend who tried to talk sense into me in the mall, I finally located his home address in Provincetown, Massachusetts. I was surprised that Griff, being an artist, didn't have an online presence and was unsure if it was him. Like a stalker, I maneuvered through satellite images and saw a blue car parked in the driveway with a rainbow Pride sticker on the bumper, and my heart swelled with joy. It had to be the correct Griffin Barfield. I sent him a certified letter through the post office with an apology for not heeding his advice and for saying I would pray for him all those years ago. After all the good times and secrets we shared, would he still be angry with me after thirty-three years?

For two whole days, I tracked the scheduled delivery through the post office. I had warm visions of our friendship rekindled, images of how much he had grown and the accomplishments he had made with his talent. By the end of the second day, a notice with a red exclamation point popped up on the tracker that read, "The recipient has refused to accept the letter."

He signed for it twice to prove it was him, and then he handed the unopened letter back to the mail carrier. It was a crushing slap in my face, which I'm sure gave him some satisfaction. If only his approach to me in the mall had been compassionate and informative all those years ago, instead of him going on the attack, I might have listened and not ruined half of my life. At least I can go to my deathbed knowing I took the upper hand and tried to mend fences.

A quote by an unknown author said it best:

"Four things you can't get back:
The stone after it's thrown.
The word after it's said.
The occasion after it's missed.
The time after it's gone."

CHAPTER 41

THE day everything unraveled in my pretend marriage, I was up late working on another novel, living vicariously through my stories, when Holly got up from another restless sleep. She awoke several times during the night due to her health problems, losing another job, and sheltering at home for two years with the COVID pandemic. I jokingly accused her of prowling, but she practically shadowed my every step out of maddening boredom.

"We need to get you to a doctor and see if there is something wrong with your prostate or something. I can't remember the last time we made love," Holly said, sitting in her chair and turning on her computer. All I could hear were echoes of people wanting to send me to a gay-conversion camp. I was done with people trying to fix me.

"There is nothing wrong with me physically. Sweetheart, I think you know why we never have sex."

"No," said Holly with a naïve expression, which I sincerely doubted.

I turned to face her in my recliner.

"I'll tell you if you truly want to know," I said as my nerves chilled and traveled through my body. I thought I would pass out. I couldn't believe I was about to confess everything after thirty-two years of marriage.

After hours of crying and slamming her fists on the computer table, I had never felt so awful in my whole life. I must have explained everything fifteen times.

"And to think I actually thought someone found me attractive, and even that was a lie."

"I'm sure lots of men think you are attractive. Please don't take it personally. I've never been sexually attracted to any female."

"You wasted thirty-two years of my life! Just think what I could've done with my life," Holly said with a bitter laugh.

"I know—I know that I wasted your life. I wasted my life as well. I gave up having any life or friends for you. Do you realize that for over three decades, I have never been one place on my own overnight? That's why I spent most of those years writing books and painting. I could only live a fantasy. But I'm done letting others control, manipulate, or shame me. I can't do it anymore. I'm not willing to waste what little is left of my life." I realized, which was more shackling, harmful, or "sinful" for myself and my wife? Living a genuine gay life or faking a relationship and sexual orientation?

"Tell all your friends whatever you want about me. Tell them I was a lousy husband if you want, but please make sure they know that I warned you that I had only ever lived a gay lifestyle when you met me. I don't want anyone to think I blindsided you or cheated on you. With that confession, most women would have run for their lives, yet you still wanted to be with me. You mentioned marriage first. You were persistent in pursuing me."

CHAPTER 42

THE day of our divorce came faster than I had expected. It was late July 2022, and I anticipated nature, the elements, and even the neighbors to be in some sort of protest, an upheaval, because I was about to break the "Till death do you part" agreement in my wedding vows to be myself. But that morning, as I drove Holly to the courthouse, the sun glistened peacefully through the towering oaks as we passed one historical home after the other on our slowly decaying street.

We arrived at the courthouse within five minutes. The room appeared cheaply built in the seventies and was stuffed with furnishing that looked as though it had been stolen from a stately old capitol building that was now too expensive to repair. We sat beside one another in the front row, and I tried to pace my breathing. It was just as I had feared. We were the only couple there wearing COVID-19 masks and the only couple there for a divorce. Most of the people in the packed room were there for cases involving property rights. I was glad I was wearing a mask to conceal my identity and hide any emotions that might show, especially since everyone was eyeing us, trying to figure out the story behind our divorce. Whom was I kidding? Like my clients who admitted it, they probably all judged me to be gay and knew exactly why we were ending the marriage. From what I had been hearing, Mississippi had the largest population of gay people married to opposite-sex partners—because it was expected of them, and they wanted a fair chance at life without fear of being fired or targeted.

The judge called us to approach the bench. We signed the papers in front of him, and that was that.

As I exited the courthouse and followed the concrete walk beside the confederate soldier statue under the towering magnolias, I began looking back at many events leading up to such a tragic mistake. I recalled the first time I had attempted suicide when I had dreamed about the cat and mouse chase with the UFO that morphed into a car, and the similar UFO dreams I had throughout my life. I realized the dreams represented my wasted life. I had been running from and chasing the supernatural in the sky, and when I thought I had found it, it was merely the clever workings of man.

Years earlier, a prophet, who had worked for a major Christian network, prophesied that God would give me three hair salons and Holly and I, as a married couple, would become prolific ministers when all I wanted was to be heterosexual and healed from a hiatal hernia. Years later, I never received my answered prayer, but the prophet had received multiple free and discounted haircuts. I now own my fifth hair salon, and never more than one at a time. I once asked the prophet what he thought of psychics.

"They're always helping police catch killers and locate bodies and stuff," I added.

The prophet shook his head and quickly hid his face behind a magazine in the waiting area.

I now see no difference in the dim abilities of psychics and the masquerading of biblical spiritual gifts as Divine in origin. Perhaps that is why men wrote the Bible warning of divination and consulting the stars and mediums. Because the ignorant might discover that it is all the same. That discovery would crumble pious kingdoms.

While thinking about the UFO dream, I remembered the earlier dream about the Book of the Dead at the onset of my parents' vanishing into the wilderness. The Psychic Fair instructor didn't know what to make of that dream, but it occurred to me that perhaps it was a foreshadowing, and the dead people wrapped up like mummies were not only my friends who eventually died young but the life I eventually lost as well. A sense of healing washed over me. That journal I had burned in the mountains would resurrect as my memoir. I had to tell my story to help others remove their death shrouds and live their lives.

Now that I, like countless others, have abandoned religion and am finally free to be myself, religion became jealous and dug its greedy claws and double standards into the state and federal government. American democracy is falling under a fascist rise in Christian Nationalism. The Supreme Court just ended abortion rights—rights that I had known all my life. Florida passed the "Don't Say Gay" law. Federal judges are ruling that HIV prevention medicine is unconstitutional because they think it only keeps gay men from dying. Apparently, these Christian insurers are eager to deny their employees lifesaving drugs if their lifestyles go against their religious beliefs. Besides various pastors calling for the murder of gay people, there has been talk of the Supreme Court undoing all gay rights. I can't believe Americans and their fifteenth spouses are willing to take children away from loving gay couples and end gay marriages. If authorities snatched their spouses and children away from these same straight people, they might have a little compassion for the pain they gleefully caused.

The famous saying "When Fascism comes to America, it will be wrapped in the American flag and carrying a cross," is proving true, and many of the insurrectionists who attacked the United States Capitol Building in their effort to overturn the election on January Sixth, 2022 were carrying American flags, Christian flags, and giant crosses as props for their fascist agenda as they stormed past an enormous gallows where their comrades chanted, "Hang Mike Pence." The most telling and shocking thing was nearly everyone I knew in my conservative Christian state never uttered one disparaging word about this deadly and unprecedented event. It is all I can do to watch the news. Thanks to the rising homophobia and manufactured outrage trended by conservative news outlets, Republicans, who claim they are against cancel culture and want limited government, are burning and banning LGBTQ and "woke" books everywhere. Conservative parents and school leaders are banning any songs that even mention a rainbow. With anti-drag laws, states are banning men from dressing as women—entertainment that's been around for thousands of years. Basement radicals armed with assault rifles are showing up to stop Gay Pride events, library book readings, and even drag queen brunches. Terrorist groups used similar tactics when schools were integrated, and the National Guard had to step in to save human rights.

Due to bigoted leaders and fascist news organizations fearmongering because they have nothing beneficial to offer society, the world seems to have a renewed problem with men crossdressing for entertainment. But since the late 1940s, high school and college football teams and other alpha boys have cross-dressed in beautiful ballgowns, flawless makeup, jewelry, and high heels for what various institutions advertised as "Womanless Beauty Pageants."

"I think men who dress like women should be beaten and locked up," my father once said at a family reunion.

I had nearly gnawed a hole in my tongue from biting it. I remembered seeing such crossdressing events in Father's school yearbooks in the 1950s, in which he no doubt wanted me to remain unaware that he had participated. Even churches joined in with the highly attended tradition in the United States, namely in the South, after the "Womanless Wedding" events and the traditional school powderpuff football games, in which boys dressed as girls, had lost their glory.

Between sharing offensive jokes against LGBTQ people on social media, and *Old Testament* scriptures warning the ancient Jews against wearing clothes pertaining to the opposite gender, many of the beauty boys' moms, who were sometimes draped in confederate flags, bragged about how pretty their sons were between pics of them hunting and dirt-bike racing. But if gay, non-binary, or transgender men cross-dressed independently of these school-sponsored events, they'd risk imprisonment, being killed, or being accused of grooming children.

Even though straight women now wear boots, pants, t-shirts, and short hair, proms are being canceled, and gay girls are barred from wearing tuxedos for their senior yearbook photos because Christian "conviction" suddenly took precedence over the fact that no state policy dealt with the yearbook photo issue. Apparently, it's okay for boys to violate scriptures if they're bait-and-switch trolls, as long as they switch.

And then there is the push by way too many conservatives and Christians to do what they used to do and use the magic words to accuse gay people of grooming and sexualizing children to become gay.

"How many girlfriends do you have yet, Milan?" countless adults asked me in preschool, thinking it was "cute" in front of mixed company.

I learned quickly that I had better hold up at least one tiny finger.

"Just one? Well, you need to get on the ball, boy."

Now there is the school-sponsored "Promposal" trend, also called "practice weddings," where yearly boys are groomed to lavishly woo their mid-teen proxy brides to go to prom with them. Growing up in a world saturated with heterosexual sex and gender roles being "shoved down my throat" didn't make me turn straight in the least. I had never read or heard of one case where a drag queen had sexually harmed children, but I could publish a catacomb of books documenting church officials who had sexually abused children. Imagine if drag queens showed up at Christian establishments wearing tactical gear and identity-obscuring face masks, carrying bombs and machine guns, while screaming that churches are harming children. With a hypocritical society eager to forget its dark history, one that demonizes progress and education, that reverse scenario would cause World War Three.

Homophobes have always been desperate to find a sinister reason why so many gay people exist because they refuse to believe gay people are born that way. They are now trying to ban LGBTQ counseling for bullied children, endangering them in every way out of conjured fears of sexual manipulation. But what most people have forgotten or don't want people to remember is that the United States was never that concerned about sexualizing children. Many people blame the odd mix of modern feminism, helicopter moms, and religious Fascism for working to erase history that they are embarrassed for people to discover. They strive politically to return America to an idealized time that never really existed.

Universally, while girls are still given baby dolls and groomed on how to become mothers, boys were once forced to swim and play water polo completely nude. In fact, boys couldn't enroll in most U.S. schools until they passed a mandatory naked swim test. And if they didn't know how to swim, they had to take nude swimming until they passed the class, regardless of who was watching them in the stands. The first mandated nude swimming for boys in the U.S. started in 1885.

I thought being forced to strip my shirt off in front of teachers and girls in gym class was humiliating. But for about sixty-five years in America, boys were forced to parade fresh from the communal showers and swim naked according to the guidelines of the American Public Health Association. Forced nude swimming didn't occur as much in Southern states partly because the Civil War left such devastation that schools were too poor to have swimming pools. If men who experienced forced school nudity have the nerve to talk about it, the people who didn't experience it will laugh them outta Texas—claim they're making it up. It doesn't suit their narrative that America was more conservative back then. And the best way they shut people up is to treat them like they're perverts with some sexual obsession or agenda to groom children.

Everyone got an eyeful back in the "good old days." Any boy who tried to cover himself was made to feel unmanly or like a nerd. Towels were strictly for drying off after showering, not for wrapping around their waists. Children and young men were photographed naked in six hundred or more public, private, and religious schools from elementary to college, namely between 1913 to the late 1970s. One newspaper published an image of a nude boy on a diving board and printed the boy's name and home address in the article. It didn't print the names of the other naked boys sitting around the pool because there were too many of them.

Video documentaries such as the swim meet at Fernden School in 1939 featured grainy clips of young teen boys standing around or toweling off balls naked around the pool with women and girls packed in the audience of titillated spectators. Countless vintage ads, home goods, tourist guidebooks, school swim team yearbook photos, town newspaper articles, paintings and illustrations, and popular magazines, including *The Saturday Evening Post,* once featured large images of naked boys of all ages swimming or playing in their articles and covers that would be criminalized today. In 1909, *New York Times* published a news article covering a city-wide swimming competition and detailed how the boys swam nude in front of public spectators. *Life* magazine published naked images of the New Trier High School swim team in full color action. A 1915 archived capture of the YMCA Swimming Championships in Toronto showed boys trying to hide their nakedness with white towels while one boy's towel was off a few inches.

But for nearly a century, nude public swimming for males wasn't considered newsworthy because it was so prevalent. Many movies, such as "Heaven Help Us," dared to show forced nudity in schools. Documentaries captured naked schoolboys showering, playing, swimming, and enduring genital hygiene inspections. Boy Scout troops and Quaker camps back then required boys to swim, play sports, and sleep nude. These institutions had dutifully adopted the nude swim requirements of the Young Men's Christian Association, YMCA. They wanted to expand the deeply moral practice they had enforced in most of these organizations for forty years.

I find it shocking that the YMCAs held Bible studies and prayer meetings where they taught boys about the first married couple, Adam and Eve, and how the sin of their nakedness required God to make them a more modest set of clothes than the fig leaves they first had to wear. All the while forcing boys to be naked for body inspections, swimming, or using exercise equipment in front of clothed female assistants and instructors.

To groom boys for military duty, schools led boys to think it was their patriotic duty to let their stars and stripes unfurl. Nobody questioned it. Boys endured so much humiliation that they tried not to look at one another. The coaches made them get ass naked, thinking they'd be swimming, only to do jumping jacks or learn how to do mouth-to-mouth resuscitation and other close and personal lifesaving techniques. Before swimming, they had to walk through trays of bleach and got their balls and asses blasted with powerful jets of water that shot up from the floor in the showers—apparatuses they called ball washers. Many boys weren't even allowed to get dressed if they got called into the principal's or coach's office because they had to be swim-ready once they returned to the pool. It always brought smiles to the girls' faces when they passed them in the halls. Teachers and students reportedly made fun of the uncircumcised boys and would ask them if they'd gotten their tallywackers pinched in their locker doors. Even female swim instructors made boys line up in the pool with their legs wide open and take turns swimming between another boy's legs like fish. The boys who couldn't see because they had to swim without their glasses sometimes ended up getting a faceful of wedding tackle. Others reportedly worried about penis fractures after teachers would whop their whoppers with a pool skimmer if their periscopes accidentally popped up while swimming the backstroke. If a boy got an erection, the instructors would humiliate and call him a pervert, then make him run laps around the gym or climb a rope naked while everyone taunted him. In the winter, they would bust their nuts high diving in cold water without swim trunks. If one forgot his gym shorts in Phys Ed, they had to go naked there, too.

Often the girls' swim class deliberately arrived at the pool early before the boys could even climb out and retreat to the locker rooms. Female teachers and girls were constantly stumbling into the gym for one reason or the other, and girls were caught checking boys out through doors, behind bleachers, and through all the windows. Female teachers would barge into the boys' showers and toilets to check for smoking or hand file folders to the coaches and such. I can only imagine what would've happened if grown men or boys received excuses to stroll into the girls' showers, gym lockers, or underage pageant changing rooms. They'd be in jail for life—or go on record as sex offenders … unless they were the president of the country and pushed anti-gay legislation.

At one point, schools started removing the privacy stalls around the toilets in the boys' restrooms and forced boys to pee side-by-side in a trough on the wall.

Are the conspiracy theories true? Have chemtrails made everyone dumb and apathetic to the glib hypocrisy and psychosis within institutions for children? Girls were finally allowed to swim publicly but only in modest swimsuits. If the girls and teachers weren't forced to be nude while swimming all of those decades, then it proves nudity has meaning; it proves how humiliating and violating it is to be forced to expose yourself. It's also more evidence that the people who think gay people and rainbow flags are sexualizing children are full of shit.

Did forcing boys to be boys backfire? It gives me the willies just thinking about the pornography of power that people hold over the weaker. In one old photo, I was shocked to see naked boys sitting around the edge of a pool with their legs spread wide while both men and women coached them on various swimming techniques.

"That's how you do the dog paddle, boys. You have to let those puppies breathe!" I imagined the team of instructors telling the children.

Many men who lived to tell and author books of this history swear there were times when mothers, aunts, nuns, sisters, female cousins, and classmates joined in watching the nude action like ancient Olympic spectators. They recount on forums and discussion groups how the swimmers had to get over their shock and humiliation as the entitled guests watched them from packed bleachers, viewing galleries, balconies, or behind one-way viewing windows to see boys swim, relay race, and dive in the buff. When the crowds grew too large, some of these organizations required spectators to be invited by the swimmers' parents, while others started charging small fees for family, friends, and the general public to watch.

Swimming was also known as bathing. Why would crowds gather to watch budding teen boys bathe? I don't wish to imagine an entire city squeezing into my bathroom while I'm in the tub. Did the whole country need to entertain themselves by watching boys unrelated to them exercising naked when there was at least one coach and lifeguard on duty for emergencies? There are innumerable videos online where classmates have pantsed other boys at backyard parties in front of girls, even with mothers looking on and joining in the fun. The whole party would be in prison if they had stripped and revealed any girls' nakedness.

I came to understand the culture that had been handed down: The belief that nature dictates that boys need to be boys and must never babysit children that aren't their own, that mothers and women can't possibly be perverts, and that healthy boys secretly enjoy dominance and being exhibitionists. I'm all for sex and nudity, but only consensual and nothing by force, coercion, or intimidation. Unfortunately, the religious society that has thrived on violence will eventually go to the other extreme and force everyone to wear sheets over their entire body, like the Taliban.

The boys from that time knew that spectators seemed mesmerized by the lewdly revealing dives such as the armstand. They could smell the anxiety on their swim team, knowing the spectators were sitting on the edge of their seats, ogling them as they marched one by one up to the ten-foot diving platform like skinned lambs expected to be Mount Olympus gods. Then, like sexual submissives, they bent over with legs apart, stood upside down on their hands on the concrete edge until their genitals collapsed near their belly buttons, and then they jumped. The second favorite swim event, which brought the audience to dead silence, was the back dives on the bouncy diving board, where bashful teen boys turned red-cheeked from humiliation. After several genital helicopters, they flipped in the air, thrust out their organs for all to inspect, and prayed they didn't bellyflop as they plummeted toward the water.

Back then, the athletic organizations allowed them to wear something besides their birthday suits—they could wear award medals around their necks, which were presented to them during the "Family Nights." After swimming, diving, and begging God they wouldn't get raging boners, the boys stood naked in line to be photographed and receive certificates. They were mere inches away from spectators sitting in the bleachers and at crotch level on the sidelines. Many men later documented that, as boys and teens at these events, especially on "Test Days," they were not warned that even their female classmates would attend the naked swims. They were given no choice but to go along and let them have an eyeful of everything they had. I find it a special kind of double standard that these sex-shaming spectators would dare sit in the stands and glue their eyes on teenage and college boys, knowing they constantly risked getting throbbing hard-ons and deep humiliation from it, just as many boys do while wrestling. Anything for the manly institution of sports and the military. But if a boy wants to put on a dress and lip-sync in a drag brunch for fun, people want to send in armed protesters.

Several women who were young girls during those decades admitted that they loved watching the boys through cracks in the school doors as they lined up for their daily naked role calls and lectures that seemed to last forever. These women swear their female instructors never prevented them from their anatomy lessons. They went around, whispering to every girl in school detailed descriptions of each boy's ass, testicles, and penis—how thick, long, hairy, or which way they curved. The running joke they confessed during those many decades was that these public swim meets should actually be spelled "swim meats" to serve community notice of the next college, high school, and middle-school-aged sausage fest.

Countless archival photos going back to the late 1800s show naked men, boys, and military crews swimming, playing, and posing for group photos completely nude, often with clothed women in the

THIRTY-SEVEN-YEAR ABDUCTION

mix.

What was the psychological motive behind deeply humiliating so many boys? Why did adults, mothers usually, exploit boys and objectify their sons, forcing them to strip to satisfy the curiosities of the girls and the entertainment of adults? Why did they claim boys shouldn't be allowed to keep their secrets from the girls? Did they think this would keep them from turning gay?

Men from those "puritan" times spoke of occasions where girls and women bullied shy boys into taking off everything near ponds, creeks, and other public swimming areas. But the adults prohibited girls from being naked in front of boys, depriving them of the female anatomy lessons they desperately wanted. I remember feeling icky and embarrassed when my mother encouraged me to take off my swim trunks six feet away from her and swim naked in the Ross Barnett Reservoir in sixth grade. I did this to avoid being considered a chicken, but it was just family and my heebie-jeebies there at the time. As I had as a child, these lads and teens felt betrayed by their fully clothed parents who raised them to be godly and modest and then suddenly withdrew protection from them on a whim.

In an era where institutions fear being sued and targeted, most school boards of education and boys' organizations will stonewall people from searching for this information, hoping the world will forget entirely. By the end of the 1950s, when forced nude male swimming was in decline, several conservative moralists started attributing the deterioration of morals to innocent children seeing naked animals, so they started joining SINA, The Society for Indecency to Naked Animals. Their noble goal was to put clothes on naked animals from domestic pets to dangerous wildlife. For years, hyper-reactionary conservatives used widespread media to push this movement to "save the children." Until, that is, they discovered the entire movement was all a satirical hoax to prove how gullible they were. Sadly, if this movement had happened during this day and time, the followers would still swear it was legitimate even if the founder himself confessed it was a joke. "It's easier to fool people than to convince them that they have been fooled," —Mark Twain.

Ironically by the 1990s, when most people had forgotten this history, speedos on men started vanishing and men's shorts went from scanty to near their ankles.

The Phalliban—modern puritans who are sinking their fangs in government and trying to out-prude one another against male bodies are suddenly behind the campaign to "protect children from turning gay"—until these prudes are caught molesting the very children they claim they are protecting. Phallic architecture has been around for millennia, but the outraged Phalliban now demands the destruction of any stone column, tower, or piece of architecture that looks anything close to the human penis. Recently, a Florida principal was fired after showing sixth-grade students a picture of Michelangelo's naked David statue that has been on display for five hundred years. Maybe if weapon manufacturers made guns more penis shaped, the Phalliban would finally do something that actually protect the children.

By the late 1980s, when American Talibangelicals and gangster rappers combined their moral influences, tight jeans, men's shorts above the knees, speedos, and naked male swimming had ended and was considered gay. While France and the rest of the world still have nude swim meets and nude beaches, American men started covering up. It was not really a human modesty issue or to protect children because girls started wearing miniskirts to church and dental-floss thin swimsuits to the church pool party the minute the sermons ended.

I see more and more news headlines where Talibangelicals use guns and death threats to remove rainbows from public and private buildings. They are stopping Gay Pride and other fun events where comical drag queens host bingo parties or theatrically read books to teenagers who choose to be there.

"It's sexualizing the children, and I'm sick of it," they scream their learned catchphrase.

Talibangelicals don't, however, want to remove the Bible from schools or libraries. They don't mind their kiddies reading pornographic scriptures, including Ezekiel 23:20, about a horny woman who had sex with men who had penises the size of donkeys and spewed cum like horses. Not to mention her fantasies about them groping her young breasts and how God became jealous and threatened to strip her clothes so everyone could ogle her naked body. Neither do they want to ban children from reading biblical stories about how God's chosen twelve tribes captured concubines as young as six to keep as sex slaves. Pornographic poetry about King Solomon and his many lustful descriptions of towering naked titties. The story of God ordering a pack of bears to rip children apart for laughing at a prophet's bald head. The story of the sex slave concubine who was gang raped all night, her body cut into twelve pieces, and sent as morbid gifts to the tribes of Israel. And these examples don't begin to scratch the hardcore surface. I constantly have book reviewers who feel a need to warn that my books have mature content and are not for children. But the same reviewers, whose literary powerhouses make millions from Christian fiction in dozens of subcategories, would never dream of adding the same warning to a review of the Bible which is infinitely worse—if they've ever actually read it.

To me, child abuse is telling children they were born inadequate and sinful, and God is watching their every intimate moment and will torture them for eternity in the flames of Hell if they don't let Him possess them.

Buckle your seatbelts because there is much to be said here. These same people who want to censor children's stories that feature an intersex character or two loving moms wouldn't dream of keeping their children from sporting events where inappropriate things actually take place: Bloody fights, streakers, naked wrestler weigh-ins, drunken brawls, not to mention the vast history of accidental nudity where players' genitals become exposed and flop around until they score a goal or reach the finish line in a race. Or the endless wrestler boners from pro-level to middle school—a sport where coaches have been known to signal or yell to their team wrestlers to "Check of the oil" of their opponents, which is a clue to violently finger-rape the assholes of the other boys in hopes to stun them for the win. There are whole blogs and chatrooms full of video and photo captures of this for fun and fetish. Other sports stadiums go wild when extra balls start bouncing on the field.

With the invention of high-definition and widescreen television, many women, too, admit they now love to watch … the players' asses as they bend over in huddles. And for the uncensored versions, they pack in the stadiums to see all of the dick-slips and fondlings, the player getting pantsed so the world can see their genitals and asses, the ass slappings, and after the games, the ultimate show of gratitude where players have been known to flash their junk for the patient fans who linger. The men want their boys there and are glad their wives and daughters have learned to share their enthusiasm for sports.

The world has culturally established a love affair for death, weapons, war, and violence front and center in everything from old nursery rhymes, Holy Bibles, patriotic anthems, and revered hymns with crucifixions, skull-crushing Judgment Days, and fountains filled with blood. But anything less familiar done with the reproductive organs between the legs, that, to many, is the real terror.

Let's cut to the chaste: Talibangelicals want to ban sex education and then wonder why there is such a high teenage pregnancy rate. These are the same folks, who have, in times past, locked constricting chastity belts and spiked or electrical urethral rings on children's sex organs. They've applied blood-sucking leeches or borax solution on little labium. The same pure-minded prudes who once forced penile piercings on children or recommended severing all nerves to the offending organs. Almost daily during many children's upbringing, they were fed what I call "scornflakes," cock-blocking breakfast cereals created by famous anti-masturbators, one of which recommended no anesthesia during circumcisions so the boys would feel the pain if they defied nature and touched their wicked willies.

Do-gooders today still don't think it was child abuse when they used to sneak erection-killing saltpeter in their boys' food. Many parents caused less disfigurement by tucking their children in tight at night, making sure their prayerful hands were awkwardly above the covers or, in some cases, the crossed position to simulate death in a coffin. Other boys in the good old days were put in straitjackets or had their hands and feet tied to their bedposts. Proper sleep positions were believed to exorcise lusty thoughts and turn children away from perdition.

"If I should die before I wake, I pray the Lord my soul to take," was cauterized into my brain like a life-altering infibulation. Of course, modern prudes, such as my parents, remain militant about parents' right to enforce their values but are desperate for much of its past to be forgotten or downplayed. That way, current society won't be on guard when they succeed at doing it again.

"Stay positive and no complaining, Milan."

I can't believe people still circumcise and mutilate boys and girls to keep them from the heinous carnal sin of self-pollution. Instead of letting the children decide what they are, parents even choose which sex to quickly "fix" their intersex infants born with both male and female sex organs.

I can hear these parents say: "I think I'm in the mood for a girl this time, Doctor Kwiksnip. Hurry and lob off the extra organ before anyone asks what sex the baby is. I already have pink balloons for the gender reveal party, so—"

Like countless parents before, my parents had repeatedly shamed or spanked me for exploring my own body. The same ignorant sorts who used to send their little wankers off to institutions to receive experimental medicine or electroshock treatments also recommended beating children to stop what they considered the evilest sexual practices that slowly shredded the soul. They traumatized the kiddies with tales of dementia, spinal cord concussions, premature death, blindness, paralysis, impotence, epilepsy, hairy palms, and nymphomania, especially if the young female masturbator was blonde. And when all else fails, they terrorize the little tee-tee-touching tikes with threats of a good old everlasting roasting in the unquenchable fires of Hell for the sin of Onanism.

"Ashes, ashes, we all fall down."

There isn't enough room in any book to list the tortures and experiments done on millions of gay children throughout history. If it were, the new moralists who fear empathy (the one-word summary of woke) would burn it in their bonfires of boneheadedness.

As I watch all of this happen, I realize it takes a unique mix of hate, religion, and ignorance for these people not to question how twisted and hypocritical they are. Only now, they seem to celebrate these facts.

Many people still tell me that I am bitter. There is no use trying to get them to see the truth of what many gay people still go through. But in the words of Assata Shakur: "Nobody in the world, nobody in history, has ever gotten their freedom by appealing to the moral sense of the people who were oppressing them." Blinded by their privilege, they don't have to fear being murdered for being themselves. They don't seem to know or care that it is legal to murder gay people like me in most parts of the United States because of the gay/trans panic defense.

We live in a shallow new world based on ultimate achievements using the latest glut of positivity secrets and memes. Sunshine and daisy people who only want feel-good, conscience-soothing people surrounding them, gaslighting and shutting out anything and anyone bitter, needy, or suffering. And money forbid you dare bore brightsided people by complaining with the details. Toxic positivity—privilege—a disconnect from the harsh reality shut out by their locked doors and mute buttons.

Privileged bullies and their beneficiaries don't want victims getting revenge, no matter how badly the victims were treated. Don't dare remind them in history books, or they'll ban or burn them, especially if the content makes them uncomfortable. They want to bottom-shelve the multitudes who were rounded up like livestock, tortured, and thrown into mass graves. Those victims couldn't believe something so diabolical could happen to them to the point that they became immobilized in sheer disbelief. Positivity only got the dead so far, and positivity will silence the emotional responses needed for paying proper respects.

Underneath the sanctimonious façade of superiority everyone projects, they are animals—the only animals on the planet who are afraid of their hidden natures being discovered, the only animals ashamed to be themselves.

I don't know what awaits the remaining years of my life now that I am a free and well-matured adult. In the handful of years I had been myself in the late 1980s, gay men had AIDS to fear, but now the rise of Monkeypox has society wanting to blame gay men for that as well. People chose to fight and vilify LGBTQIA people; otherwise, there wouldn't be anything obvious to identify them as Christians.

I wish I could go back over three decades ago and have a talk with that manipulated, demonized kid that I was and tell him that the only way he would genuinely have a liberated life and true healing is by having an honest and authentic relationship with himself and with the person to whom he is genuinely sexually attracted. But I can only go forward, and I'm going to do it authentically. I don't want to be anyone's back-alley buddy, only communicating in private emails. I plan to live out loud and expect potential friends to be okay with it. That way, I'll know which ones are worth my devotion.

At Pine Belt Pride.

Since I hadn't done anything by myself in over three decades, I took baby steps on a beautiful October morning and sold my books at Pine Belt Pride at Town Square Park in Hattiesburg, Mississippi. Another first is showing my bare legs. I hadn't worn shorts in over thirty years because of the religious programming and shaming, from which I am now completely free. Remember, I said "baby steps." While my wonderful neighboring vendors kept an eye on my booth for me, I went to the restroom in my new rainbow-cuffed shorts and somehow tripped on the uneven sidewalk. When I stood to my feet, feeling like a bumbling lug, I realized I had skinned my hands, knees, arms, and elbows. I was a bloody awful mess. In the back of my head, I could hear sanctimonious voices gloating, "This is what you deserve." "Pride goes before destruction and haughtiness before a fall." But I picked myself up with what little dignity I had left, dabbed as much blood off me as I could with the remaining toilet tissue in the filthy porta potty, and learned to walk on my own, so to speak. I didn't know a single person at the Gay Pride event. Still, I felt like I had finally returned home and met some of the nicest people ever—parents who, instead of abandoning their gay children, were there supporting the event and embracing their children.

The second big step for me was to find the only gay club in Jackson where my old friends might still go. For years during my abduction by the church, I often reminisced and dreamed of the fun times I had in the gay clubs. Foolishly, time had paused in my head,

263

and I imagined that all the people I remembered (those who hadn't died) were still waiting for me to come back, burst out of the closet and resume a free life. That Saturday night, I got dressed up in my hippest shirt, did my hair all fierce, and drove to the new bar that had recently replaced several other short-lived bars since my heyday at The Limelight. The location had moved from hip downtown to a run-down neighborhood. Crime had significantly increased in Jackson, so I was on high alert until I made it safely inside the new club. It was refreshing to see more diverse races, especially with the bar employees, but I was immediately stunned by the lack of friendliness.

Perhaps they're on edge because of the rise in far-right attacks on gay establishments, I reasoned.

Workers at the ticket booth had to scan my driver's license before I entered the nearly empty club. The TV screens everywhere advertised the drag show and dance party that night, so I was looking forward to something close to what I remembered.

Like divas, the four drag queens came from the back of the club and huddled close. For twenty minutes they took selfies by the bar without speaking to any of the guests. I had seen this trick before: Their social media pages would show a different reality of the night. I was struck by how the queens had gone from humor and minimal padding to looking like strippers who had emptied a cement truck inside their bottoms.

I ordered a drink from the bartender and took a barstool near the back. I didn't recognize a single person, but only about thirty people were in the club, and it was minutes before showtime. When I used to go out as a liberated teenager, Saturday nights were so packed you could hardly move about the club, and it was hard to have a single conversation with new people competing for your ear. Back then, in fact, a little person had bitten my ear while I was trying to tune out his questions and dance. Now, many of the guests chose to stand around in the crumbling parking lot. The huge dance floor remained empty, and the music sounded like a broken record stuck on repeat until a moment of ecstasy when the DJ played Lady Gaga. Then it went back to disposable repetition. *Weren't the owners getting the hint?* Everyone there resembled bored misfits who would rather be in their own niche club, wherever that might be. In my black jeans and alternative boutique shirt, I realized I had grossly overdressed. Many bearded, balding men dressed like they might be heading out camping for the weekend. Half the guests seemed to be straight couples, and as soon as guests entered the club, they huddled in their secluded corner with their friends. Cell phones were brandished everywhere; instead of cigarettes, everyone lugged around clumsy vaping devices. Nobody mingled with strangers like they used to do. *Was it true? Had cell phones crippled our social skills?*

An hour and a half passed, and the promised drag show hadn't started, so I went to the restroom just in case anything fun might actually occur later. After sanitizing my hands, I looked in the mirror and saw every wrinkle on my face under the harsh light. Whom was I kidding? I realized at that moment that four decades had passed, and time had moved on without me. The older men I remembered as a teen back in the eighties were either dead now or in nursing homes. And more shockingly, many of the younger ones had passed away as well.

Milan, you are going to have to restart your life from scratch.

I touched up my thinning hair and, for a change of scenery, decided to sit on the padded seats around the dance floor. I was determined to stay positive and adapt to the times. After I realized that five more hours could pass and nobody would talk to me, I decided I would rather go home and watch the paint dry, so I left, convinced I would never return and a new club would soon be replacing this one. But the real problem would never be addressed.

Within days after I finished writing this memoir, Pastor Whittington died at an old age. I remembered the dream about him the night he had baptized me—where he died, and nobody grieved at the funeral, and then when he came out of the coffin, nobody cheered. When I told him about the dream that following Sunday, he seemed spooked and quickly said, "It represents a sort of spiritual rebirth."

I don't know if this was the case at his four-hour funeral because I had no desire to attend or watch the live streaming of it. No one reported him resurrecting, but I have come out of the coffin. I was a twenty-three-year-old gullible boy when that awful man baptized me. I'll be fifty-seven in a few weeks. As I write this, I'm listening to Dusty Springfield sing "Yesterday When I Was Young." When I was a teen, I occasionally heard older people encourage the younger generation not to waste their fleeting youth, but what they were really saying went over my head. I wish I had listened.

Also, after finishing this memoir, I learned, through endless internet searches, that my mother had died three months earlier. My intuition was right yet again: My parents wanted a private burial ceremony. I expected them to avoid telling me, but I never anticipated my extended family to keep my mom's passing from me. All of this waste and loss because my parents chose to cherry-pick ancient scripture written for people from a primitive time. I assume my father is still alive. I overcame my fear of him a few years ago, and my nightmares of him abusing me ended after learning to control my dreams, a practice confirmed by a professional dream therapist I consulted. Now that I'm free in my old age, I'm not going to waste the remainder of my time.

If you've suffered any of the religious oppression that I have, just remember that morality is up to personal interpretation, and no religion invented morality, as many adherents proudly claim. Michael Sherlock said it best: "Christianity did not become a major religion by the quality of its truth, but by the quantity of its violence." I'm for freedom of all or no religion even though religion isn't usually for my freedom. Yet, instead of fighting against Christian Dominionism and its endless misuse, many privileged moderates find it easier to scream that victims like me are painting their faith-based establishments with too wide of a paintbrush. I cannot imagine the cognitive dissonance they must squelch to tell that to the infinite victims of the Crusades, Inquisitions, Witch Trials, and gay-conversion camps. Moderates have a recorded reputation for helping extremists achieve their goals, not by yielding the sword necessarily, but by silencing any criticism needed to keep their siblings from the dominion on which moderates, too, ultimately live richly. "Those who can make you believe absurdities can make you commit atrocities." —Voltaire. And those who can keep you quiet or nonjudgmental about the absurdities and atrocities have carried out the gravest injustice.

Even if you were born nailed to a cross as I was, you can pull yourself off of it. You can refuse to exist under prophecies of fear and doom, no matter if ancient sheepherders from the Middle East wrote the cancerous and highly divisive riddles.

You don't have to crucify who you are in order to live.

About The Author

Multi-Award-Winning Author Milan Sergent studied creative writing in college and began writing the novel series *Candlewicke 13* in 2007, a year after featuring some of the series' characters in his solo art exhibition, titled "Outsiders and Apparitions," near Rockefeller Center in New York City.

An artist and poet since adolescence, Sergent's poetic works also won an international book award.

To learn more about the author or his works, visit http://www.milansergent.com. While there, join the mailing list for important news updates and notifications about future novel releases.

Also Available by Milan Sergent

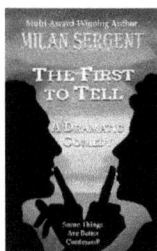

THE FIRST TO TELL: Cooper Pearmain has big plans for a quiet and cushy retirement on the ocean. He has a secret about his wife that would prove devastating to her. Though Lilibet's acting career has long expired, she is determined to remain relevant at all costs. She, too, has a secret that could destroy her husband's hard-earned work. They both abhor one another, and the only bond the couple has left is these secrets. People are starting to question whether their shocking public wars are all just acts of eccentrics trying to revive Lilibet's career, or they are locked together in some sadomasochistic codependency. When the Pearmains suspect the Mayfields, a psychology undergraduate and her husband, are threatening to expose both of them before either Cooper or Lilibet get to use their weapons of reckoning, the young couple becomes embroiled in a horrifically hilarious vacation that will change everyone in ways they never could imagine. Unfortunately, they all learn the hard way that some things are better confessed.

"With his unique style of writing and ingenious syntax, Milan Sergent effortlessly tells a tale so dark and serious with humor that lightens the mood at just the right moment. This story has some of the most interesting and well-spun characters that I have ever come across in a novel. An absolutely exciting and intriguing story that will catch you off guard at almost every turn! I highly recommend this book for anyone who wants an outside-the-box experience. I can't wait to read the rest of his work."
—Anne-Marie Ledo for *Readers' Favorite*

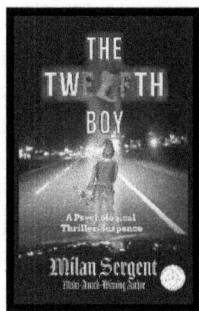

THE TWELFTH BOY: After years of waiting, Savannah Graysen finally finds love and has a miracle baby on Christmas Eve. The boy child, Noel, is a sign from the heavens that being a subservient wife and lover of Christmas has finally paid off until Noel, believed to be an abomination, ends up dead in a manger with a scripture carved on his little chest. Savannah learns the hard way that some institutions cannot be touched, especially when they're ancient and sacred. Even God said so Himself: "Touch not mine anointed, and do my prophets no harm." What starts as a mother seeking justice soon entangles her in a web of deceit so divided, so brainwashed, yet still so intent on its mission, that it cannot be reasoned with. If Savannah loses everything dear, will her bravery, she never knew she had, be enough of a reward in Hell?

"The Twelfth Boy by Milan Sergent is a fast-moving, page-turning novel that took my breath away…. I read this book in one sitting, glued to the pages, and I can't recommend it highly enough. It poses many questions about our perceptions of society and the ideas we are subjected to from our early years. A beautifully crafted book that deserves to do very well."
—Lucinda E Clarke for *Readers' Favorite*

DANG NEAR ROYAL: When the Gurneys receive a visit from a reality show producer, bringing news of a life-changing inheritance, they must choose to go down with their crumbling shack in rural Mississippi or try to pass themselves off as British aristocracy. Will the dangerous conspiracy theories the elusive Gurneys cling to prove true when many try to convince them that they are victims of human trafficking being exploited in a snuff film?

"[Dang Near Royal] is comedy at its finest …. This is all go right from the first page, a truly down-to-earth comedy with a touch of the bittersweet to it. Milan has written a story that you can only truly appreciate if you understand British humor. I do and I think this would go down a treat as a made-for-TV series in the UK."
—Anne-Marie Reynolds for *Readers' Favorite*

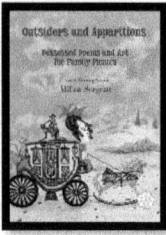

OUTSIDERS AND APPARITIONS: The Pitrick family picnic went off without a hitch until Patty drove the unwelcome wagon into a roadside ditch. Her daughter cried out with maddening dread while apparitions appeared high overhead. She didn't take it as a sign that Patty was dead, but that the crash had mashed her sauerkraut sandwich. This is an eclectic book of poetry and art by an easily bored author and artist who broke free from gross boundary violations, conformity demands, and abandonment as a youth. The past now only apparitions: he is currently possessed with a mission to encourage expression without dull traditions, rules, or shackling expectations. The soul can be possessed, but the product it produces must be free to protest.

"This superb collection of poetry and art, Outsiders and Apparitions by Milan Sergent, cleverly confronts societal opinions on outward success, happiness, and inner fulfillment …. Each poem is illustrated with the most extraordinary and exceptional artwork. I was absolutely captivated by this collection. Milan is such an inspirational artist and writer. His talent for provoking thought and change in human behavior is superb …."
—Lesley Jones for *Readers' Favorite*

MARTYRS AND MANIFESTATIONS: This is an eclectic book of poetry and art by an easily bored author and artist who broke free from gross boundary violations, conformity demands, and abandonment in his youth. With oppressive forces still clawing from the grave, and people who try to shame or silence victims and embarrassing history, Sergent is currently on a mission to encourage expression without dull traditions, rules, or shackling expectations. Authoritarians can leave us feeling hexed, but you can break the spell.

"As a fan of Milan Sergent in general, I anticipated getting into another excellent collection of verses and art, and I was once again thoroughly impressed …. There is a really quirky mix of traditionalism and celebration of the poetic form which Sergent cleverly subverts and twists into new rule-breaking permutations to delight and surprise his readers …. The underlying themes, empathy, and emotional quality of the work are second to none, clearly coming from a real place within the author which we marginalized folk can all relate to. Overall, I would highly recommend … to poetry fans, surrealists, and the oppressed seeking freedom the world over."
—K.C. Finn for *Readers' Favorite*

"Engaging storytelling … bursts with odd, witty, playful incidents and characters. The narrative continually surprises … charming … laugh-out-loud funny."

— The BookLife Prize by *Publishers Weekly* for Book Two of the Candlewicke 13 Series.

"Whether you're a younger reader or just young at heart, this is a very immersive, high-quality fantasy series that never ceases to amaze me with its imaginative quality and new twists to the plot."

— K.C. Finn for *Readers' Favorite*

"Vibrant and funny …."

— The Booklife Prize by *Publishers Weekly* for Book One of the Candlewicke 13 Series

Ingram Content Group UK Ltd.
Milton Keynes UK
UKHW020032240623
423977UK00015B/129/J

9 781954 430143